Structuration Theory

TRADITIONS IN SOCIAL THEORY

Series Editors: Ian Craib and Rob Stones

This series offers a selection of concise introductions to particular traditions in sociological thought. It aims to deepen the reader's knowledge of particular theoretical approaches and at the same time to enhance their wider understanding of sociological theorising. Each book will offer: a history of the chosen approach and the debates that have driven it forward; a discussion of the current state of the debates within the approach (or debates with other approaches); and an argument for the distinctive contribution of the approach and its likely future value.

Published

PHILOSOPHY OF SOCIAL SCIENCE: THE PHILOSOPHICAL
FOUNDATIONS OF SOCIAL THOUGHT
Ted Benton and Ian Craib

CRITICAL THEORY
Alan How

STRUCTURATION THEORY
Rob Stones

Forthcoming

FEMINIST SOCIAL THEORY
Sam Ashenden

STRUCTURALISM, POST-STRUCTURALISM AND POST-MODERNISM
David Howarth

MARXISM AND SOCIAL THEORY
Jonathan Joseph

MICRO SOCIAL THEORY
Brian Roberts

DURKHEIM AND THE DURKHEIMIANS
Willie Watts Miller and Susan Stedman Jones

Further titles in preparation

Structuration Theory

Rob Stones

First published 2005 by
PALGRAVE MACMILLAN
Houndmills, Basingstoke, Hampshire RG21 6XS and
175 Fifth Avenue, New York, N.Y. 10010
Companies and representatives throughout the world

PALGRAVE MACMILLAN is the global academic imprint of the Palgrave
Macmillan division of St. Martin's Press, LLC and of Palgrave Macmillan Ltd.
Macmillan is a registered trademark in the United States, United Kingdom
and other countries. Palgrave is a registered trademark in the European
Union and other countries.

ISBN–13: 978–0–333–79377–0 hardback
ISBN–10: 0–333–79377–3 hardback
ISBN–13: 978–0–333–79378–7 paperback
ISBN–10: 0–333–79378–1 paperback

This book is printed on paper suitable for recycling and
made from fully managed and sustained forest sources.

A catalogue record for this book is available from the British Library.

A catalog record for this book is available from the Library of Congress.

Library of Congress Catalog Card Number :2004056952

10   9   8   7   6   5   4   3   2
14 13 12 11 10 09 08 07 06

Transferred to Digital Printing 2009.

For Ja

Contents

List of Figures

Acknowledgements

My colleague and friend Ian Craib, in his role as editor of the *Traditions in Social Theory* series, asked me to write this book some four or five years ago. I initially said no, and then wavered, and finally he convinced me that I should say yes. I'm both delighted and relieved that Ian did persuade me and I hope that he would have been pleased with the result. I think he would but will never know for certain as Ian died just before Christmas 2002 after living with cancer and the shadow of its possible return for nearly ten years. It is to Ian that my greatest thanks must go.

I would also like to thank the many students and academic colleagues who have engaged with me in discussion and exploration of themes in structuration in courses, graduate boards and seminars through the years. It is difficult to exaggerate the importance of these encounters. Kaoru Aoyama, Ana Cuevas, Sung Kyung Kim, Berenice Rivera Macias, Maria Rassokhina and Ake Tangsupvattana have, in the process of grappling with the implications of social theory for their own doctoral field work, helped more than they might imagine to clarify some of my own thoughts about application and theoretical coherence.

It is apparent from the pages of *Structuration Theory* that I am indebted to a legion of formidable intellectuals who have developed, used, criticised and clarified dimensions of the approach. I see the book as drawing together and building upon their insights. A central position in this distinguished constellation has to be given to the founder of the tradition, Anthony Giddens, but the project of 'strong structuration' I outline in these pages is also heavily indebted to many others, most prominently Pierre Bourdieu, Ira J. Cohen, Nicos Mouzelis, Ewa Morawska, Margaret Archer, William Sewell Jr, John B. Thompson, Nick Crossley, Gregor McLennan, William Outhwaite, Ian Craib, Andrew Sayer, Chris Shilling, Richard Whittington, Tony Spybey, Nigel Thrift, John Urry, Richard Kilminster, Chris Bryant and David Jary. The last two mentioned, Chris Bryant and David Jary, have played a particularly important role in the formation of structuration's credentials as a tradition, compiling, editing, sorting, chronicling, and critically appraising scores of theoretical and empirical contributions over the past fifteen years. It would have been impossible for me to have written anything approximating the same book if I had not been able to draw on the fruits of their scholarship.

I am grateful to the Fuller Bequest Fund in the Department of Sociology at the University of Essex for sponsoring my attendance at various conferences, and for the generous study leave the university provides. Aspects of arguments presented in the book have been presented in talks at a number of venues including: the American Sociological Association's annual conference, Chicago, August 2002; the Department of Sociology at Trento, Italy (thanks to Carlo Ruzza for arranging this); the Department of Arts, Humanities and Social Sciences at University College Worcester; the Department of Social and Communication Studies at University College Chester; the Old Theatre at the London School of Economics; and my own department at the University of Essex.

I would particularly like to acknowledge the support and encouragement given to me in various ways by Ken Plummer, Ira J. Cohen, Miriam Glucksmann, Andrew Sayer and John Scott, amongst others. Thanks to Mike Stones for producing all the original figures for the book, and for much else besides, and to Catherine Gray for continuing to be a consummate editor, combining tact, skill and steel in equal measures.

My family, as ever, provide nourishment and purpose, and they combine this with a healthy disrespect for academic deadlines. Special thanks to my daughter Klong and my son Pim for not at all resenting the hours a worthwhile project requires. Finally, I dedicate the book to my wife, Ja.

ROB STONES

Introduction: Structuration Theory

This book is intended, in part, as an introduction to structuration theory. At the same time it aims to provide a revised, stronger, framework for structuration theory. This framework is a synthesis that draws from and builds upon criticisms, debates, defences and refinements within the field of structuration, whilst also drawing lessons from the many applications of the theory at the substantive level. The resultant 'strong' project of structuration should thus be seen as a bringing together of the insights and contributions of a formidable group of intellectuals who have engaged with structuration at both the theoretical and empirical levels.

The reader will doubtless be aware of the crucial part played by social theorist Anthony Giddens in the creation and development of structuration theory as a distinct analytical and conceptual resource. Whilst responding to, and incorporating, significant criticisms of Giddens's seminal version of structuration into the stronger structuration project, I have also made a point of hanging on to the core strengths of his presentation of the theory. I have only relinquished elements where the case against hanging on to them was more powerful than any argument I could muster in defence. I have looked for the chance to modify, refine and develop aspects of Giddens's theory much more often than I have relinquished them completely. On the other hand, I do argue in the course of the book that many dimensions of Giddens's early and middle period writings that were presented as aspects of structuration bore little relationship, in fact, to the core defining features of structuration. One needs to be clearer, tighter and more systematic than Giddens has been about structuration theory's distinctive and defining characteristics. The revised project of structuration I argue for here thus incorporates central elements of Giddens's original exposition, and continues the spirit of that project, but it also advances and consolidates that spirit: by more carefully delineating the scope of the structuration project; by developing and reconfiguring some of the older concepts that fall within these parameters; by adding a substantial number of new complementary conceptual categories; and, finally, by thinking more systematically about the relation of each of these elements to questions of methodology, evidence, and the specificity of research orientations.

1

Structuration theory has reached a decisive point in its trajectory, a point that could see it fade as a distinct approach or, alternatively, establish itself more strongly than ever as an integrated perspective able to offer invaluable kinds of systematic explanatory power and critical insight to social theory. There has been a certain paradox or irony in the fate of structuration in recent years, at the theoretical level it has been the negative target of sustained and detailed criticisms, whilst at the empirical level its history, at least on the surface, has been one of overwhelming success as scores of researchers have found that its concepts have allowed them to gain critical purchase on empirical phenomena in fields as diverse as accounting systems, archaeology, demography, organisational and political culture, the sociology of technology, the management of inter-firm networks, migration studies, the analysis of sport and leisure, and of gender and patriarchy (see Bryant and Jary, 2001b, pp. 43–61).[1] A central reason behind structuration's uneven fortunes has been the absence of any concerted and systematic attempt to respond to criticisms at the theoretical level. The person one might most have expected to undertake this task, Anthony Giddens, defied any such expectations. Structuration theory was drawn together from a number of influences and crystallised by Giddens in a whirlwind of production that lasted for a long decade from the mid 1970s to the late 1980s. During these years, he wrote a string of books, some in the form of systematic and sustained book length arguments setting out the major tenets of structuration, others in the form of collections of one-off engagements with individual authors or themes that were given the 'structuration treatment'. After this period, Giddens turned his hand to other things, to broad questions of modernity and globalisation, and to issues of politics and the 'Third Way', moving from his position as Professor of Sociology at Cambridge to the post of Director of the London School of Economics, and for good measure self-consciously styling himself anew as a 'publicly engaged intellectual', being vaunted not only as Tony Blair's 'guru' but also as an influential voice in the development of political agendas from South Korea to Brazil.[2] Perhaps one should not be surprised that during this period of transformation and change the amount of energy that Giddens had to devote to demanding and nuanced questions of social theory in general, and to structuration in particular, was less than it had been.

Giddens had, in any case, often complained about the ways in which most of the authors who have drawn on structuration theory for empirical research had employed his concepts (see Giddens, 1989, p. 294; 1990b, pp. 310–11). He complained that they tended to import his concepts *en bloc* into their research in a way that merely served to unnecessarily burden and clutter studies with an excess of abstract concepts. The works applying concepts from the logical framework of structuration theory that Giddens approved of were those that used them more selectively, 'in a spare and critical fashion' (Giddens, 1991b, p. 213, also see 1991b, pp. 213–16; and 1989, p. 294).

A second objection Giddens had to the attitudes taken up by both researchers and critics to the relation between structuration theory and empirical research was that they seemed to want 'detailed guidelines for research procedure'. He, on the contrary, felt that the concepts of structuration theory should only be seen as 'sensitising' devices for research purposes or as helping to 'provide an explication of the *logic* of research' (Giddens, 1990b, pp. 310–11, my emphasis; and 1989, p. 296). One could agree with Giddens on the first point about selectivity and parsimony whilst disagreeing with his preference for the abstract concepts of structuration to be used only as rather loose conceptual orientations rather than as ideas that should be closely integrated with issues of methodology and empirical research. This is a point I will return to frequently during the course of the book.

For a time Giddens retained an interest in defending structuration at the theoretical level, with aspects of the theory supported and upheld as part of lengthy replies appearing in influential collections devoted to the exposition and analysis of various aspects of his work by respected theorists and commentators in an array of relevant fields (see Held and Thompson, 1989; Clark *et al.*, 1990; Bryant and Jary, 1991). As late as 1993 in a preface to the second edition of *New Rules of Sociological Method*, originally published in 1976, Giddens also engaged directly with Nicos Mouzelis's criticisms of structuration. This could have heralded the beginning of a renewed interest in developing those parts of structuration that either hadn't stood the test of time or had never quite been adequately developed in the first place. But what might have looked like a new beginning in fact turned out to be more of an ending. In more recent times Giddens has shown little interest in defending the theoretical aspects of structuration against critics. Moreover, he has at times been quite negative about his previous association with structuration theory, comparing it on one public occasion to one of those youthful indiscretions that follow people around wherever they go in later life.[3] Of course, it would be unfair to read too much into an off-the-cuff remark, but what I think we can quite safely infer from such a comment is the absence of a profound continuing engagement with structuration.

Nobody, of course, can do everything, and it is quite understandable in some sense for Giddens to have left some of his earlier preoccupations aside as he has moved on to other things. He has after all left a valuable legacy behind him. On the other hand, I believe that the impression Giddens sometimes gives of dismissing structuration is a misjudgement. If one is tied up with other things, engaging with practical demands and writing about other more substantively oriented subjects one can well see the temptation, as structuration came under critical fire from some very heavy guns, to dismiss it as a youthful indiscretion. Yet, one can decline to immerse oneself personally in the challenge this time around whilst still acknowledging that there is indeed a challenge to be met and that the target of that challenge is something worth defending. To deny the latter is to do an injustice to the quality of conceptualisation and critique produced by the youthful (and, it should be said, by the not so youthful) Giddens, and also to the intrinsic power and value of structuration.

Structuration theory is certainly worth defending. Having said this, however, it remains at a crossroads nevertheless. In his original remit to the *Traditions in Social Theory* series to which this volume belongs my late and much missed friend and colleague Ian Craib asked authors to outline 'the distinctive contribution of (their) approach and its likely future value'. It is clear to me that for structuration theory, the latter half of this request is closely related to the first half. The likely future value of structuration theory will depend heavily on what its distinctive contribution can be said to be. It will also depend upon whether a framework can be produced that can integrate or defeat the various criticisms that have been aimed at structuration, and that can convince readers of its attractions as an explanatory and critical perspective of significant power.

The Distinctiveness of Structuration Theory

A characterising feature of structuration theory is that it goes beyond just looking at structures or just looking at agents, or of giving an *a priori* primacy to one or the other. It emphasises both. This is one of its characterising features but it is not, by itself, what makes structuration distinctive. Its distinction lies in the particular way that it conceptualises structures and agents. Firstly, it places phenomenology, hermeneutics and practices at the heart of the interrelationships and interdependencies between the two. These provide the hinge, if you like, between structure and agency. Secondly, it is not only that the hinge between external structures and agents is affected in large part by these things, for phenomenology, hermeneutics and practices are always also at the very heart of both structures and agents themselves. Social structures almost always either have agents within them and/or are the product of the past practices of agents. And agents, for their part, have social structures within them, not least in the guise of particular forms of phenomenological and hermeneutic inheritance. Social structures are not reified entities denuded of human beings and their irreducible qualities, just as the views and experiences that prompt the thoughts and actions of social agents are not those of beings who are islands unto themselves, secreted away from social currents. The phenomenology and hermeneutics of practices play an indispensable role in structuration's conception of social structures, just as social structures play an equal role in the understanding of the phenomenology, hermeneutics and practices of agents.

Giddens captured this emphasis in his conception of the 'duality of structure' which I will treat, along with Giddens and a range of commentators, as constituting the very core of structuration theory (Giddens, 1979, p. 5; 1984, p. 25; and see, for example, McLennan, 1984, p. 126; Sewell, 1992; pp. 12–13; Sydow and Windeler, 1997, p. 462). Giddens argued that structure enters into the constitution of the agent, and from here into the practices that this agent produces. Structure is thus a significant *medium* of the practices of agents. There is a complex and mediated connection between what is out-there in the social world and what is in-here in the phenomenology of the mind and body of the agent. Structure is also, however, the *outcome* of these practices of agents, whether one is talking about the knowledge produced by reading books, the reproduction of a living language through speech, the convening of a regional Parliament, the building of a house, or the institution of a national tax system. Giddens calls this notion a 'duality of structure' in order to indicate the dual role of structure as both medium and outcome. Taking a lead from McLennan (1984, p. 126), I would argue that it often makes things clearer to emphasise that both the moment of medium and the moment of outcome in fact contain 'a duality of structure-and-agency' (see p. 16). Either way it is presented, the notion of duality draws attention to structuration theory's distinctive focus on what I call a 'structural-hermeneutic' core in its characterisation and understanding of social processes, practices and relations.

Limits to Structuration Theory

Giddens himself sometimes underestimated the significance of the duality of structure for structuration theory. As I indicate in chapter 1 this was behind his overestimation of the appropriate and effective scope of the theory. In arguing for a 'strong' project of structuration I want to distinguish quite rigorously between theoretical approaches that pay little attention to duality's structural-hermeneutic core and structuration theory itself. Thus, for example, I will follow John B. Thompson and others in arguing that structuration's conceptualisation of structure as the medium and outcome of practices needs to be distinguished from more conventional notions of social structure (Thompson, 1989; Jary and Jary, 1995/1997). These more conventional notions of structure tend to eschew or radically minimise the role of phenomenology and hermeneutics. They typically use the term to refer to macro and meso clusters of institutional, group or systemic properties and practices; their distribution, inter-relations and tendencies. These are conceptualised at a greater or lesser level of abstraction or concretisation, and refer to a range of types of phenomena from entities as broad as 'the capitalist system' through class structures and structures of inequality, poverty, income and such like, to specific sets of functionally specialised institutions within the spheres of, for example, the family, education, the military, politics, culture or big business.

Whilst these conventional notions of structure are to be distinguished from structure as medium and outcome, they are still important to the structuration project. This is because, to use and deepen C. Wright Mills's invaluable rendering of the task of the sociological imagination, these conventional structures are able to act as framing devices that can help to situate the biographical experience of individuals and groups at the intersection of the forces of history and of social structure. Structuration theory itself is focused directly on the processes and practices involved at the point of this intersection. It is focused on the structural-hermeneutic nexus of immanent circumstances in which – now to paraphrase Marx, with an amendment from the structurationist geographer Allan Pred – people make history and produce places, not in circumstances of their own choosing, 'but in the context of already existing social and spatial structures which both enable and constrain the purposeful conduct of life' (Pred, 1990, p. 119). Giddens has noted that this Marxist theorem about praxis is 'simple to set out but extremely complicated to elaborate' (see Gregory, 1984/1997, p. 28). Taking up this challenge structuration theorists, and those engaged in debates around it, have fought, successfully in countless areas, to elaborate, refine and develop the basic insights of Marx's maxim. But it is essential to recognise not only the strengths of structuration theory but also its limits, and the way that it relies on other theories and approaches. Thus, framing structuration case studies of the immanent moments of circumstance and agency, of medium and making, in terms of wider, more conventional, macro and meso structures allows one, not least, to retain that invaluable sense of how these processes intersect with the greater forces and movements of history, geography and social structure. Structuration theory needs other theories and perspectives to provide such frames, just as other theoretical approaches would often do well to call on the resources of structuration.

Between large historical, spatial and social forces, on the one hand, and the situated practices of individual agents, on the other, it is useful to identify meso-level networks of relations and practices. It is about the causal significance of such networks that Pierre Bourdieu writes when he argues that television's coverage of current affairs displaces newsworthy events from the networks of social relations in which they are embedded, denuding them of any context in which they could be adequately comprehended. The 'litany of events' that we see on television are 'reduced to the level of the absurd . . . cut off from their antecedents and consequences' (Bourdieu, 1998, pp. 6–7). Without the framework afforded by such networks, argues Bourdieu, television news cannot:

> make events (say, an outbreak of violence in a high school) really understandable, that is, they cannot reinsert them in a network of relevant relationships (such as the family structure, which is tied to the job market, itself tied to governmental hiring policies, and so on) . . . This vision is at once dehistoricized and dehistoricizing, fragmented and fragmenting (Bourdieu, 1998, pp. 6–7).

Although this is specifically about the forms of knowledge offered by television, the same points could apply to all forms of social knowledge. These 'networks of relevant relationships' can be researched and investigated more or less 'conventionally', or more or less on the basis of the structural-hermeneutic diagnostics at the heart of structuration. Whether or not the latter strategy is necessary will depend upon the nature, depth and detail of the understanding required, and whether it is possible will depend on practical questions to do with the existence of relevant evidence and the exigencies of gaining access to it.

Ontology-in-General and Ontology-*in-Situ*

Giddens's own very particular orientation to structuration theory meant that he could not help much with a number of issues that are central to the way I have introduced the promise and the distinctiveness of the approach. His conception of structuration was pitched very much at the philosophical and abstract level. He failed to dwell sufficiently upon the distinction between the philosophical and the substantive levels, and upon the logical implications of the distinction. The absence of clear links to substantive circumstances meant that structuration theory was too free-floating. Depending upon where the emphasis was placed, structure or agency, it could be presented as either an overly voluntaristic theory – one that overestimates the knowledge and power of agents and their consequent ability to 'make a difference' – or an overly fatalistic and deterministic theory, where the structures make all the running. Giddens's treatment of the key concepts of structure and agency, and of other related concepts such as time and space, was overwhelmingly at the abstract and generalising levels. He was concerned with understanding what social structures and agents, for example, can be said to be at the abstract level. He wanted to know what their characteristics are, what sorts of things or entities they are, what features they have and what features they don't have. He developed his notions of them in abstract terms so that the conceptual definitions he settled for would encompass all structures and all agents, the very nature of time and space. In other words, he wanted to capture the general characteristics of these entities so that the concepts would be useful to the widest possible set of circumstances across times and places. They would be 'trans-situational'. The concepts he produced were 'ontological' concepts – concepts about the very nature of social entities over and beyond any particular empirical manifestation of them in specific social circumstances, time and place.

As I see it, a key advantage of the strong theory of structuration that forms the framework for this book, is its refusal to remain focused upon only the philosophical level, to the neglect of the conceptual and methodological links between the abstract and the particular. Instead, strong structuration is determined to develop bridging concepts between the philosophical and substantive levels of structuration, to develop not only what we might call 'ontology-in-general' but also 'ontology-*in-situ*', ontology directed at the 'ontic', at particular social processes and events in particular times and places. This commitment rests on the belief that structuration theory contains within it a deep mine of untapped potential at the empirical, substantive level, and that it is only by shifting focus that this potential can be exploited.

It is worth itemising in summary form, including some things that have already been mentioned and some that will be introduced more fully at a later stage, the claims that will be made in this book for the advances made by the synthesis of strong structuration over Giddens's version of structuration. I will argue that strong structuration possesses a superior grasp of:

• the implications of the centrality of the duality of structure to structuration
• the need to develop a greater sense of ontology-*in-situ* against an overly exclusive emphasis on ontology-in-general pitched at the philosophical and abstract level
• the many areas of ontology within the province of the duality of structure that have previously been inadequately developed and insufficiently specified.
• the importance of epistemology and methodology to the structuration project
• the scope of purpose and question-types appropriate to structuration theory
• the forms of methodological bracketing (agent's conduct and agent's context analysis) necessary to unlock the empirical potential of structuration theory;
• the need for structuration case studies to be framed and mediated by other approaches, something that follows naturally from the acknowledgement of the limits to structuration theory's scope.

Finally, strong structuration insists that attention to all these factors is required for the formulation of research strategies. The contents of such strategies would build on existing work to lay more systematic foundations for a fruitful and distinctive research paradigm necessary to consolidate structuration theory's position anew as an essential and invaluable part of the theoretical landscape.

Outline of Chapters

Chapter 1 reviews Giddens's seminal contribution to structuration theory. Particular attention is paid to what he himself felt he was trying to achieve and to the various theoretical influences on his writings. The most important concepts in his version of structuration are outlined and some of the strengths and weaknesses of his approach are indicated. There are, by now, several book-length secondary accounts either of Giddens's work as a whole or of his writings on structuration theory, and for more extensive treatments of those aspects that are broached only fleetingly here I would direct readers to one of these sources.[4] The focus of this chapter is on sifting through those aspects of Giddens's work that could be said to have made an enduring contribution to structuration theory as a distinctive tradition in social theory. Chapter 2, 'Critics of Structuration', looks in detail at, and assesses the arguments of, some of the most widely cited and powerful critics of Giddens's version of structuration. These include the fiercely critical account of Giddens in Margaret Archer's *Realist Social Theory*, and John B.Thompson's and Nicos Mouzelis's incisive but more discriminating assessments. The chapter also reviews and assesses the historian William J. Sewell's influential article from the *American Journal of Sociology* that sympathetically but critically attempted to revise structuration theory. Also included in the chapter are discussions of particular contributions made by Ira J. Cohen and Chris Shilling to the positive elaboration of underdeveloped areas in Giddens's work on structuration. Cohen's notion of 'position-practice relations' is outlined as a basis for giving definition and detail to the conceptual space indicated by Bourdieu's 'networks of relevant relationships', and to do so from a structurationist perspective.

Chapter 3 builds on the lessons drawn from the critics of structuration to conceptualise a more developed, refined and adequate ontology of structuration. The notion of a quadripartite cycle of structuration is introduced in order to elaborate upon and clarify the variety and nature of the elements involved in the 'duality of structure'.

The quadripartite cycle involves:

1. *external structures* as conditions of action;
2. *internal structures* within the agent;
3. *active agency*, including a range of aspects involved when agents draw upon internal structures in producing practical action ;
4. *outcomes* (as external and internal structures and as events).

The arguments for the strengths and advantages of the quadripartite framework are set out alongside a series of important and complementary concepts drawn from Mouzelis's *Back to Sociological Theory* (1991). The detailed elaboration of each of these four parts is carried out in dialogue with writers who have either criticised or applied structuration theory. The second part of the cycle is itself analytically divided into two types of internal structure. One of these, the *general-dispositional*, corresponds closely to Bourdieu's notion of habitus and to Mouzelis's notion of the dispositional. The emphasis here is on aspects of internal structure as media that can be used by the same agents across different situations. The other type, the *specific-conjunctural*, refers, instead, to agents' more specific knowledge of particular settings and contexts. The chapter ends with a look at the relations between specific *in-situ* agents and external structures. The emphasis here is on the contribution of such situated agents to wider structures and on the extent to which external structures can be said to exert independent causal power over situated agents.

The first part of chapter 4 draws out in detail the implications of the strong structuration ontology for various strategies of research and for the methodological steps within such strategies. This includes an explanation of 'methodological bracketing' and an account of the roles of *agent's context analysis* and *agent's/strategic conduct analysis* in strong structuration. The second part of the chapter looks at the kinds of 'framing' relationships that can exist between the wider macro and meso structures, on the one hand, and the particular focus of various structuration research strategies, on the other. Studies drawn on to illustrate the ways that such framing can help to position the experience of agents involved in structuration processes at the intersection of wider historical, spatial and social structures include:

- Michael Mann's analysis of the French Revolution in the second volume of *Sources of Social Power: The Rise of Classes and Nation-States 1760–1914* (1993);
- Richard Whittington's structuration account of managerial agency and social systems, originally published in the *Journal of Management Studies* (1992/1997);
- Eamonn Carrabine's account in *Theoretical Criminology* of the effects of changing and competing governmental regimes on micro-interactions in Manchester's Strangeways prison (2000);
- Joan Scott's post-structuralist feminist analysis of the discourses of the Parisian garment workers of 1848 from *Gender and the Politics of History* (1988);
- my own structuration informed analysis of the room for manoeuvre allowed by the international financial system for Harold Wilson's Labour Government of the 1960s (1988, 1990 and 1992).

Chapter 5, 'Two Empirical Case Studies', provides detailed and extended examples of structuration theory 'in action' in ways that embrace many of the different methodological steps outlined in chapter 4. This means, *a fortiori*, that they also involve, and therefore illustrate, aspects of each of the four parts of the quadripartite character of the duality of structure. In each case one can see how a developed structurationist ontology can shape empirical insights, and can also show the researcher what is missing from an account, can point to the limits of what she knows. The first, lengthier, case study, focuses on Ewa Morawska's magisterial *Insecure Prosperity: Small-Town*

Jews in Industrial America 1890–1940, a rich and detailed historical and sociological study, theoretically informed by structuration theory, of the emigration of East European Jews and their resettlement in Johnstown, Pennsylvania. The second case study involves a critical analysis of *A Doll's House*, the late nineteenth century play of Norwegian dramatist Henrik Ibsen, in terms of strong structuration. Whilst Morawska's study deals very much with routines and their relative durability, it is also about change, but this is slow change over years as the migrants gradually blend the socio-cultural patterns of life inherited from the old (Eastern European) country with the traditions and lifestyles of the dominant host society of the USA. Ibsen's play, by way of contrast, is much more about contingency, instability and the unsettling of routines. As such it brings different issues and emphases to the fore than the ones highlighted in the study of Johnstown's Jews.

The conclusion briefly summarises what the book hopes to have achieved in terms of outlining a stronger and more powerful framework of structuration theory. It also draws some lessons for intra-theoretical debate and co-operation, and suggests that the project of strong structuration outlined here is an open one, both corrigible and capable of being extended and elaborated in many directions. Finally, it offers some brief thoughts on the critical relationships that structuration theory can forge with key dimensions of the civic imagination, politics and ethics. From abstract ontological concepts through methodological steps and bracketings to issues of theorised empirical evidence, the account offered here only begins to scratch the surface of what structuration theory promises to those with a mind to take advantage of the resources it has to offer. It provides an array of 'structural-hermeneutic' tools and insights that, used skilfully in concordance with other theoretical approaches, make it possible to significantly increase the sophistication of the sociological imagination. It allows us to make meaningful and nuanced links between large historical, geographical and social forces, proximate networks of social relations and practices, and the sung and unsung phenomenological experiences, opportunities, perceived and actual constraints, sufferings, routines and triumphs of diversely situated human beings.

1

Giddens's Structuration Theory and its Influences

This chapter focuses on Anthony Giddens's seminal and enduringly valuable version of structuration. I start by outlining the main ideas and concepts of his approach, highlighting the pivotal role played by the hermeneutically informed 'duality of structure'. The strong version of structuration that will emerge in the course of the book takes as its most unequivocal point of reference the structural-hermeneutic concepts related to this term. I argue that Giddens's concepts often require further development and refinement, as well as supplementation by other concepts from other writers, sometimes, but not always, writing in response to his work. Nevertheless, it is this original set of structuration concepts and especially the conception of the duality of structure, that remains pivotal.

The extended account of these concepts will be informed by two particular kinds of orientation or preoccupation within Giddens's treatment of structuration. One of these is an ontological preoccupation, an emphasis on developing the various concepts that can articulate and delineate the most significant aspects of the nature of social entities and processes. These concepts, which I will describe at length below, stretch from structures to agents, from practical to discursive consciousness, from hermeneutics to power, from time and space to normative sanctions, from praxis to structuration, and embrace many more besides. The second, related, orientation – within which the ontological preoccupation is couched – involves the pitching of the concepts of structuration at an abstract, philosophical, level rather than at a more substantive, empirically directed one. Put simply Giddens's conception of structuration theory and its contribution to social thought is focused primarily upon issues of ontology at an abstract, philosophical, level of analysis. This translates as a preoccupation with what I will call 'ontology-in-general' rather than with the alternative, more substantive, possible focus of 'ontology-*in-situ*'. The latter, which I will place at the heart of strong structuration, doesn't neglect 'ontology-in-general', but is concerned with ontological concepts at this general level as a prelude to an equal concern with how such concepts can inform analysis directed towards specific processes involving structures and agents in particular, situated, contexts.

After outlining the key concepts of Giddens's structuration I will go on to investigate a little more directly the two preoccupations just outlined. I will note particularly how the orientation towards abstract ontology is accompanied by a relative, and self-conscious, neglect of epistemology and methodology. The relative lack of importance given to methodology follows logically from Giddens's lack of concern with ontology-*in-situ*. The result of all this taken together is that Giddens's view of the relationship between the ontological concepts of structuration theory and empirical research is excessively minimalist. Finally, I will argue that Giddens has to some extent presented the theory of structuration in a misleading way, allowing himself to be carried away with the thought that it is grander and more global than it really is. Consequently, he has extended its nominal remit into areas in which it cannot perform. I will argue that the majority of Giddens's broad-ranging substantive explorations of historical sociology, the institutional processes and contours of modernity, and of the trajectories and possibilities within the political spheres of late modernity, are not in fact, despite what Giddens himself suggests, studies that draw on structuration theory in any significant sense. Rather, they are best characterised as pluralistic and non-reductionist studies that do indeed draw from various ontological insights but ones that have little, if anything, to do with the structural-hermeneutic nexus at the heart of structuration. I will argue, thus, that the scope of structuration is much narrower than is suggested by Giddens. Nevertheless, I will also argue that, once settled within its narrower domain, structuration theory provides a much more powerful and incisive set of tools than it has been given credit for. Indeed, the global ambition encouraged by Giddens has had the negative effect of deflecting attention away from the real strengths of structuration, dissipating the energies of defenders of structuration to all points of the theoretical compass instead of allowing them to be concentrated in the territory most worth defending and most easily defended.

Ontological Concepts and the Duality of Structure

Giddens's approach to the ontological concepts of structuration theory, and to the inter-relations between them, can be easily grasped once it is seen in terms of his overarching aims. Giddens sets out to build a social theory, to build an approach to the causes, processes and movements of history and society, that avoids two pernicious misconceptions prevalent in social thought. These two traps from which social theorising needs to free itself are objectivism and subjectivism. The first, objectivism, places all the emphasis on impersonal forces and subject-less structures, in which agents, if they are considered at all, are no more than the playthings or puppets of reified social systems. The second, subjectivism, reduces the whole of social life to the actions of individual agents or groups, their actions, interactions, their goals, desires, interpretations and practices. Subjectivism uproots agents from their socio-structural context, treating them as deracinated, free-floating, individuals, whereas objectivism treats them so derisively that they sink without trace, conceptualised as if they lack the autonomy to cause even the slightest ripple of disturbance on a social surface determined wholly by powerful and impersonal systemic tides.

Giddens wanted to find a way of avoiding the voluntarism involved in subjectivism and the reification involved in objectivism. To do so he developed concepts by drawing from what he considered to be the best from the insights of both objectivist and subjectivist social theories. His strategy was to engage with particular theorists and their major theoretical statements, and to reveal both the worth and the one-sidedness of their contributions. Thus, whilst the legacies of classical nineteenth- and early twentieth century theorists such as Comte, Marx, Weber and Durkheim were drawn upon, they were drawn upon critically. Giddens took what he felt to be their key insights and contributions but reconceptualised them in a way that would avoid the misguided and outmoded nineteenth century commitments to various types of determinism, and to forms of naturalism such as functionalist and evolutionary thought drawn rigidly and over-literally from the natural sciences. The aspects that Giddens felt were worth keeping were integrated into structuration theory. *New Rules of Sociological Method*, for instance, published in 1976, engaged with various 'interpretative' schools of thought in philosophy and social theory in 'an exercise in clarification of logical issues' (Giddens, 1993/1976, p. viii). This 'clarification' was always driven by, and directed towards, Giddens's own project of theoretical reconstruction. In *New Rules* the aspects of this project of reconstruction that he had clearly in his sights were those concerning the issues of the conceptualisation of agents and agency, with a particular emphasis on the significance of self-reflection and of language as 'the practical medium' through which humans actively contributed to the ordering of social life. In *Central Problems in Social Theory*, published three years later, the same strategy was employed but this time in relation to structuralism, post-structuralism and functionalism. The engagement with structuralist traditions here enabled Giddens to develop and expand upon the conception of structure that he had introduced in chapter 3 of *New Rules* (1993/1976, see pp. 125–32), here importing terms from the tradition of post-structuralism to further develop the idea, explicated below, of structures as 'virtual', as in a certain sense existing 'out of time', a notion at the heart of structuration.

A collection of essays, *Studies in Social and Political Theory,* appearing in 1977 but containing essays written over a long period, contained major papers on functionalism, positivism and hermeneutics, developing structuration theory as a distinctive approach on the back of the same strategy of the 'logical clarification of conceptual issues' in the work of others, from Durkheim to Schutz, and from Merton to Habermas. *A Contemporary Critique of Historical Materialism,* published in 1981, expanded the interest in the subject of time that had appeared in *Central Problems,* giving it a much more central place in Giddens's approach. Structuration theory is much in evidence in this book but, to my mind, it is by now increasingly apparent that there is a significant tension between structuration and wider issues of historical sociology and societal and inter-societal systems writ large; a tension that was only noticeable – and this perhaps in retrospect – in the chapter on Historical Materialism in *Central Problems.* This is a tension that continues in the 1984 summation of Giddens's contribution to social thought, *The Constitution of Society,* in the second volume of *A Contemporary Critique* published in 1985 under the title, *The Nation-State and Violence* and in his later books on modernity and politics. I will say more in a subsequent section about the nature of this tension and its relationship to the strong project of structuration.

Giddens's mode of proceeding in these writings consisted of both negative and positive moments. The negative moment entailed a critique of theories that modelled themselves too closely on the natural sciences, ignoring the differences in the subject matter of the social sciences. Giddens stressed the centrality of human social activity and intersubjectivity to the subject-matter of the social sciences (for example, Giddens, 1993/1976, p. vii). As already noted, it also entailed a critique of theories that were too one-sided, that emphasised one aspect of social relations to the exclusion of other, equally important aspects. The positive moment entailed, firstly, a commitment to acknowledging the meaningful, normative, nature of social relations along-side the natural and material dimensions, and secondly, an attempt to combine many different aspects of social ontology into an approach that would recognise the contribution of each but not to the detriment of any of the others. Thus, whereas Marx and many Marxists were said to have often emphasised the economic over other aspects of social life, Weber to have emphasised power and especially administrative power, Durkheim and Parsons to have emphasised the normative dimension and the internalisation of values, Giddens wanted to keep open a place for all of these in his ontology. And also, whereas structuralists and post-structuralists – from Saussure through Barthes and Derrida – were said to have emphasised the importance of language systems over other determinants of social life and practices, and interpretivists and ordinary language philosophers – from philosophers such as Winch and Austin, to phenomenologists, symbolic interactionists and ethnomethodologists – to have emphasised hermeneutics, shared understandings, and/or ordinary language over all else, Giddens wanted to combine their emphases with an equal emphasis on the institutional, material and power dimensions of social life. He also wanted to bring in from other disciplines novel aspects of ontology that he felt had been neglected by social theorists working in the domains that most interested him. Thus, for example, he enlisted the aid of geographers, historians and philosophers in bringing notions of time and space into the central heartlands of social theory.

Giddens described his task of building a repository of ontological concepts as one which subsequently enabled him to fire conceptual salvoes into social reality (Giddens in Gregory, 1984/1997, p. 24). It was within this framework that the idea of the duality of structure emerged as the most fundamental conceptual building block for the theory of structuration (see introduction, pp. 4–5). Giddens defines the duality of structure in terms of:

> the essential recursiveness of social life, as constituted in social practices: structure is *both medium and outcome* of the reproduction of practices. Structure enters simultaneously into the constitution of the agent and social practices, and 'exists' in the generating moments of this constitution (Giddens, 1979: 5, my emphasis).

Structures serve as the 'medium' of action as they provide, through memory, the bases upon which agents draw when they engage in social practices. As Gregor McLennan has observed, it would perhaps be more appropriate to speak of this moment in the structuration process as a 'duality of structure and agency' as both are involved when agents draw on structures as 'medium' (McLennan, 1984, p. 126). Meaningful and ordered social action would be impossible without this 'medium'. Structures are also the 'outcome' of these actions. Giddens doesn't make the distinction but there are two dimensions to such outcomes. The first is that the surface patterns of social practices in various areas of social life are the outcomes of agents drawing on structures in order to produce these practices. The second is that these interactional patterns and the hermeneutics of their production also have consequences – phenomenologically mediated – for the structures *within* agents at the beginning of the next cycle of structuration.

Giddens's Conception of Structures and their Role in Social Practices

To overcome subjectivism and objectivism Giddens thus focuses on 'duality' and in the process combines the subjective and the objective *within* his basic conceptualisation of structure, and also *within* his conception of the agent. There are a number of dimensions to his conceptualisation of structures and their role, and I will say more about other dimensions below, but there are some that are pertinent at this point. Thus, Giddens sees agents not only as always rooted in a structural context, but also as always and inevitably drawing upon their knowledge of that structural context when they engage in any sort of purposeful action. He also argues that agent's 'capabilities' will be drawn in large part from their ability to harness aspects of structures to their projects (1979, pp. 88–94). The possibility of agents actually being able to draw on such potential capabilities will rest, at least in part, on the agent's perception and understanding of their availability and inherent potential. Giddens analytically divides these structures-within-knowledgeability into three different types: the structures of domination [power], signification [meaning] and legitimation [norms] (for example, Giddens, 1979, p. 82). These structures involve phenomenologically inflected 'stocks of knowledge' about the external context and conditions of action. This is knowledgeability about the distributions and configurations of power, meaning and norms within the terrain of action. Giddens notes that this is only an analytical distinction and that all three dimensions would inevitably be involved in any social action. The analytical distinction allows one to focus on any one of the structures independently, and also, in principle, to examine the particular ways in which they are combined. Giddens also uses the term 'resources' to refer to the structure of domination, within which he includes both control over economic, or allocative, power resources and control over people or authoritative resources. He uses another term, that of 'rules', as shorthand to refer to the structures of both signification and legitimation. Thus, he often refers to agents drawing upon rules and resources.

Giddens also makes a distinction between, on the one hand, the structures of domination, legitimation and signification themselves, existing as knowledgeability in memory traces, and, on the other hand, what he calls 'modalities', the ways in which agents in particular circumstances can draw on or employ these structures as rules and resources in interaction (see figure 1.1). Thus, he distinguishes, for example, between the overall structure of domination that is potentially available within the memory traces of individuals and then the more limited and task-specific 'facilities' on which

INTERACTION	communication	power	sanction
(MODALITY)	interpretive scheme	facility	norm
STRUCTURE	signification	domination	legitimation

Figure 1.1 Structures as employed in social practices

Source: A. Giddens, 1979, *Central Problems in Social Theory*, London, Macmillan, p. 82.

these agents subsequently draw, on the basis of the prior availability, when they engage in a definite interaction.

It is worth mentioning, in passing, that there is a certain lack of analytical clarity here with respect to two issues. The first regards the relation between 'structures as memory traces' and 'structures as resources'. Giddens seems to be unsure himself about what he wants to say on this point. On the one hand, he sometimes appears to include certain material elements of context and capability in the notion of structure as resources. Thus, in *Central Problems* he writes of resources as the 'material levers' of all transformations of empirical contents (1979, p. 104). But at other times, as in the definition he gives to structure in *The Constitution of Society*, he sees structure as resources as existing only as memory traces and as instantiated in action (1984, p. 377). The latter definition logically rules out structures as resources having any prior material content, a conclusion that Giddens would be hard put to defend as consistent with many of the points he makes about power and transformative capacity.[1] It is the first, earlier, definition that is ultimately more coherent. Thus, whilst noting the ambiguity in Giddens's writings I will, for the rest of the argument of this book, work with the assumption that 'structure as resources' has both phenomenological and material dimensions. I will return to this issue in the next chapter.

There is also a lack of clarity about where one should draw the boundaries between the agent and the structures that are available to be drawn upon by the agent.[2] If these structures are to be seen as being in one way or another *within* the agent, either as memory traces or capability then one needs to be clear, for example, whether or not any particular material resources beyond the human body itself should be said to be either 'part of' or 'belonging to' a particular agent. Should, for example, material objects employed by an agent in the performance of an action – from tokens of exchange through clothes and weapons to technologically sophisticated means of transportation or communication – be thought of as part of the agent's embodied capability informed by the hermeneutic structures within that 'body', or should they be thought of as material things external to the agent?[3] This would need clarification before we could ascertain which material resources should be seen as internal to the agent and which as external to the agent but as available to be drawn upon as part of the external structure of domination. The difference is highly significant as it is the difference between power being in the hands of one's own agency and it being dependent upon the compliance of others.

In a further distinction, related to figure 1.1, of the different stages of the process by which agents draw on structures – a distinction to add to those of structures *per se* and the modalities by which they are drawn upon – Giddens refers to the moment of the practice or interaction itself. In the case of the 'structure of domination', in which 'facilities' are used as the modality, the interaction itself is said to be an exercise of 'power'. The sequence is that agents draw on the structures within them in the form of specific facilities through which they exercise power at the surface interactional level. Similar distinctions are made for the other two structures, so that specific 'interpretative schemes' are used to 'communicate' meaning in interaction on the basis of the signification structures, whilst specific norms of action (conformist or transgressive) are employed against the background knowledge of the prevailing situational norms provided by the structure of legitimation. The individual's preferred norms are drawn upon against a knowledge of the wider legitimation structures, which indicate what is and isn't the appropriate thing to do, and their resultant practices produce negative sanctions or rewards at the level of interaction. Issues of power and communication will also clearly be involved in the determination of whether negative sanctions or positive rewards ensue from the individual's (or the group's) norm-related practices. The distinction, to repeat, is only an analytical one.

Giddens places great emphasis on the fact that when interacting agents draw from particular aspects of the wider structures of domination, legitimation and signification by means of the various modalities, they are at one and the same time engaged in the process by which whole social systems are reproduced. This link between the praxis of variously situated agents and the reproduction of the larger societal structures is essential to his generalised perception of society as being characterised by what we might call 'structured-praxis'. Social relations are conceptualised as being draped from head to toe in praxis, a praxis that is structured and patterned whilst it also – starting from these conditions not of its own choosing – itself structures and patterns subsequent practices. Giddens explains this relationship between individual actions and the wider structures – mediated by structures as the medium of action – by reference to Saussure's discussion of the production of an utterance. Giddens writes:

> When I utter a sentence I draw upon various syntactical rules (sedimented in my practical consciousness of the language) in order to do so. These structural features of the language are the medium whereby I generate the utterance. But in producing a syntactically correct utterance I simultaneously contribute to the reproduction of the language as a whole ...The importance of this relation between moment and totality for social theory can hardly be exaggerated, involving as it does a dialectic of presence and absence which ties the most minor or trivial forms of social action to structural properties of the overall society, and to the coalescence of institutions over long stretches of historical time (Giddens, 1982, p. 37; cf. Giddens, 1979, p. 114).

The three levels of conceptualisation used by Giddens in explaining what is involved when agents draw on structures are extremely useful in that there is often good reason to distinguish between these different moments. Some aspects of this will become more apparent when I discuss what Giddens means when he labels his novel conception of structure as a 'virtual' conception. Having said that distinguishing between the levels is useful, I find the precise terminology that Giddens uses here to be somewhat cumbersome and unduly restrictive, and I will not adhere to the letter of it in subsequent chapters. This is because, for the purposes of both clarity and fluency, it often makes sense to swap the terms around and so to talk, for example, of power, meaning or normative structures, and of drawing on power resources rather than always having to insert 'facilities'. The context will usually make it clear which moment of the sequence one is referring to, and when it doesn't this can be spelled out.

The Structuration Process and the Limitations of Analogies

In pursuing their purposes and goals, drawing on structures within interaction, we have seen that agents also help to either reproduce or change the structural context that allowed them to act in the first place. Thus, agents in structural contexts draw on these structures within the context in order to act, and these actions, in turn, work not only to satisfy, more or less, their own wants and desires, they also reproduce or change the structural context. In other words, agents draw on structures to produce actions that change or reproduce structures. This is the cycle of structuration. It is what is meant by the term 'structuration'. Neither structures nor agents are given primacy. Both require the other. It is not one or the other but both that are involved in social processes. More than this, however, Giddens wants to say that even when one has accepted that both structure and agents are involved in the causal process, it is still important to be wary of seeing the sequence in terms of a discrete structural moment being succeeded by a discrete and entirely separate moment of agency, which is then succeeded by another discrete moment of structure, and so on. Giddens believes that this is what is wrong with those ideas of social structure that envisage its role in causal processes in terms of a model of the skeleton of a body or the walls of a building. Such models, splitting anatomy from physiology, splitting the bricks and mortar from the flesh and blood human activities that are carried on within them, are very misleading analogies to use as a guide for thinking about the relations between social structures and social agents at the philosophical, abstract, level of ontology-in-general.

It is certainly the case that those analogies are misleading if they are used in an exclusive, all-encompassing manner. As analogies meant to convey part of the human and social condition they are fine, for it is quite true that some kinds of social and material constraints analogous to the walls of a building can be found to exist for most situated agents in most places and in most times. If it is used as an exclusive analogy, however, it fails, because it is at least equally the case that conceptions of the things that are 'out-there' in social relations also enter 'in-here' within the agent, informing what she does and how. Conceptualising the latter is, in fact, essential to being able to understand when and why a situated agent experiences something as a constraint, for this will depend upon their hermeneutic mediation of the 'walls'. If she is happy to live within them, happy that they keep her metaphorically safe, warm and dry then she will not perceive them as constraints. She will, at one and the same time, perceive them in-here as enabling and also as having an external existence that is separate from her, like the walls of a building. It should be remembered, also, that those metaphorical social 'walls' will be partly made up of people, people who will themselves also have hermeneutically mediated perceptions of the walls as they appear to *them*.

Given his aims of overcoming the twin excesses of objectivism and subjectivism at the level of ontology-in-general, Giddens believes that the sole reliance on mechanistic, inanimate, analogies results in each of the two parts of structure and agency being treated too exclusively. There is too much of a *dualism*. Giddens wants to argue that the mutual affecting, the intermingling, shouldn't be left out of the equation. For, as we have seen, in the very process of acting agents draw on social structures that have entered into their understandings of, *inter alia*, socially legitimate and illegitimate actions, distributions of power and potential sanctions. They draw on their knowledge of social structures as they produce the social practices whose purpose is to realise their variously motivated wants and desires. The structures, in this sense, must first enter into the agents before they can be drawn upon. Agents have structures within them. Equally, the structures – the perceived configurations of legitimate and illegitimate actions, conventionally accepted meanings, and distributions of economic and authoritative power – are seen both to have agents within them and to be the product of agents. The configurations of norms, the conventional significations and the possessions of power that are perceived by agents exist only because of the involvement of agents in producing them and continuing to produce them. Structures and agents intermingle, structures are within agents and agents continually help to constitute structures. There is a *duality* at work in which agents and structures are not kept apart but in which they are mutually constitutive of one another.

Structures as Virtual

Giddens's distinctive conception of structure is derived 'transcendentally' in the following sense. He begins from something in the social world that can reasonably and without controversy be agreed to exist. He then works backwards to ask what other things must also exist as preconditions for this something whose existence is uncontroversial. The latter, in Giddens's case, is simply the fact that people engage in actions and interactions. His notion of structure attempts to capture the key social dimensions of the 'capabilities' that agents must possess given that they engage as they do in social actions and interactions. He argues that regarding structure as a 'virtual order' of differences implies recognising:

- the existence of agents' knowledge of 'how to go on' in social relations
- their possession of the capabilities required to so 'go on'
- the recursive mobilisation of both knowledge and capabilities in the production of social practices and organisation (Giddens, 1979, pp. 64–8).

Structure, in Giddens's sense, thus exists 'virtually' in the form of: (i) the knowledgeability that is based on memory traces (Giddens, 1979, p. 64; 1984, p. 377); and (ii) the material or physical conditions or levers (such as a relatively functioning body, a kitchen, gas hobs, a pan and utensils, garlic, onions, chillies, tomatoes, lime and some beans, soaked overnight) required as 'capability' preconditions for that action (cooking a meal) or interaction (subsequently eating that meal with friends) (Giddens, 1979, p. 104). Structure in the first sense must be 'internal' to agents, even if the objects of knowledge are external, whereas structure in the second sense may be internal, as in the body, or external, as in the gas hob and the garlic, although in the second case the designation of internal or external will, as mentioned earlier, depend partly upon how one decides to define the boundaries of the agent in a particular case.

I should say in parenthesis here that the term 'virtual' has caused more trouble than clarity for structuration and that it is the concepts it denotes rather than the term itself that are important for structuration theory. This having been said, the 'virtual' qualities of the two dimensions of structure are clearly different in that one exists in memory traces whereas the other exists only in inanimate material form (the body itself presumably occupying a position that somehow combines the two, but this is left unremarked by Giddens). What they have in common is that they represent latent capabilities that remain just that, latent capabilities, until they are drawn upon by agents for whom they become temporarily relevant as they engage in a particular activity. They are drawn on, and thus transported from the condition of latency or virtuality to that of the manifest or the actual as, to use Schutz's term, the agent makes practical use of them as they appear to her within the particular 'horizon of relevance' thrown up by a specific activity (Schutz, 1962, pp. 11–12; 1970; Heritage, 1984, pp. 51–61; Crossley, 1996, pp. 83–4).

Structure exists 'virtually' in one further, related, sense. It is virtual in this sense at the very same time that it also has a manifest existence. For once an agent has acted, has drawn both on her knowledgeability and on the material levers of action in order to act, then the structures now not only exist as the capabilities they were, but also they exist in a more specific sense as the prior conditions that made this particular action or interaction possible. They could be said to exist instead of the prior conditions, in the case of – to take one kind from a number of possible examples – the handing over of the material embodiment of five dollars, where the structural capability that existed before the handing over has now been relinquished. In part they have an actual or manifest existence because they are there in the words chosen, the energy expended, the movements made, the performance produced, in all the ideational and 'material levers' involved in the actions, in what Giddens calls the 'instantiation' of structures in action. They are only there partially, however, because when structures are employed as means of informing and guiding agents to 'go on' in the right sort of way, much of their input is not laid out in time and space like china and silver across a dining table or strides across a drawing room floor. For example, the successful use of courteous words and courteous behaviour towards others in interaction depends not only upon the immediate 'work' manifested in the 'doing' of an interactional performance but also upon the precondition of having knowledge and understanding of many things – to do with such conditions as what is appropriate at this social moment in this room with these people, and why that would not be appropriate in the same room at another moment with the same group of people, or in the next room with the same or another group, and so on – that won't be visible in the actual production of a courteous performance.

This notion of structures as virtual is not as exotic as it seems to have appeared to many. The 'absent' facilitating capacities and knowledge involved in such interactional performances are presupposed by much of what Schutz says about typifications, by what Goffman says about situational proprieties and by what Garfinkel says about accountability (see Schutz, 1962, 1970; Goffman, 1963, pp. 23–4; Manning, 1992, pp. 79–82; Garfinkel, 1967, pp. 1–34). They can also be said to be part of what Bourdieu talks about as habitus, with the added advantage here that Bourdieu pays greater attention to the nature of the particular social fields in which such capacities were originally nurtured and nourished. These leave their traces in the form of the transposable dispositions embedded and embodied within an agent as a matrix of perceptual and linguistic schemas, competencies, appreciations, typifications, morals, sentiments, know-how and so on (see Bourdieu, 1972/ 1977, pp. 82–3; 1980/1990, pp. 52–65; Crossley, 2002, pp. 171–8). Many of these capacities are 'transposable' in the sense that they are adaptable and adjustable to the various social conditions in which they are called upon by the agent. On the other hand, the adaptability is limited precisely because the conditionings and exercises from the past have already predisposed the agent to do certain things as 'second nature', with ease, and without pause for reflection (see Bourdieu, 1980/1990, pp. 56–7; 1999, pp. 340). In the terms of post-structuralism all these capacities and forms of embedded knowledge exist in the background as *paradigmatic* sets of capabilities ready to be drawn upon by agents involved in particular activities. The part played by these structures in the production of an interaction remains in large part a virtual one, invaluable and necessary to the production of the action but not manifest within it. This is what Giddens means when he writes that: '[S]tructures exist paradigmatically, as an absent set of differences, temporally 'present' only in their instantiation, in the constituting moments of social systems' (Giddens, 1979, p. 64).

Time, Space and the Stratification Model of the Agent

Central to the mediation of structures, to their use as the 'medium' of the production and reproduction of practices, is Giddens's stratification model of the agent (see below, figure 1.2). This model has been implicit in much of the discussion so far but it is worth making it explicit and linking it to some of the notions of time and space central to Giddens's thinking. There are three dimensions to Giddens's conception of the agent:

- motivation of action;
- knowledgeability and the rationalisation of action; and
- the reflexive monitoring of action (see Giddens, 1984, p. 5).

I will look at each of these in turn. The dimension represented at the foot of figure 1.2 is that of motivation which involves the wants or desires of the agent that give them the impetus to engage in practices. This motivation may be direct, intense and purposeful, or indirect and much more routine, as in the difference between an earnest and focused attempt to impress in a maiden speech in Parliament and the walk up the stairs and along the corridor for the start of just another day in the Ministry. The motivation may be straightforward and clear or more opaque and complex; and, a related point, it may also be conscious or unconscious, or a combination of the two (Giddens, 1979, p. 58). Giddens harnesses his version of structuration to particular versions of psychoanalysis, drawing especially on the notion of ontological security first coined by R. D. Laing (1960), on Freud's psychology of critical situations, and on Eric Erikson's (1977) version of ego-psychology (see Giddens, 1979, pp. 120–8; 1984, pp. 51–64).

Ian Craib has provided what seems to me to be a powerful critique of Giddens's use of these sources, arguing that he presents an overly simplified notion of the personality. There is a misleading picture, for example, of ontological security as synonymous with 'feeling safe'. This ignores the point that in Laing's work and more widely in psychoanalysis it refers to the inner ability of a personality to deal with threats, anxiety, ambivalence, and so on, whether in situations of the familiar routines that Giddens emphasises or in times of rapid and turbulent change. Craib calls for a more complex and

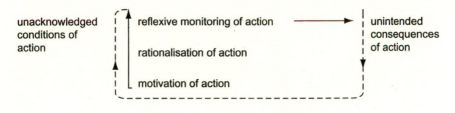

Figure 1.2   Giddens's stratification model of the agent and action

Source: A. Giddens, 1984, *The Constitution of Society*, London, Macmillan, p. 5.

dynamic notion of the personality, more autonomous, much less reducible to the impact of social forces, and with more emphasis on the processes and mechanisms of integration and of the inevitable, important and disappointing failures of integration (Craib, 1992, pp. 24–5, 37–40 and 171–77; 1994, pp. 112–32; see also Loyal, 2003, pp. 60–2 and 68). There is something more important, however, than agreement or disagreement with Craib's specific criticisms of Giddens's use of psychoanalysis. This is to accept that whilst it is vital that structuration provides a conceptual space for the unconscious within its model of the agent, the particular form and content of how that space is then filled out need not be determined once and for all. I would argue that the core, most distinctive, hermeneutic-structural features of the structuration approach need not be tied *a priori* to any one version of psychoanalysis, and that to accept a degree of openness and debate in this area is the most constructive and potentially fruitful position for structuration to adopt.

The rationalisation of action, the second element of figure 1.2, is a link between the agent and the structures employed as the medium of a particular action. It refers to the process by which the agent draws on her knowledgeability of the social structures we have discussed above. This includes what Giddens refers to as 'the technical grounding or empirical content of the knowledge of the social and material context that is applied as "means" in purposive acts to secure particular outcomes' (Giddens, 1976/1993, p. 90). Knowledgeability and its quality are central to the structuration process. It is also closely related to the issue of unacknowledged conditions of action and unintended consequences of action. On one level, and leaving aside the various necessary caveats, it is important to agents, from political decision makers to gamblers at the races, that the more adequate their knowledgeability of context – that is, the fewer the relevant conditions of action that have gone unacknowledged – then the less likely they are to engage in actions that may lead to unintended consequences. On another level, however, it may matter little to agents about to get married or on the verge of suicide that they will also contribute their bit, unintentionally, to the reproduction of the heterosexual character of the family on the macro societal level or to an upturn in the annual national statistics for suicide.

The rationalisation of action thus involves degrees of knowledgeability, with various implications for immediate outcomes and the reproduction of the wider social structure, but it also embraces a further significant dimension. This is a tacit, or more explicit, sense of the interweaving and interlocking of different purposes and projects so that something like a 'hierarchy of purposes', more or less coherent and consistent, will characterise an agent's approach to the range of pursuits she is involved in (see Giddens, 1993/1976, pp. 84 and 90–1). This means that not only does an agent engaged in a particular action draw on the three different types of structures when she orients herself to an immediate context of action, it means that she must also keep in mind her other projects, their likely contexts, and what is likely to be required to fulfil them.

Thus, as she manages, more or less well, to ground her actions in an adequate knowledge of the structural context, the agent will typically be doing this whilst engaged in 'multiple roles', or what in Robert Merton's more careful categorisation are known as 'status-sets'. Merton points out that it is not uncommon for each of the various statuses in which people find themselves to be in different institutional spheres – 'for example, one person might have the diverse statuses of physician, husband, father, professor, church elder, Conservative Party member and army captain' (Merton, 1967, p. 42; cf. 1957b, pp. 368–9). The stances taken up with respect to each of the different status positions will have to be integrated with each other as the person goes about his or her life. In addition to this, each of these individual statuses will often have a whole cluster of role-prescriptions (more or less well defined, more or less contested) attached to them. In Merton's terms these are 'role-sets' and taking the position of school teacher as an example he notes that this 'relates the teacher not only to the correlative status, pupil, but also to colleagues, the school principal and superintendent, the Board of Education, professional associations and, in the United States, local patriotic organisations' (Merton, 1967, p. 42; see Giddens, 1979, pp. 118–19). The agent's rationalisation of action is seen to be no easy thing, and seems to confirm Giddens's insistence, following Garfinkel, that social practices are not the product of 'cultural dopes' but are the skilled accomplishments of knowledgeable agents.

The way in which agents draw on their various structural contexts and more or less successfully order and integrate their various practices into more, less and equally important concerns is monitored reflexively by the agent (the topmost element of figure 1.2). Such monitoring is usually tacit and taken for granted and is connected by Giddens, firstly, to ethnomethodology's emphasis on the intrinsic sense of accountability that agents bring to their ongoing actions, such that the stock of knowledge they draw on when they give accounts of why they did something is the same knowledge they drew upon when they engaged in the practices in the first place. He also connects agents' monitoring to Heidegger's insistence on the irreducibly temporal character of human existence. Being is said to necessarily involve 'movement between', in which agents are 'thrown' into a ceaseless flow of temporality in which present practices are reaching out to, and opening up, the conditions and memories produced by past practices during the same flow as they are reaching out to, and opening up, future outcomes (Giddens, 1981, pp. 29–34; also see Urry, 1991, pp. 161–2). Human beings are able to, and are condemned to, 'transcend the immediacy of sensory experience through both individual and collective forms of memory; through an immensely complex interpenetration of presence and absence ' (Urry, 1991, p. 162), and Giddens's emphasis on the importance of memory traces as the locus of structures should be seen in this context. In more prosaic terms Giddens writes that:

> (o)ne's life activity does not consist of strung-out series of discrete purposes and projects, but of a continuing stream of purposive activity in interaction with others and with the world of nature: a 'purposive act' . . . is only grasped reflexively by the actor, or isolated conceptually by another agent (Giddens, 1993/1976, p. 89).

Giddens also draws on Hägerstrand's (1975, 1976) time-geography to emphasise that the flows of action through time, phenomenologically linked to much that is absent as well as to what is present, will necessarily be affected both by the embodied nature of agents and by their being situated in particular physical contexts (Giddens, 1981, pp. 37–41; 1984, pp. 110ff; Urry, 1991, pp. 161–6). In Giddens's hands such factors can be both enabling and constraining depending upon circumstances and upon what the agent wants to do. The types of determinants involved here include:

- the movement of the body across time towards death, bounded by the life span;
- the indivisibility and corporeality of the body;
- time as a scarce resource;
- the limited capability of human beings to participate in more than one task at once or to be in more than one place at one time;
- the fact that movement in space is also movement in time;
- the limited 'packing capacity of time-space' such that no two human bodies or physical objects can occupy the same space at the same time (Giddens, 1984, pp. 111–12).

All of these things can impose 'capability constraints' on agents, including the need for regular sleep or food, and 'coupling constraints' as regards the activities that can be undertaken with others. One can see how these emphases would cross-cut the three analytically distinct kinds of social structures involved in the duality of structure. The structures within agents will be more or less inflected with time-space considerations, and this will affect the degree to which the actual conditions of action are acknowledged or unacknowledged, just as it will also affect the ways in which structures are drawn upon as a medium of action. The temporal and spatial exigencies of the external structures will also clearly make some projects more feasible than others.

Giddens also either incorporates or develops a number of spatial categories that serve similar functions when thought of in relation to the duality of structure:

- *locales* that provide the immediate setting for interactions;
- the *regionalisation* of such settings as distinct zones, perhaps for different activities as with the different rooms of a house;
- issues concerning the *presence availability* of other actors;
- the notion of time-space distanciation that draws attention to the ways that social activity increasingly involves interactions with those who are physically absent (Giddens, 1984, ch. 3).

A phenomenon related to the latter is 'time-space convergence', the shrinking of distance in terms of the time needed to move between, or to communicate between, different locations. Giddens compares, amongst other things, the four months it would have taken by stagecoach or wagon to travel from the East Coast to the West Coast of the United States with the four days by rail in 1910, and with the five hours it would take today by regular air services (Giddens, 1984, p. 114).

Giddens's notion of *practical consciousness* should be seen in the light of these observations on tacit knowledge and temporal flow. For practical consciousness refers to the knowledgeability that an agent brings to the task of 'going on' in everyday life, a practical type of knowledge that is usually so taken for granted that it is hardly noticed, if at all, by the person exercising it (Giddens, 1979, pp. 24–55, 57–8; 1984, p. xxiii). It is what Heidegger called 'ready to hand' knowledge, the kind of knowledge that one only notices when something goes wrong, when what usually works doesn't, for some reason, work this time, as when a carpenter hits her hand and not the nail with her hammer or when someone has moved the pedal bin to the other side of the kitchen. For Giddens, as for Bourdieu, this kind of practical consciousness is the most important, and the most prevalent form of social knowledge. Giddens distinguishes this from what he calls *discursive consciousness*, which denotes the ability of agents to give verbal expression to their knowledge about the social conditions of their action and the way that they 'go on' within these conditions. Whereas with the unconscious there is a bar of repression that prevents its articulation, the boundaries between practical and discursive consciousness is potentially more fluid and shifting. On the other hand, there is a relation of tension between the two in that the stocks of knowledge that agents draw on in their production of everyday practices is 'usually not known to actors in an explicitly codified form ... [t]he accounts actors are able to provide of their reasons are bounded, or subject to various degrees of possible articulation, in respect of tacitly employed mutual knowledge' (Giddens, 1979, pp. 57–8). Both practical and discursive consciousness, together with considerations of power, are closely related to Giddens's insistence that agents, to be agents, should always be able to 'act otherwise', 'to intervene in the world or to refrain from such intervention, with the effect of influencing a specific process or state of affairs' (Giddens, 1984, p. 14). This ability is, in Giddens's view, possessed by virtually all human subjects, even those in the most oppressive circumstances. This is because of what he calls the 'dialectic of control' by which there are relations of autonomy and dependence built into all social relations beyond those based purely on physical coercion. Given this, it is always possible, in situations beyond the latter category, to 'say no', to refuse to comply, and so to make a difference.

Agents' Hermeneutic Frames of Meaning: An Illustration from the British Textile Industry

At this juncture it needs to be stressed that structuration's hermeneutic and phenomenological emphasis means that it would be difficult to over-emphasise the point that all these different aspects of agents and agency should be seen as suffused and informed by an agent's hermeneutic frame of meaning. Thus, for example, when Giddens talks of the 'technical grounding' or empirical content of an agent's knowledgeability, this needs to be understood as already embedded within a particular phenomenological world-view, a way of looking at things that is culturally, socially and biographically specific to that group or person. Some sense of this can be gained from an all too brief summary of some relevant points about competing frames of meaning taken from a case study of a major company within the British wool-textile industry conducted by Tony Spybey and directly informed by Giddens's structuration theory (Spybey, 1984/1997)[4]. The study brings out well the part played by, and the central significance of, hermeneutic frames of meaning in the structuration process. At the onset of the study in the late 1970s the various activities of the organisation were based in relatively small units of manufacture located mainly in West Yorkshire but also in parts of the West of England and of Scotland. The enterprise had been employing up to 15,000 people, achieving an annual turnover of almost £100 million (Spybey, 1984/1997, pp. 550–1). The workforce contained 'a high proportion of women and of immigrants and a certain resistance to change' (p. 551), there was marked deference from the workforce and paternalistic attitudes among management. Spybey used extensive, and repeated, open-ended interviewing and observation involving a 50% sample of the thirty mill-managers in the group over a three-year period. In the course of the research a number of issues emerged that were common to all of the respondents but it became apparent that there 'were two major and quite distinctive sets of values, beliefs, norms, techniques and so on to which managers orientated and contributed' (p. 553).

Spybey defined the two groups in terms of these different frames of meaning, labelling one group the 'traditionals' and the other the 'professionals'. Of the fifteen mill-managers participating in the study, nine could be identified as traditionals and six as professionals. The two groups shared the same broad external working context – which would have provided the external basis for the structures existing in their memory traces and being drawn upon as means in any interaction – and gave similar degrees of significance to the same aspects of that context. These aspects included the ownership and control of the organisation by two brothers who held 64% of £27 million capital, the form, organisation, modes of decision-making and degrees of managerial autonomy within the group, relationships between manufacturing units, levels and types of skill, the economic recession and the future of the industry (p. 553). The *ways* in which the two groups perceived all of these aspects, however, were deeply inflected by their distinct frames of meaning. The traditionals are said by Spybey to have been the embodiment of past traditions within the present; 'wool-men' of the industry who had emerged as trusted hands selected from the rank and file for their ability to lead and organise, men without training in management *per se*, men who had 'derived their frame of meaning extensively from the work community as an integral part of the traditions of the industry' (p. 551). The brothers' attitudes to the organisation and its members were 'autocratic, paternalistic and unchanging' and the preservation of traditional patterns had nurtured among the traditional mill managers a strong, personal identification with the workforce, the craft-orientated traditions of the industry, and the distinct and unique qualities of the product itself. The managers regarded themselves as specialists in the design and manufacture of a high quality product; and they were heavily committed to what, Spybey notes, Claus Offe (1970) has called a 'task-continuous status organization', derived from the guild system, in which the controller and the controlled share common experience of the production process (Spybey, 1984, p. 552). The managers operated in a cellular structure and enjoyed a great deal of autonomy in the day-to-day running of the mills, with centralised reporting and flows of information being kept to a minimum. They liked these arrangements and felt that they worked in favour of their long-term interests (p. 552).

The 'professionals', by way of contrast, were mostly younger and had come into the organisation from a different background in terms of experience and training. This meant that they:

> derived their frame of meaning from different sources. Investigation showed that they had either formal management training or else experience in a different type of organisation. They thought that the group needed a more integrated structure

involving more control over day-to-day decision-making and that this should be the prerogative of a more dynamic and professional central management unit. They were opposed to the autocratic style of leadership of the brothers. For them the independence of individual mills represented in many cases a duplication of resources and a misapplication of investment rather than variety and creativity as claimed by the traditionals (Spybey, 1984, p. 554).

For the professionals it did not matter what the organisation was producing because there existed universal principles of management. At the heart of their management principles lay an emphasis on the primacy of financial investment and its monitoring rather than any manufacturing tradition. Much of Spybey's account revolves around the structures of power embedded in the brothers' leadership that facilitated the wants of the traditionals and frustrated those of the professionals. This situation of enablement and constraint was reversed when, during the course of the study, both brothers died resulting in a period of change propelled by the heirs' lack of concern with the operations of the group and the restriction of their interest to its status as a financial investment. This led to a division between ownership and control and meant that, 'in contrast to the brothers' era, the organisation became directly affected by the exigencies of stock market finance and its attendant principles' (p. 557). There was a clear change in operating principles with a move to 'professional management thinking', consistent and continuous monitoring of profitability, and the primacy of 'financial data' over 'wool-commodity data' (p. 558). It is clear both that the frames of meaning of the proximate actors and wider structural factors played their part in these developments.

It is worth remarking here that in looking at specific hermeneutic frames of meaning *in situ* Spybey exceeds Giddens's own brief as to the purposes of structuration theory. As noted above, Giddens is for the most part quite determined to restrict the insights of structuration theory to questions of ontology at an abstract, philosophical, level of analysis. Once this is understood then it is easy to see that from Giddens's own perspective many of the criticisms of his version of structuration miss the point as they are criticisms of his failure to engage in conjuncturally specific empirical studies, which I have referred to as studies of ontology-*in-situ*. On the other hand, many of those critiques do highlight the point that Giddens's neglect of the *in-situ* means that he is unable to even begin to approach many of the most interesting *sociological* questions (see Urry, 1991, p. 171). John Urry, for example, points clearly to what is inevitably lost by Giddens's lack of interest in *in-situ* variations in the constitution, hermeneutic perceptions and uses of time and space at different times and places within specific societies.[5] He notes, for example, Giddens's absence of interest in the hermeneutics of travel and why saving 'time' or covering more 'space' might be of any interest to people. Urry himself offers a series of possible answers to this, from the pleasures of liminal zones, through the company of strangers, to simply visiting the new (p. 168), all of which, as with more instrumental possible answers to do with the organisation of international and trans-national organisations and connections in search of profits and power, suggest a variable phenomenological dimension whose specifics will vary from situation to situation, case to case. Urry goes on to look at other dimensions of *in-situ* specificity and notes how Giddens neglects to examine, for example, how and why different structurings of time are found in various industrial countries. Thus, the weekend as a time-zone is more important, and more firmly upheld, in some countries than in others. Urry rightly notes how the production of such zoning can depend upon a plurality of *in-situ* determinants with complex interconnections between them, from the strength of the labour movement to resist the temporal flexibilisation of the workforce to the nature and strength of various religious traditions to 'protect the sanctity of the weekend (that is, the family) from commercialization' (Urry, 1991, p. 168). Similar points are made as to Giddens's lack of interest in the production of particular places as opposed to generalised points about space; mentioning specifically the literature on 'restructuring' that has 'addressed and confronted the notion of a fixed, ahistorical and functional core/periphery (Massey, 1984; Bagguley *et al.*, 1989; Urry, 1991, p. 172). Urry finds Giddens's omissions perplexing – 'curious' is the word he uses – but they cease to be curious or strange once they are situated in terms of his commitment to structuration as only an abstract and generalising theory.

The Neglect of Epistemology and Methodology

Having outlined the ontological framework of Giddens's structuration theory, I now want to emphasise his relative neglect of epistemology and methodology. As Giddens launched structuration theory in the 1970s, he presented it quite explicitly as a project that would give priority to ontology over epistemology. He argued that far too much time had been spent on the finer questions of 'knowing' when, to his mind, the logically prior questions of 'being' had still been insufficiently explored. It was, he suggested, important to spend much more time than hitherto on delineating the nature of social entities – the ontological nature of the things that were the 'objects' of knowing – rather than on the rather esoteric and sterile search for a royal road to knowledge.

Giddens's retreat from epistemology is to my mind one of the key reasons for the under-developed character of his version of structuration. By focusing only on issues of ontology at a high level of abstraction he locked his version of structuration into an overly limited space. Christopher Bryant, in an incisive critique of Giddens's indifference to epistemology, dates the decisive moment in what we might call Giddens's 'epistemological break' as 1977, presumably a reference to the article on 'Positivism and its Critics' in *Studies in Social and Political Theory*, originally written for Tom Bottomore and Robert Nisbet's classic collection *A History of Sociological Thought* published the previous year (Bryant, 1991: 139). *New Rules*, written at about the same time, also devoted the whole of one of its four main chapters to 'The Form of Explanatory Accounts', with discussions of Kuhn and Popper, paradigms, science and non-science, the epistemological grounding of science, the significance of falsification, and the problem of adequacy. But a concern with these kinds of issues was, for the most part, to disappear from Giddens's writings in subsequent years. This was not an unacknowledged drift but a purposeful neglect, one that he pugnaciously defended time and again.

My own view is that whilst Giddens may have been right in terms of a judgement about the relative expenditure of energies in the theoretical conjuncture of the 1970s, he was not right in an absolute sense to set ontology and epistemology against each other. Nor is it any longer appropriate to suggest that sociologists and social theorists should spend less time than they do on questions of epistemology and methodology. The 'ontological turn' in which Giddens played his part has by now long been massively dominant in most domains of social theory, with new aspects of ontology and, more broadly, new substantive objects of study, being discovered, rediscovered, described and redescribed in the finest of detail on an ever quickening cycle of enthusiasm and exhaustion. The proliferations of journals, and of sections within national and regional sociological associations, are just two of the most visible indicators of this.

This is not, of course, to say that enough work has therefore been done on ontology and that it is time to swing the pendulum right over to the other side with all attention now being devoted to epistemology and methodology. This would be a sterile and retrograde move. There continue to be many innovative, exciting and revolutionary developments at the ontological level (see the reviews in, for example, Thrift, 1996; Urry, 2000), and the points I will develop throughout the book about the under-development of Giddens's own ontological accounts should by themselves caution against any premature neglect of this area. Rather, it is to say that the pendulum should swing back to the centre, that a balance should be restored between ontology and epistemology. It is a mistake to allow the development of either to stray too far from the development of the other (cf. Loyal, 2003, p. 44). We shall see that the points about the inadequacies of Giddens's own ontology, for example, are brought more clearly into relief by placing them in the context of the epistemological purposes and question-types central to structuration theory. Engaging with problems of 'what to know?', 'how to know?' and 'how much can be known?' make one quickly aware of limitations in the conceptualisation of ontology – in the quality of thought about 'the kinds of things and relations that are there to be known'.

Social theory now needs to work hard at developing epistemological and methodological guidelines that are sophisticated and nuanced enough to respect the refinements of ontology produced over the last thirty or forty years. It could strive equally hard to harness the complexities of those ontologies produced before then but whose potential couldn't be released due to the combined inadequacies of empiricist orthodoxies and nascent post-empiricist alternatives whose incipient creativity was prematurely quashed by the one-sidedness of the ontological turn. Strong structuration addresses this epistemological deficit by insisting that reference be made to the whole structurationist 'package', including not only ontology but also particular question-types or problematics, methodological issues – including methodological bracketing and reflexivity as well as the identification of analytically distinct research steps – and the relations between all of these and empirical evidence (see chapter 4, pp. 116–27).

Structuration Theory and Empirical Research

It was clear from Giddens's early writings on epistemology that he was committed to a post-empiricist notion of the social sciences in which, *inter alia*, theories and substantive knowledge were always under-determined by empirical evidence. In such a post-empiricist view, one which is by now quite rightly *de rigeur* amongst social theorists, empirical evidence is always given significance by the various assumptions, models, categories, typifications, definitions and problems that a researcher brings to that evidence and to her use of it. Facts, to be facts, will always be perceived as such from within a network of assumptions and pre-conceptions. The sensory experience that gives us evidence is always already embedded in all of these presuppositions – even when it challenges some of the presuppositions, it does so from within. It was clear from his writings of the mid 1970s that Giddens saw the range of inter-related concepts of ontology he was developing under the name of structuration theory as belonging to the relatively abstract level of knowledge which establishes the internal logical coherence of concepts within a theoretical network. He distinguished the relations between concepts at this level (ontology-in-general) from another level of relations, what I think of as the level of the methodological matrix in which ontology-in-general is translated into ontology-*in-situ*. This matrix relies upon concepts couched at the level of ontology-in-general but is specifically concerned to investigate, explore and clarify the 'relation[s] between statements involving those concepts and the object-world' (Giddens, 1977, p. 79).

As we have noted, Giddens ploughed his energies into establishing structuration theory on the first of the two levels. This focus of interest and concern was what lay behind his comments, to be discussed in a moment, on the 'methodological' relation between structuration theory and empirical research. Giddens was clear that his primary task was to work out the logical coherence between ontological concepts – to create an inter-meshing organising network of concepts – that would then be available as a 'medium whereby truth as a relation between statements and the object-world is made possible, but does not provide the substance of that relation itself' (Giddens, 1977, p. 79). The substance of the relation itself, the substance of the various relations between the structurationist ontology and empirical research into the object-world, was not something Giddens regarded as the province of structuration theory *per se*.

It is a little more complicated, however, than Giddens believing that structuration theory has no implications whatsoever for empirical research. Rather, he is able to combine the conviction that the theory, '[b]eing abstract and generalized ... is necessarily at some distance from particular research projects' (Giddens, 1989, p. 295) with a parallel belief that structuration theory is, however, of direct relevance to empirical research (see Giddens, 1989, p. 296). Thus, we have distance from particular empirical projects, on the one hand, and direct relevance on the other. What Giddens means here is that whilst the ontology of structuration is, indeed, at some distance from particular research projects, it can be useful in sensitising researchers to the kinds of entities that exist in the social world (Giddens, 1989, p. 294; 1990b, p. 310). The problem I find with his notion of 'sensitising' is that in demonstrating what it means he consistently pulls up short of exploring the 'methodological relation' between ontology and empirical research with anything like the same rigour and sense of focus that he devotes to the level of ontology. Part of this is probably to do with what interests him, but it is also, I feel, down to his sheer lack of appreciation of the subtleties and complexities involved in any use of structuration theory at the empirical level.

Thus, when Giddens elaborates on the notion of 'sensitising' he typically focuses on what we have called 'ontology-in-general' rather than 'situated ontology' or the level of the ontic: the particular shape, form and content of entities at the substantive, empirical level. He doesn't seem to see that there are specific problems associated with moving from the level of a generalised abstract ontology – applicable to contexts of social practices at all times and places – to a particular practice situated in a particular time and place. It is probable that he might, on an intuitive level, acknowledge some of these problems but believe that there is nothing of a theoretical or general character that one can say about this methodological relation. This would explain the tendency Giddens has, when discussing this relation, to retreat back into questions associated with 'ontology-in-general'. For example, Christopher Pierson, in a series of interviews with Giddens, suggests to him that unemployment is a structural feature of the world that may present itself to a specific individual as a powerful external force or reality whose effect he or she feels. Pierson, in this and other questions, specifically focuses on the 'ways in which structural features of the world present themselves to individuals' (Giddens and Pierson, 1998, p. 80). Giddens replies:

I wouldn't dispute that at all – it certainly is true for an individual facing the labour market. But I don't think that in any way compromises the logic of the relation between agency and structure (Giddens and Pierson, 1998, p. 80).

Both here and in subsequent remarks in the same chapter Giddens immediately accedes to what he regards as the obviousness of there being structural constraints for situated individuals at the ontic level before moving quickly back to structuration theory's ontology-in-general: the general logic of the relation between structure and agency. When Pierson returns again to the theme of how structural forces may act upon the individual with a force as powerful and irresistible as a physical object, Giddens again refuses the invitation to think more deeply about such substantive experiences. He again couches his answer not in terms of the situated individual but in the terms of ontology-in-general:

There are only structural forces, to repeat, in so far as there are established conventions that people follow. There are structures in so far as people constantly reproduce those conventions in what they do and they give structured form to institutions. Institutions incorporate at the same time forms of power but they are simply not like physical structures (Giddens and Pierson, 1998, p. 87).

From the point of view of ontology-*in-situ* Giddens's failure to respond more adequately – seeming not even to 'get the point' that Pierson wants to address, or, at the very least, to be unwilling to concede that the point is worth dwelling upon – comes across almost as obdurate and, certainly, as exasperating.

The replies are perfectly reasonable and cogent, however, from the perspective of ontology-in-general. And it is from within this – limited – perspective that one should understand Giddens's various comments on the relationship between structuration theory and empirical research. Nicky Gregson has long since expertly excavated the logic behind Giddens's treatment of the relations between structuration theory and empirical research, and what I will argue here both parallels and concurs with her insights (Gregson, 1989, pp. 235–48). Leaving aside the most basic strategy of simply running through some ontological concepts that he regards as 'most generally relevant to social research' (see Giddens, 1990b, p. 313) his comments on the relationship fit into one of two different patterns, both reliant upon, and restricting themselves to, the ontology-in-general perspective. The first of these is evident in the concluding chapter of *The Constitution of Society* in which he draws on examples of empirical research to 'provide an empirical illumination of some of the basic elements of structuration theory' (Giddens, 1984, pp. 281–354; 1989, p. 297), showing how various researchers had been sensitive to the logical implications of those concerns. Giddens focuses his attention on four different conceptual themes that he has elaborated at the philosophical level – the duality of structure;

structural constraints; contradiction and conflict; and institutional stability and change. His strategy is simply to show the reader that there are sociological texts in existence – some that were directly and explicitly informed by structuration theory but others that were not – in which researchers have produced accounts of social relations and processes that reproduce and demonstrate the insights of one of these chosen conceptual themes of structuration theory.

Thus, for example, Paul Willis's work *Learning to Labour* (1977), was drawn upon by Giddens to reveal certain aspects of the duality of structure at work in the social world. It did not matter to Giddens that Willis's work was not directly informed by his structuration theory, for it was nevertheless sensitive to the relevant phenomena and processes in the social world, and also to the 'logical implications of studying a subject-matter of which the researcher is already a part' (Giddens, 1984, pp. 376–8; and 1989, p. 296). It is, centrally, sensitive to the ways in which the structurally mediated hermeneutics and non-conformist behaviour of working-class boys in a middle-class educational system led to the consequence of them ending up in working-class jobs. Most of the discussion here is directed towards revealing that the world Willis describes is a world that includes intended and unintended consequences, skilled and knowledgeable agents, discursive and tacit knowledge, a dialectic of control, actions with motivational content, and constraints working through the active involvement of the agents concerned; in short, many of the different components of the duality of structure. The purpose of the account is simply to reveal that these processes – explicated at the philosophical level by Giddens – can be found in the social world, and to show researchers how these concepts of structuration 'looked' when fleshed out in an empirical context (see Giddens, 1989, pp. 296–7).

The second, slightly different, pattern into which Giddens's comments on the relationship between structuration theory and empirical research fall is apparent in his extended comments on the relationship in his reply to critics contained in Held and Thompson's (1989) edited collection of commentaries on his work by major figures in specialised areas of his thought. Here, instead of looking for the concepts of structuration in already existing sociological accounts, Giddens takes one broadly defined area of actual social relations and then suggests how such an area would be likely to contain processes of structuration that the researcher could actively seek out. He introduces the general hypothetical example of 'studying marriage relationships, and the break-up of marriage, in a number of communities of varying socio-economic levels' (Giddens, 1989, p. 297). The most specific he gets in terms of a particular research problem is to say that our main interest will be in 'the nature of marital relationships and in the origins and consequences of marital separation'. The aim is to see '[h]ow ... some of the notions of structuration theory [might] be used as sensitizing devices in the pursuit of such a research inquiry' (Giddens, 1989, p. 297).

Giddens again organises his account in terms of ontological themes worked out at the philosophical level, emphasising that the researcher could or should: 'place the emphasis squarely upon the constitution and reconstitution of social practices'; '(delve) into the subtle interplay between the intractability of social institutions and the options they offer for agents who have knowledge, but bounded discursive awareness, of how those institutions work'; look for both stasis and change; think about the expectations each partner holds about the other; and think about how these expectations are sanctioned within the overarching framework of the legal system; be alert to the relative degrees of routine, traditional, behaviour, on the one hand, and skilful, strategic thinking, on the other; look at the temporally sedimented traditions and the spatial organisation of locales involved in a mother's relationship with her daughter, and so on (Giddens, 1989, pp. 298–9).

As in the first pattern this explication of the relation between structuration theory and empirical research is geared heavily towards simply finding confirmation of structuration's ontology-in-general. It is concept-led rather than question-led. It is not geared towards addressing particular sets of marriage break-ups in specified communities or, *a fortiori*, towards understanding specific questions or suppositions about such particular, *in-situ*, phenomena. If it was it would need to be more attuned to the precise relationship between, on the one hand, the general ontological concepts produced at the philosophical level and often approached discretely, one at a time and apart from each other, and on the other hand, the varied, complex, combined and overlapping, very specific, synthetic, forms that ontology-in-general takes on in particular situations. Strong structuration, by way of contrast, is not content just to look in a broadly defined manner at a broadly defined sphere of social action for evidence of social processes that parallel the core concepts of structuration. Rather, it is oriented towards theorising and articulating a range of key relationships between ontology-in-general and ontology-*in-situ* such that appropriately combined ontological concepts can be actively used to evaluate the quality and adequacy of empirical research claims. With any one piece of empirical research there will typically be a nexus of suppositions or claims about the world and then greater or lesser empirical substantiation of those claims. Strong structuration believes that ontology should play an important regulative, marshalling, role mediating between knowledge claims and their empirical substantiation. To this end it focuses on the relationship between the relevant network of ontological concepts (both in-general and *in-situ*), the particular issue addressed, the suppositions and claims made about this issue, and the empirical substantiation offered for those claims/suppositions. It is concerned with the degree to which particular accounts of situated events and processes can be assessed as valid or as invalid. It follows that methodological reflexivity in relation to all of the relationships involved in the process of 'finding out' is central to strong structuration.

All of this is in stark contrast to Giddens's particular espousal of the broad 'sensitising' approach in which 'finding out' the specifics of a situated process and assessing the validity of the attendant account are eschewed in favour of 'selectively looking for' traces of – often discrete – ontological concepts of structuration in sociological texts or in a general area of social relations. It is revealing in this respect that it is directly because Giddens's account of Willis's lads is motivated by a desire to show the strategic nature of their conduct – the skilled and knowledgeable quality of their agency, the sources of their motivation, and the impact of the dialectic of control – that the resultant account is one that emphasises that the lads are actively involved in the production of the constraints on them. This emphasis mirrors the interviews with Pierson in its concern to re-emphasise discrete themes taken from ontology-in-general rather than to rigorously explore the more complex scenarios thrown up by ontology-*in-situ*. For their active, skilled and knowledgeable, involvement is stressed at the expense of the degree to which the lads are indeed subject to structural constraints that they cannot change, whether these be the 'internal'[6] inheritances from upbringing and the resultant lack of the requisite habitus and hence cultural capital, or 'external' in terms of the daunting formal requirements of the educational and occupational systems, or of the material resources available to the parents of children from a working class background.

As far as we can tell from Giddens's account it is quite conceivable that the majority of the lads from Hammertown school would have been delivered through the closed factory doors even if their behaviour at school had been dutifully conformist and – in terms of Giddens's definition – passive, rather than actively resistant. These are, in fact, the kinds of aspects that Giddens does mention in the subsequent case study when he discusses Diego Gambetta's study of educational opportunity in Piemonte in north-west Italy (Giddens, 1984, pp. 304–10; see Gambetta, 1982). But the reason they are highlighted now is because this case study is designed to illustrate the ontological notion of structural constraint. The emphasis on ontology-in-general and on using empirical research simply to illustrate or look for discrete structuration concepts provide the criteria by means of which Giddens can safely 'cherry-pick' from his empirical material, choosing not to select the parts that don't suit his purpose. The concepts he wants to illuminate or flesh out empirically dictate what is selected. There is also selectivity, of course, in the approach advocated by strong structuration but here the purpose is different. Here the attempt to answer a question about a specific substantive phenomenon dictates which concepts are drawn upon and which other concepts they are combined with. With respect to the Hammertown lads, for example, the question could be posed in terms of investigating *both* the structural constraints upon, *and* the opportunities for, the active contribution of the lads' agency to their employment chances. Such an approach, led by *substantive explananda* (things-to-be-explained), is more prepared to be surprised by the evidence, and more prepared to work hard to analyse complex substantive phenomena that do not easily exemplify in any 'pure' sense any one of structuration's concepts. The extent to which, and the ways in which, concepts of structuration are able to be combined together, in conjunction with traces of empirical evidence, to shed light on a particular phenomenon only becomes clear after a good deal of theoretical and empirical dialogue. This is dialogue in which, as we shall see later, there is much mediating work to be done in the realm of theoretically informed methodology.

Distinguishing Non-reductionist Pluralism from Structuration Theory Proper

I hope I have made it clear that whilst I hold Giddens's account of structuration to be wanting in a number of significant respects, I still want to reserve an important place for many of his undeniably seminal contributions to the approach. Given the important role that his work would continue to play within the renewed conception of structuration for which I am arguing, it follows that if the distinctive contribution of structuration theory to social theory is to be established with some precision then one will need to be clear about which parts of Giddens's work fall into the category of structuration theory, and which do not. It is essential to distinguish the appropriate domain of structuration theory from Giddens's other writings as both he and others consistently conflate the two. Thus, whilst I am sympathetic to much of what I will call Giddens's anti-reductionist work – by which I refer primarily to his substantive work on historical sociology and on the institutions of modernity – it is important to establish that this work is not a manifestation of structuration theory.

I will first say a little more about what I mean by anti-reductionist pluralism before distinguishing it from the ontology of structuration theory. By anti-reductionism I refer to a general movement in social theory that rejects explanations of social phenomena that give undue emphasis to some causal forces at the expense of other significant forces that are correspondingly denied their due causal autonomy and efficacy. A classic case of such reductionism would be the economic determinism of some kinds of Marxism whereby the political, legal and ideological superstructures are reduced to the status of epiphenomena of the economic base. This kind of conception has been criticised over time by an array of both Marxists and non-Marxists, with, for example, Gramsci and neo-Gramscians developing conceptions of relative degrees of autonomy of the cultural and discursive spheres from the economic base (cf. Gramsci, 1971; Hall, 1980), Althusser arguing for the relative autonomy of the ideological, legal and political levels from the economic, which was said only to be determinate in 'the last instance' (cf.

Althusser, 1969/1965; Benton, 1984), and Poulantzas, in similar vein but taking things further and developing first a 'regional' and then a 'relational' account of just one of these levels, the political, that in both cases gave it a developed *sui generis* reality of its own that was irreducible to, albeit deeply influenced by, the economic (cf. Poulantzas, 1973, 1978; Jessop, 1985; cf. McLennan, 1996, pp. 55–61).

Just as Neo-Marxism stretched further and further away from economic determinism, and at its edges gave way to the 'necessary non-correspondence' and the 'discursive autonomy' of Post-Marxism (cf. Hindness and Hirst, 1977; Laclau and Mouffe, 1985), theorists working in adjacent or overlapping theoretical traditions also began to (or continued to) frame their work in terms of an explicit non-reductionism. In this sense there was a convergence of traditions. Non-reductionism *per se* was sometimes accompanied by a more or less serious and concerted attempt to look at the way in which a number of different levels, mechanisms or domains were held to be jointly responsible for the production of events, practices, social phenomena (for example, Lindblom, 1977; Giddens, 1984, 1985; Mann, 1986; Walby, 1990; Parsons, 1991). The different domains were held to articulate with each other, to interweave and interconnect in ways that combined both necessity and contingency (cf. Jessop, 1990, pp. 11–12). The emphasis of non-reductionism, however, was heavily weighted towards establishing the distinctiveness of spheres or levels rather than towards explicating precisely what was involved in the articulation itself. This was no doubt partly because of the recalcitrant complexity of the challenges involved in undertaking the latter. The consequence was that questions concerning issues of joint or plural causality, and of relational interdependencies were only broached at an imprecise and rather vague level.

In the more abstract cases there was very little attempt at all to trace through detailed sequences in which non-reductionist spheres were brought back together in interwoven chains of mutual influence. Judgements here were more a function of general philosophical intuition or belief than of a well-developed framework of conjunctural analysis of the kind whose parameters and procedures have been formulated in some detail in realist writings on the relationship between theory and method, most trenchantly in the work of Andrew Sayer (Sayer, 1984, 2000a; cf. Bhaskar, 1979). I include Giddens's substantive writings on institutional clusters in this abstract and under-specified category as so many of the concepts he employs at this level – from the more abstractly conceived institutional domains of symbolic orders/ modes of discourse, political institutions, economic institutions, and law/ modes of sanction in *Central Problems of Social Theory*, to the more 'substantive', world capitalist economy, nation-state system, international division of labour, and world military order of *The Consequences of Modernity* (Giddens, 1979, 1984, 1990) – remain either cut off from, or only very weakly informed by, the central concepts of structuration.

In *Central Problems* there is a direct transposition of Giddens's ontological account of structures onto the account of institutional domains, with each one of the latter constituted by a mixture of the universal social constituents (structures) of signification, domination and legitimation, but with one or other of them dominant depending upon the institutional domain (see figure 1.3). Thus, for example, allocative power is dominant in economic institutions but this doesn't mean that the constituents of signification and social norms are not also required to communicate the negotiations and decisions, and to make sure that those involved can be sufficiently trusted to carry out those allocative policies. The impulse towards non-reductionist pluralism can explain why Giddens would want to distinguish here between different types of institution, and between different constituent elements within institutions. What is not clear is what he thought he had achieved by the unmediated transposition of the ontological categories of signification, domination and legitimation involved in the duality of structure onto the institutional domain. The under-developed quality of the relations between the three ontological categories and any historically significant institutional categories means that the figurative and rhetorical implication of some kind of explanatory connection between them is strikingly premature. Ultimately, what we have is little more than the most preliminary sketching out of an area for future development. It is notable, in fact, that the direct transposition disappears in later books such as *The Nation-State and Violence* (1985) and *The Consequences of Modernity* (1990a) where, as I have noted, more 'substantive' categories are employed. If the institutional categories of *Central Problems* are meant to be at a higher level of abstraction than those in the later books then work also needs to be done in spelling out both the connection between these two levels of analysis and the explanatory pay-off one might expect from taking the trouble to formulate any such connection. Neither is self-evident.

S–D–L	Symbolic orders/modes of discourse
D(auth)–S–L	Political institutions
D(alloc)–S–L	Economic institutions
L–D–S	Law/modes of sanction

S = Signification
D = Domination
L = Legitimation

Figure 1.3   Giddens's classification of institutions

Source: A. Giddens, 1979, *Central Problems in Social Theory*, London, Macmillan.

Thus far, it is clear that Giddens's lack of attention to the relations between his abstract ontology and his substantive socio-historical theoretical categories leaves his non-reductionism highly under-determined by notions of structuration. The connection between the two, already weak, is entirely severed by a move Giddens goes on to make at the methodological level. Here, he characterises his approach to the broad institutional categories as fitting within the methodological brackets, or focus, of what he calls 'institutional analysis'. This form of analysis he defines as:

> Social analysis which *places in suspension the skills and awareness of actors*, treating institutions as chronically reproduced rules and resources (Giddens, 1984, p. 375, my emphasis).

Giddens himself somehow never draws the logical conclusion from the use of this form of bracketing, namely that it is fatal to any pretence to structuration given that it is impossible to even begin to address the duality of structure from within it. Institutional analysis, according to Giddens's definition, is not interested in the interpretative or hermeneutic ways in which actors draw upon their perceptions of the structures of signification, domination and legitimation, as they go about their social interactions. This is confined to another methodological moment, that of 'strategic conduct analysis', one not thought appropriate to the realm of the large sweep of historical sociology. Strategic conduct analysis, which I would argue approaches the heart of structuration theory, and which I will return to many times later in the book, is defined as:

> Social analysis which places in suspension institutions as socially reproduced, concentrating upon how actors reflexively monitor what they do; how actors draw upon rules and resources in the constitution of interaction (Giddens, 1984, p. 373)
>
> ... the focus is placed upon modes in which actors draw upon structural properties in the constitution of social relations ... The analysis of strategic conduct means giving primacy to discursive and practical consciousness, and to strategies of control within defined contextual boundaries. Institutionalized properties of the settings of interaction are assumed *methodologically* to be 'given' ... It is to concentrate analysis upon the contextually situated activities of definite groups of actors (Giddens, 1984, p. 288, my emphasis; also see Giddens, 1979, p. 80).

Giddens suggests that in the analysis of strategic conduct researchers should avoid impoverished descriptions of agents' knowledgeability; should attempt to provide a sophisticated account of motivation; and should attempt an interpretation of the 'dialectic of control' (see above, p. 29).

Institutional analysis, by way of contrast with strategic conduct analysis, retains no effective space for the 'structural-hermeneutic' nexus of structuration theory. Rather, it is said to treat the universal social constituents of domination, signification and legitimation (rules and resources) 'as chronically reproduced features of social systems' (Giddens, 1979, p. 80). This would seem to be a clear acknowledgement by Giddens that the form of analysis he uses in most of his broader writings on politics and historical sociology, the form of analysis, that is, he uses to investigate non-reductionist institutional clusters, brackets out the phenomenology of agents, brackets out the way that agents perceive and draw upon their structural context.[7]

Given the axiom we started out with regarding the centrality of the 'duality of structure' for structuration theory it is clear that Giddens's approach to non-reductionism leaves him unable to grasp the process of structuration *in situ*. It cannot grasp structure as a 'medium' of agent's practices, it cannot grasp what is involved in agent's conduct. Neither can it know about the frame of meaning from within which an agent perceives external structuration processes, or whether an agent perceives those structures accurately or inaccurately. Neither can it know which structuration 'outcomes' are intended and which are unintended. Even with more developed ontological links between structures at the most abstract level and more substantive notions of institutions, the methodological bracket of institutional analysis would still place in suspension crucial components of every one of the four parts of the quadripartite process of structuration (see chapter 3) intrinsic to the duality of structure. Consequently, any writing produced loyally within the confines of this form of bracketing will not fall within the parameters of structuration theory. Institutional analysis simply does not allow for any of the bridging concepts, procedural methodological guidelines, or substantive historical detail that would denote the movement *from* the non-reductionist insistence on the distinctiveness of institutional clusters and practices *to* sequential and interlocking accounts, informed by notions of hermeneutics and duality, of the articulation or mutual influencing of different clusters in the production of social outcomes. This is a non-reductionist pluralism, to be sure, but it is a non-reductionist pluralism that has very little to do with structuration theory.

Indeed, it is worth noting in conclusion that it is not only the institutional clusters that are cut off from both the ontology of structuration and the *in-situ* process of structuration but also, for the same reasons, a whole array of other concepts – intersocietal systems, structural principles, structural sets, contradiction, time-space edges – in the terms in which they are discussed by Giddens in *Central Problems* and *The Constitution of Society*. None of these concepts listed are in and of themselves concepts of structuration, and Giddens's uses of them at a substantive level, likewise, are not instances of structuration-*in-situ*. To be instances of structuration they would have to be more closely articulated with the duality of structure and its structural-hermeneutic nexus, and to be of use in the analysis of *in-situ* processes of structuration they would, in addition, also have to be explored in a manner unconfined by the methodological parameters of institutional analysis. In Giddens's hands they are neither of these things. With the centrality of the duality of structure in mind the next chapter turns to Giddens's critics to evaluate their contribution to debates about structuration theory.

2
Critics of Structuration:
Friends or Foes?

This chapter reviews some of the most influential criticisms of structuration. I attempt to draw out what is most incisive from these critiques, at the same time rejecting those arguments that are insufficiently persuasive or too extreme in their conclusions. The purpose is twofold. The first aim is to provide a clear and concise summary of the main arguments against Giddens's version of structuration. The second is to prepare the ground for the next chapter's attempt at a creative synthesis that will take into account both the strengths of Giddens's structuration and the most trenchant contributions of his most powerful critics.

I do this against a background in which structuration has been under attack from many quarters and in which the critiques launched by Margaret Archer and Nicos Mouzelis, in particular, have led some commentators to go so far as to write its obituary. In a recent book on structuration for the Open University's Concepts in the Social Sciences series, John Parker stated his belief 'that the moment of 'structuration' theory passed some time ago. It still figures prominently in routine social theoretical talk, but its force is only that of a tired conventional wisdom' (Parker, 2000, p. x). Parker proposes the superseding of structuration – within which he includes the work of both Giddens and Bourdieu – by what he calls 'post-structuration',[1] an approach built on the work of Archer and Mouzelis which emphasises the *dualism* of structure and agency. This approach is said to acknowledge both the difference between structure and agency and their interdependence. This is contrasted with structuration theory of which the stress on *duality* is said to entail an 'identity' between structure and agency. 'Identity' here means more than interdependence, it means a debilitating impossibility of distinguishing one from the other, and it is in this respect above all that structuration theory represents a dead-end.

In what follows I try to show that the positive contributions of Archer, Mouzelis, and other influential critics, such as John B. Thompson and William Sewell Jr can be fruitfully accommodated within an amended and refined framework of structuration theory. I also outline the contribution of two avowedly sympathetic, albeit not uncritical, writers on structuration, Ira J. Cohen and Chris Shilling, through their development and use of the conceptions of 'positions' and 'position-practice relations'. In the course of my exposition I also attempt to undermine too easy an equation between the work of Mouzelis and Archer by indicating that there are tensions between their stated positions. Mouzelis, for example, accepts and works within the broad notion of duality central to structuration theory, whilst Archer, by way of contrast, places a rejection of the notion at the heart of her critique.

I believe that to reject structuration theory rather than to build on its productive and fertile, and still incipient, insights would be to do the cause of social theory a great disservice. It is no doubt true that Giddens's and Bourdieu's ontologies are a little 'flat' in some respects, but so are those of Archer and Mouzelis in other respects. Practical social analysis needs more connections, more alliances, not more disconnection and division. It seems to me that all of these writers share an estimable project in common. It makes no sense for structuration not to remain the name we give to that endeavour.

John B. Thompson on Giddens's Notion of Structures

John B. Thompson, a close friend and colleague of Giddens at Cambridge University and a co-founder of Polity Press, is the author of one of the most widely cited and influential critiques of the theory of structuration. In looking at this critique I will leave aside his discussion of constraints as I will consider the most general conceptual points on this topic in looking at Archer's work. Also, the force of Thompson's more specific criticisms in this respect dissolve once one accepts, as I will, his point that structuration theory requires a more conventional notion of social structure (although I will insist that this should be placed alongside the distinctive and innovative conception of structure that Giddens rightly places at the heart of structuration) (cf. Jary and Jary, 1997/ 1995, pp. 145–7). In any case, I will concentrate here on Thompson's other criticisms of Giddens's account of structuration.

Thompson begins his critique by drawing attention to what he calls the 'looseness' of Giddens's account of structures as rules and resources. In fact, he focuses, for reasons that are left unexplained, almost exclusively on rules rather than resources. He argues, rightly I think, that Giddens has not provided a sufficiently clear and consistent account of what he means by 'rules', and nor has he provided 'clear and consistent examples of what would count as a relevant "rule"' (Thompson, 1989, p. 64). There are two points to be made about this. Firstly, I share the view of both Thompson and of William Sewell Jr (who, in turn, draws on Bourdieu's forceful critique of the notion of rule in *Outline of a Theory of Practice*) that Giddens affords structuration theory, and himself, no favours by equating the complex idea of drawing on the internal structures of signification and legitimation in the production of interaction (by means of interpretative schemes and a conception of norms) with the misleading, confusing and, however conceived, overly formalistic idea of following a rule. Secondly, even if one dispenses with the notion of 'rules', Thompson's point about the vagueness of what is involved in drawing on structures is, I believe, still valid and I will attempt to develop this area in the next chapter.

After his initial comments, and working with an intuitive sense of what it means to follow a rule, as he must in the absence of a clear definition from Giddens, Thompson goes on to address the very concept of structure that lies at the heart of structuration theory and the duality of structure. He provides four arguments as to why it is not 'useful and satisfactory to identify social structure with rules (and resources)' (Thompson, 1989, p. 64, original bracketing). Firstly, he argues that the identification of rules and resources with social structure doesn't allow Giddens any means of clarifying the relative importance of different types of rules or aspects of rules. Giddens is well aware, says Thompson, that some rules are 'more important than others for the analysis of, for example, the social structure of capitalist societies' (p. 64). But the implicit framework that suggests the importance of particular rules for the analysis of capitalist societies is, in fact, an implicit conception of social structure (that is, capitalist social structure, in this case) that is separate and different from the concepts of rules and resources that Giddens has identified with social structure. In other words, whatever his ambitions for structure as rules and resources, it is apparent that Giddens cannot do without a more conventional conception of social structure.

Thompson's second and third points call attention to issues of what he calls *structural differentiation*. The second point refers to the semantic or significatory aspect of rules. He notes that there are indeed rules governing the application of an adjective such as 'bloody' or a noun like 'the Left' in contemporary Britain. However, to study these semantic rules 'is not *in itself* to analyse part of the social structure of Britain' (p. 65, original emphasis). An analysis of the ways in which such semantic rules are indeed relevant to social structure would need to demonstrate 'that the rules are differentiated according to class, sex, region and so on' (p. 65). But, again, to study such differentiation would require a prior framework, 'some structural points of reference, which are not themselves *rules*, with regards to which these semantic rules are differentiated' (p. 65, original emphasis). Thompson's third point focuses on the differentiation of opportunities available to variously situated individuals. He takes the example of an institution, such as a school or a university, in which certain individuals, classes or groups have restricted opportunities for entry and therefore for participation:

> It seems evident that such restrictions cannot be adequately conceptualized in terms of 'moral rules' or 'sanctions', since such restrictions may operate independently of the rights and obligations of the agents concerned ... what is at issue is the fact that

the restrictions on opportunities operate *differentially*, affecting unevenly various groups of individuals whose categorization depends on certain assumptions about social structures; and it is this differential operation or effect which cannot be grasped by the analysis of rules alone (p. 65).

The fourth and final argument against Giddens's notion of structures is that it provides no way of formulating what Thompson calls the idea of *structural identity*. He explains what he means by this through asking us to reflect upon two enterprises in different sectors of the British economy, for example the UK plants of the Ford Motor Company and the various establishments of the Macmillan Press. He notes that each of these enterprises is a complex institution possessing vast resources of machinery, stock and capital, and that each is organised, operated and characterised by a range of different rules and resources. However, beyond these rules and resources:

> there are certain features which Ford and Macmillan have in common, namely the features which define them as *capitalistic* enterprises. These features are not additional 'rules' which are 'drawn upon' by actors within these institutions, in the manner that a supervisor might 'draw upon' a rule in the contract in order to fire a worker who failed to turn up. The common features are of a different order altogether; they are better conceptualized, I believe, as a series of elements and their interrelations which together *limit* the kinds of rules which are possible and which thereby *delimit* the scope for institutional variation (pp. 65–6, original emphasis; also see Thompson, 1981, pp. 145ff. and 1984, part 3).

The core of the argument here rests again upon the idea that social structure conceived as rules and resources cannot capture the shared broader framework within which the rules and resources exist and are drawn upon. A different notion of social structure is required for this. For Ford UK and Macmillan to be seen as having in common the structure of capitalistic enterprises one needs to think of them in terms of sharing 'a series of elements and their interrelations'. These elements and their inter-relations are characteristic of all capitalist enterprises. The institutional character of all capitalistic enterprises will, as long as they remain as capitalistic enterprises, stay within a certain range of variation. This framework will, in turn, place limits on the 'kinds of rules which are possible'. The implication is that it is only by first delineating the wider, more traditional conception, of social structure that one can situate and understand the structural pressures on agents within each enterprise to draw on certain rules and resources in some ways and not in others. And it is only by sketching out the wider sense of social structure that one can identify similarities between different institutions and between the sets of structural pressures bearing upon agents situated within them.

Taken together, Thompson hopes that his four arguments demonstrate that Giddens's proposal to conceive of structure in terms of rules (and, in brackets, resources) 'is deficient, for it presupposes but fails to address some of the most important concerns of structural analysis' (p. 66). Consistent with this argument, Thompson goes on to praise Giddens's introduction of wider more conventional notions of structure in *A Contemporary Critique of Historical Materialism*. These are concepts at different levels of scope and abstraction such as *structural principles* and *sets and elements/axes* that between them cover everything from types of entire societies, through *sets of transformation/mediation relations* – such as the set implicit in Marx that Giddens sets out as 'private property: money: capital: labour contract: profit' – to so-called *proximate axes of structuration* such as the division of labour within the capitalistic enterprise (see Giddens, 1981, pp. 54–5; Thompson, 1989, pp. 66–71). It is clear that Giddens here is much closer to some sort of engagement with the broader structural dimensions that Thompson approaches by means of the notions of 'the social structure of particular types of society', 'structural differentiation' and 'elements and their interrelations'. Nevertheless, Thompson is still critical of Giddens for continuing to adhere, 'somewhat tenaciously', to the 'rules and resources' conception of structures at the same time as he works with the newly introduced, more conventional, notions of structure, without sufficiently distinguishing one conception from the other (Thompson, 1989, pp. 68–71 and 75).

Thompson is right, I think, to suggest that Giddens never makes sufficiently clear the relationship between what I would see as his meta-theoretical notion of structures (as rules – norms and interpretative schemes – and resources) and his more conventional substantive notions of structures. Gregor McLennan made some similar points very soon after the publication of *A Contemporary Critique of Historical Materialism* (1981). In a discussion of Giddens's general writings on domination, legitimation, allocative and authoritative resources, which in themselves he thought 'acute', McLennan nevertheless came to the austere conclusion that 'Giddens's contributions to these questions strike me as having relatively little to do with the theory of structuration' (McLennan, 1984, p. 127). Thompson notes that Giddens continues to insist in *The Constitution of Society* (1984) that structures as rules and resources is the 'most elemental' meaning of structure. For Thompson this is inevitably confusing because, for example, a *structural principle* applying to 'class-divided societies' (city-states, ancient empires and feudal societies) which 'operates along an axis' relating urban areas to rural hinterlands:

> is not a 'rule' in any ordinary sense: it is neither a semantic rule nor a moral rule nor a 'formula' which expresses what actors know in knowing how to go on in social life. To insist that a structural principle *must* be some such rule, or must be analysed in terms of rules, is to force on to the material a mode of conceptualization which is not appropriate to it ... Similarly it seems unhelpful

and misleading to interpret Marx's account of the structural relations involved in the capitalist system of production in terms of 'sets of rules and resources' (Thompson, 1989, pp. 68–9).

Giddens's reply to this is that he never suggested that a structural principle was equivalent to a rule. Rather, a structural principle is said to cover at least some of the features of social systems with which Thompson is concerned and which he characterises in terms of social structure. Giddens writes that he sees the structural principle of a social system as a 'mode of institutional articulation' that is connected both with a range of institutional orderings and with time-space distanciation (Giddens, 1989, pp. 257–8).

Whilst Giddens is right, of course, to say that he never explicitly suggested that a structural principle was equivalent to a rule, this doesn't weaken the crux of Thompson's argument which is that he leaves conceptual confusion in his wake. For he does speak of structural sets as sets or combinations of rules and resources (see Giddens, 1984, pp. 302–4; p. 377), and these are presented as a mid-way point between the structural principles of entire societies, on the one hand, and axes or elements of structuration such as the division of labour, on the other. He also clearly sees all of these more traditional notions of structure as being underpinned by the 'more elemental', ontological, concept of structure as rules and resources. This is attested to, not least, by his invocation of the methodological bracket of 'institutional-analysis' to look at what I've called the more traditional notions of structure. As noted above (chapter 1) this methodological move brackets the ways in which agents draw upon structures as rules and resources in the course of interaction and looks only at the chronically reproduced properties of social systems. As Thompson quite rightly notes, this invocation side-steps rather than solves the conceptual problems; Giddens has still failed to provide a clear analysis of how the different levels of structural analysis relate to each other (Thompson, 1989, p. 71).

I am in agreement with Thompson that Giddens's ontological conception of structures 'fails to address some of the most important concerns of structural analysis' (p. 66). I disagree, however, with the suggestion that one could and should dispense with structuration's innovative notion of structures altogether. There are two specific points I want to make in this regard. Firstly, the problem lies not in the ontological conception of structure itself but, on the one hand, in a misunderstanding about what sort of work it can reasonably be expected to do, and on the other hand, in Giddens's failure to spell out exactly how he believed this conception was related to the wider notions of structure that he juxtaposed with it. It must be conceded that there are many concerns of social structural analysis, of the kind highlighted by Thompson, that need to be approached with an eye for broader patterns, for larger networks, for longer sequences, and for huge comparisons. Thompson's argument reveals very clearly how an analysis based on structuration's ontology of structures as norms, interpretative schemes and power resources radically limits itself if it does not frame and locate itself within a more broadly conceived notion of social structures (see chapter 4). One must, that is, accept that there are limits to the work that the ontology of rules and resources can do on its own. This having been said, there are still, nevertheless, many highly significant social questions for which Giddens's distinctive ontology of structures and its associated conception of the duality of structure would provide the most powerful and effective means of analysis. Any such piece of practical social analysis would, at the same time, benefit from being located and framed on the basis of more traditional conceptions of structures.

Secondly, Thompson at times underplays the value of structuration's ontology at the same time as he overestimates the explanatory power of his more traditional conceptions of social structure. Thus, take his example of the restricted opportunities for entry into schools and universities experienced by certain individuals, groups or classes of individuals. As noted above he writes that such restrictions cannot be grasped by rules alone: 'It seems evident that such restrictions cannot be adequately conceptualized in terms of "moral rules" or "sanctions", since such restrictions may operate independently of the rights and obligations of the agents concerned' (p. 65). I would, of course, accept the importance of locating any structuration-informed analysis of particular restrictions within a broader socio-structural frame that provided information about such things as the entrance requirements, the number of available places, alternative opportunities for education, the socio-cultural and economic characteristics of successful and unsuccessful applicants, and so on. It is not at all clear, however, that the proximate restrictions on a particular group of individuals would operate independently of the moral rules – the hermeneutic sense of rights and obligations – of the agents with the power to make the decisions as to who will gain entry and who will not. It may be independent of the agents who wish to enter, but they are clearly not the only agents situated in this particular configuration of agents related to each other by norms, interpretative schemes and power resources.

Once one addresses questions of causation to do with processes involving agents acting within particular social contexts then structuration's ontology of structures is invaluable. It is an ontology that would profitably inform any understanding of the status of, and the legitimate uses of, the more conventional conception of structure. Take, for example, a social issue such as the propensity of children from a particular housing estate to do less well in school examinations than other children. It would no doubt be judicious and illuminating to frame this phenomenon within, say, a socio-economic structural frame and within the broad parameters of a middle class educational system. On the other hand, neither the systemic formation of local economic conditions, nor the construction of a middle-class educational system, with its middle-class mores and practices, nor the family and neighbourhood socialisation and schooling of the children happen all by themselves. All involve the situated actions or interactions of agents on the basis of structures that they draw upon, whether routinely or creatively, whether pre-reflectively or reflectively. In other words, even traditionally conceived social structures don't work by themselves; they work on the basis of agents acting *in situ*, drawing upon and being influenced by interpretative schemes, conceptions of values and norms, and power resources.

Margaret Archer's Critique of Structuration[2]

In a series of publications Margaret Archer has strongly and consistently criticised structuration theory for what she has dubbed the 'conflation' or 'elision' of structure and agent (for example, Archer, 1982, 1988, 1995, 2000). Here I concentrate on the detail of her most recent sustained argument against Giddens's work, the argument contained in *Realist Social Theory: The Morphogenetic Approach* (1995). Archer argues that Giddens's stress on duality, whereby structures exist as memory traces and in the instantiation of practices, means that one cannot tell where structures begin and agents end, or *vice versa*. The two are mixed together and confused such that any analytical value possessed by the concepts in the first place disappears. Instead, she argues for 'a dualism between structure and agency' that she believes to be both superior to and incompatible with structuration's notion of duality. Archer's definition of 'structure' emerges in this context. She uses it to distinguish between the material and cultural conditions in which action takes place, on the one hand, from the action itself, on the other hand. She then employs this distinction as a basis on which to trace out the respective roles played by structure and agency in sequences stretching over time. This is at the root of her commitment to the notion of 'dualism', a distinction between two things – structural conditions and action within the limits allowed by those conditions. It is vital for Archer that the two be kept apart to the extent that we are able to discuss them separately, and that we recognise that their separation, far from being just a methodological, analytical, ploy, is a highly significant aspect of reality.

Archer's morphogenetic approach is based upon a combination of a realist ontology and a methodology of practical social analysis that she labels 'analytical dualism'. In fact, the combination is said to be a necessary one. Archer argues that the very ontology of realism is itself predicated upon this 'analytical dualism' in which structure can be separated from action (Archer, 1995, p. 151). This must be the case if society, following the realist philosopher Roy Bhaskar, is to be *both* the ever-present pre-condition *and* the continually reproduced, post-dated, outcome of human agency (Archer, 1995,

p. 150). It must be the case simply because there is an implicit temporality involved in this characterisation, in which structure precedes action which, in turn, leads to a more or less attenuated structural outcome or elaboration which, in turn, provides the preconditions for action, and so on. For Archer, 'the distinctive feature of the morphogenetic approach is its recognition of the temporal dimension, through which and in which structure and agency shape one another' (Archer, 1995, p. 92).

The liberating aspect of this analytical dualism for practical social analysis, argues Archer, is that it allows one to investigate the temporally defined interplay between structure and agency – between structural conditioning (time 1), social interaction and its immediate outcome (times 2 and 3), and structural elaboration (time 4) (cf. Archer, 1995, pp. 157–8; pp. 192–4). The fatal weakness of structuration theory for Archer is precisely that it doesn't allow one to investigate this interplay, to trace or unpick the linkages and interconnections between:

1. structural conditions, with their emergent causal powers and properties;
2. social interaction between agents on the basis of these conditions;
3. and subsequent structural changes or reproductions arising from the latter.

Archer argues that the seeming resemblance between realist social theory and structuration theory is a superficial and misleading one. For whilst structuration theory, too, argues that society is both the condition and the outcome of human agency, it does so in a manner that is flawed.

My own view of Archer's critique can best be approached by distinguishing between two aspects of her argument. Firstly, and on this point I agree, on the whole, with Archer's criticism and feel that an incorporation of her insights into structuration would be an advance, structuration theory is said to neglect the temporality involved in the sequence of relations between structure and agency in the production and reproduction of society. Secondly, and on this point I do not agree at all with Archer's criticism, structuration theory is presented as ruling out, in its very essence, both the desirability and the possibility of paying more attention to the temporal dimension, and hence to the interconnections between structure and agency, between pre-conditions and post-dated outcomes. The grounds on which this judgement is made are, to my mind, not very convincing. Archer labels Giddens as an 'elisionist' with textual support from prominent but, at best, equivocal commentators on structuration theory, namely Ian Craib, John B. Thompson and Derek Layder (Archer, 1995, p. 93ff and 1996, pp. 687–91; cf. Willmott, 1997, pp. 100–3 and 1999, pp. 5–21).[3] He is an 'elisionist' because, as noted, his idea of the 'duality of structure' is said to effectively collapse structure and agency together in such a way that it is impossible to disentangle them from one another. Accordingly, Archer uses the term 'inseparability' as a shorthand term to denote the basis of the limitations of structuration theory (Archer, 1995, pp. 93–101):

> Because 'structure' is inseparable from 'agency' then, *there is no sense in which it can be either emergent or autonomous or pre-existent or causally influential.* Instead, 'structural properties' (i.e. defined as 'rules and resources') are 'instantiated' in social practices and have no existence outside this instantiation by agency. In this consistent ontology of praxis, structural properties exist and have any efficacy only by courtesy of agents (Archer, 1995, pp. 97–8, original emphasis).

The problem with this is that it is a mixture of truths and inaccuracies, such that the resultant effect is a highly misleading picture of structuration theory.

The prominence we have already given to the duality of structure, with its emphasis on structure as both medium and outcome – where those outcomes then become the medium for subsequent actions – should alert us to the exaggeration involved in Archer's representation. Whilst there are certainly aspects of structure that are left undeveloped or ill-defined, and hence indeterminate, in Giddens's work – and the explicit emphasis on the temporality involved in the sequence of relations between structure and agency is indeed one such aspect – it is only on a highly selective and doggedly unsympathetic reading that one could believe that Giddens means structure to have no 'pre-existent or causally influential' role. For even conceding the point that in Giddens's writings there is a certain under-theorisation and lack of clarity over what it means for structures to have a 'virtual' existence until instantiated in action, it is still clear that for an agent to be able to draw on the internal structures – that is, on their internal perceptions of the external conditions – of domination, legitimation and signification (cf. Giddens, 1984, p. 29 and *passim*) then these structures must either pre-exist the moment in which the agent draws upon them or, at the very least, exist at the moment the agent draws upon them. It is only by quoting Layder's unsympathetic and inaccurate characterisation of structuration theory – 'structures *only* exist at the point when they are produced and reproduced by actors in concrete instances of instantiation' (Layder, 1981, p. 64, cited in Archer, 1995, p. 99, my emphasis) – that Archer is able to suggest that structures in Giddens never pre-exist actions. In fact, one need delve no further than Giddens's central and oft-repeated distinction between *systems* (which are those aspects of external structural outcomes that *do* only exist in concrete instances of instantiation; that is to say, as the result of actual social practices) and *structures* (which agents draw upon recursively in order to produce the recurrent social practices that constitute social systems) in order to undermine such an interpretation (cf. Giddens, 1979, pp. 65–9).

There are certainly areas within structuration that are underdeveloped and could benefit from criticism and elaboration, and the domain of the boundaries – the 'edges' – between structure and agency is just such an area. By the very act of highlighting this area Archer prompts a whole series of questions as to the ways and the extent to which structuration does and/or should conceptualise it. In order to judge whether other aspects of Archer's criticisms of structuration with respect to these 'edges' are justified, and to draw out the strengths and the limits of her critique, I will focus carefully on Giddens's treatment of these boundary issues. I will also review and draw in the acute contributions made by the Greek theorist Nicos Mouzelis to these issues. In doing this it is necessary, for the sake of analytical clarity, to distinguish between the boundary between external structures and agents, on the one hand, and the one between internal structures and action, on the other. It is important to recognise that the issues Archer raises about pre-existence, causal influence and autonomy are relevant to both, even though Archer's own target is the first boundary between external structures and agents. Mouzelis engages with both sets of boundaries.

Giddens and Nicos Mouzelis on Internal Structures and Agency

Let us look first at what Giddens writes about the boundaries and relations between internal structures and agency. When he speaks of agents drawing on virtual structures to produce practices he is always, in the first instance, referring – at least in large part – to internal structures, to the ideational and/ or perceptual grasp of the social context. We can look at what this might mean for an agent drawing on the structure of domination (power resources, transformative capacity), and how it relates to the other moments of the structuration process. The agent-in-focus will have a more or less clear, more or less explicit, sense of the power she has at her disposal. She will also have an equivalent sense of the power that others within the relevant context of action have at their disposal. Both of these senses – of the power perceived to be available to self and also to relevant others – are part of the internal structures; they are virtual senses of the power relations that attain at any one time in relation to a particular goal, desire or such like. When the agent acts, if she acts, then she will draw on this 'knowledge' (and the 'knowledge' may be more or less accurate) in order to produce her action. In saying that these 'virtual' structures become 'instantiated' in the action itself, Giddens just wants to say that there is a clear sense in which the knowledge that is drawn on – recursively, from stocks that pre-exist their use – to produce the action is in a certain sense also 'present' in that action. The knowledge of what the situation promises as possibility and requires as tribute will be carried through into the action, in the sense that the action is carried out on its basis. It informs and guides the action itself; it is a necessary immanent constituent of the action. It is, *pace* Archer, causally influential.

It is important to note that in following through the logic of this we have not made any definitive presumptions about either the relations between the internal structures and the external conditions of action, or between the internal structures and the subsequent external consequences or outcomes of action. In other words, we have said very little about the boundaries between, and the relations between, the internal and the external structures. The focus has been on just two parts of the structuration process: the internal structures and the agent's conduct in drawing upon them. Even here, however, there has been a clear sense not only that the internal structures are causally influential but also that they can pre-exist (time 1) the moment of their being drawn upon (time 2). I will usually be expected to have the sense that I have a $10 note before I decide to spend it. I will also know – more or less well – about my other forms and sources of wealth, income and likely calls on these within a relevant time horizon, and this background knowledge will play its part, virtually, in the action that is the spending of the $10 note.

In this specific realm of relations between internal structures and agency there is undoubtedly something to be said for Archer's lament about the inseparability of structure and agency. For it will often be the case that the agent-in-focus employing taken-for-granted knowledge of context and of 'how to go on' in the routine enactment of routine tasks will, herself, hardly be aware of any boundaries between the internal structures that are drawn upon and the agency that draws upon them. A situation such as this, in which the agent's orientation to the context of action is primarily what Nicos Mouzelis labels as 'natural/performative',[4] rather than one of critical distance and reflection upon that context, is, however, a limit case at one end of a continuum of possible relations between internal structures and agency (Mouzelis, 1991, p. 28; 2000, pp. 748–9). Mouzelis talks about this continuum in the same language that Giddens uses to talk about internal structures, the structuralist and post-structuralist language of the 'paradigmatic' axis that underlies the latter's characterisation of structures as 'virtual'. Just as a speaker of language draws on the available grammatical and substantive linguistic reservoir, or paradigm, of language at her disposal in order to utter a sentence, so agents draw on their 'paradigmatic' reservoir of internal social structures in order to engage in social action and interaction. Mouzelis has no problem in accepting this language and its implications. The introduction of the notion of a continuum, however, is an important qualification and refinement to what Giddens has to say about the relation between the virtual and agency. At one end of the continuum is the relationship between the two that is the one just mentioned of habitual, relatively unreflective, symbiosis in which the two merge into one another in the unfolding process of routinely getting on with life. This is very close to what Archer means by 'inseparability', and it is difficult to see why the close, almost seamless, interweaving of internal structures and agency in these cases should be held to signify a weakness for structuration theory. This is how things are in these cases and structuration theory represents this conceptually in a way that isn't in any obvious way unfaithful. The boundaries are indeed simply not clear to the agent-in-focus. The issue is naturally more complex when it comes to considering the ability of a third party, such as a sociological researcher, to identify separate aspects of structure and agency within the habitual, routine, practices of the agent-in-focus.[5]

In labelling this habitual, routine, end of the continuum (and the same will be true for the other extreme) I will not use Mouzelis's own term as it overlaps in a potentially confusing manner with other terms already used in my exposition.[6] Instead of his preferred term I will refer to it as the 'taken-for-granted duality' and I will contrast it with the 'critical duality' at the other end of the continuum. The latter, as already implied, refers to instances in which the agent has a degree of critical distance from the internal structures, such that she is able to take up a strategic-monitoring relationship to them, or to reflect upon them theoretically. The distinction is a valuable one at the most general, abstract, level of ontology. Mouzelis, however, goes further than this and makes the more theoretically substantive claim that the further the 'analysis shifts from individual to collective action, from micro to macro actions'[7] then there will be a tendency for more critically reflective attitudes towards received internal structures to come to the fore (Mouzelis, 1991, p. 30). Clearly at the 'critical duality' end of the continuum the agent herself has a sense of the difference between her own agency and the relevant internal structures which she both draws upon and responds to – creatively or otherwise. At this end of the continuum, therefore, structure and agency are not as inseparable as Archer feared, even as we are still focusing upon what I would feel is the 'harder case' of duality as medium, of the relation between agency and internal structures.

Mouzelis notes that the overall structuration process will be the result, *inter alia*, of a variegated mixture of types of critically distant and taken-for-granted relations between agents and their internal structures. Thus, the reproduction of the institution of marriage will typically involve a range of both habitual, routine and strategic-monitoring attitudes to the perceived 'rules' of marriage. Mouzelis usefully draws out the concrete implications of his conceptual distinctions as he argues that the critical distance sense of duality becomes:

> particularly salient as one moves from the partners of individual marriages to collective actors who, in a variety of ways, are concerned with the maintenance or transformation of marriage rules and resources. I have in mind here feminist groups championing women's rights, religious leaders trying to boost traditional family values, legislators wishing to transform the rules that apply to divorce or abortion, finance ministers considering the rules on inheritance, and so on. All the above, and many other strategic/monitoring orientations and concerns, are as crucial for understanding the reproduction and transformation of marriage rules and resources as are the day-to-day routine activities of husbands and wives (Mouzelis, 1991, p. 30).

One significant point upon which I diverge from Mouzelis is his belief that his conceptual innovations are somehow at odds with Giddens's account of structuration theory. Thus, Mouzelis presents Giddens's notion of duality as intrinsically equivalent to his own category of taken-for-granted duality, as if the implication is that agents in structuration theory always just 'take' the internal structures that are given to them by society and reproduce them in an acritical, routine, manner (Mouzelis, 1991, pp. 27–31; 1995, pp. 137–8; 2000, pp. 748–9) On my reading this was never Giddens's intention. There is too much emphasis on agents as skilled, knowledgeable, interpretative, reflexive, and able to do otherwise, for this to ring true. Indeed, in Giddens's rejoinder to Mouzelis in the preface to the second edition of *New Rules of Sociological Method,* he argues as much, accepting the 'sort of distancing Mouzelis has in mind', emphasising that this is endemic in the institutionalisation of investigative and calculative attitudes towards system reproduction in the 'post-traditional' conditions of modernity (Giddens, 1993/1976, p. 6). It is clear that he agrees with Mouzelis that the degree of distancing is variable. At the same time he re-emphasises the more general ontological point that, whatever their place on the continuum, agents still cannot step outside the 'flow' of action and the flow always involves agents in drawing upon and reconstituting structures – creatively or otherwise (Giddens, 1993/1976, pp. 5–7). It seems very clear to me that it is better to acknowledge Mouzelis's innovations here not as contradicting structuration theory but as insightful conceptual refinements at the level of ontology-in-general that immediately enhance the critical potential of structuration theory as it becomes ontology directed towards the *in situ* and empirical level.

External Structures and the Agent

Giddens and Archer on External Structures and Constraints

If we add the moment of the external conditions of action to the picture then we add Archer's notion of external structures at time 1, the external structural moment that is the basis for being able to identify structural conditions independently of the actions that are possible within the limits of those conditions, and the moment that precedes social interaction and its immediate outcome (times 2 and 3). I would agree with Archer on the importance of this moment for social analysis. I would also say that Giddens leaves this area of structuration badly under-developed at the level of ontology. Nevertheless, and paralleling what we have already seen with internal structures, we can state categorically that Archer goes too far in her strong claim that there is no room in Giddens's version of structuration for pre-existent and causally influential external structures. That this claim is unfounded can be seen very clearly from looking at two sets of his comments on the nature of constraints upon agency, firstly in his introduction to the second edition of *New Rules of Sociological Method*, and secondly in *The Constitution of Society*. In the first case Giddens could not be more direct: 'It is perfectly obvious that every situated actor faces an environment of action that has an "objectivity" for him or her in a quasi-Durkheimian sense' (Giddens, 1993, p. 7). The second example of the same stance is more elaborately theorised. Here he distinguishes between three aspects of constraints posed for the actor by the environment facing him or her: material constraints, negative social sanctions and also 'structural constraints' that derive from the 'given' character of structural properties *vis-à-vis* situated actors (Giddens, 1984, p. 176). Giddens, as usual, explicates these concepts – the three different types of constraint – in terms of ontology-in-general, but it is not difficult for us, in addition, to draw out the implications for ontology-*in-situ*, and also to elaborate on what is logically entailed by them. 'Structural Constraint', says Giddens:

> stems from the 'objective' existence of structural properties that the individual agent is unable to change. As with the constraining qualities of sanctions, it is best described as *placing limits upon the range of options open to an actor, or plurality of actors, in a given circumstance or type of circumstance* (Giddens, 1984, pp. 176–7, original emphasis).

This notion of 'objective existence' refers to external structures[8] in Archer's sense. The example Giddens discusses in this context is that of the labour contract which often confronts the worker-in-focus as a feature of an external reality that he or she cannot change. When such objective existents make it impossible for the agent-in-focus to do certain things then they have the character of external constraints. Giddens's example makes it evident that normative considerations (in this case encoded in law) may well play a decisive role in creating and sustaining the relevant constraint. In many, perhaps most, cases the external situation will contain objective existents that are resistant to change by the agent-in-focus but which are not experienced in this way as they don't prevent her from doing what she wants to do – they may even enable, facilitate, desired actions. For example, the labour laws that are on the whole inequitable, and that are resistant to change, can nevertheless still facilitate, in their unchanged form, a desired action against a category of unfair treatment at work that is in fact covered by them. In this latter case, external constraints may still make themselves felt in the form of normative sanctions after the event as managerial agents within the external context react punitively to what they perceive as trouble-making, the transgression of what they considered to be acceptable 'deferential' behaviour. In this case the agent-in-focus would thus have sanctions applied during time 3 or at time 4.

The latter example draws attention to a distinction between the type of constraint that renders certain actions literally impossible and the type that doesn't make the actions impossible in the first instance but, instead, poses a constraint in the sense that such actions, once performed, would probably incur a punishment of some kind. This is the distinction that Giddens makes between constraint as normative sanction and constraint as structural constraint. In an important sense the label that Giddens gives to these different forms of constraint is misleading. It would be better to have labelled them as, say, structural sanctions and structural constraints, as this would have avoided the implication that negative sanctions somehow don't involve structures. For it is important to be clear that both structural constraints and the likelihood of normative sanctions are both aspects of the external structures that face the agent-in-focus, just as, also, are material constraints.[9] The examples of the labour contract and of potential management reaction to 'trouble-making' as different types of structural constraint both point to the fact that the constraining external structures are socially produced and sustained by agents. These agents, of course, are themselves socially situated agents, no doubt themselves subject to various pressures and constraints. In the face of Archer's critiques it is necessary to emphasise and insist upon this point. Namely, that the very notion of external constraints, or, in Archer's wider terms, of the structural conditions at time 1 (or at time 4), has itself to be conceptualised as containing agents, and thus as containing internal structures within these agents. Another way of expressing this is to say that the combination of structure and agency within the person or agent – where structures within agents are the *medium* of social practices – that Archer attacks in structuration is itself a necessary component of an adequate conceptualisation of the external structures that are the basis of Archer's notion of dualism. To be fair to Archer it is also the case that Giddens never makes this sufficiently clear as his preoccupation with internal structures entails a consequent failure to sufficiently explicate the notion of external structures that logically underpins his notion of structural constraint (see Stones, 2001).

Logical consistency with Giddens's structuration theory would necessarily, it seems to me, entail the following. The external structures facing a particular agent-in-focus at time 1 would provide a range of possibilities for, and/or constraints on, action. At a minimum, any notion of external structures would have to recognise their threefold impact on the agent-in-focus's ability to act:

1. by enlisting the aid of 'objectively existing' structures of *domination/power* in order to pursue certain goals, or by being subject to the constraints entailed by the distribution of power amongst non-compliant others;
2. through successfully deploying *normative* sanctions and rewards on the basis of more or less mutually acknowledged social norms embedded in the 'objectively existing' structures of legitimation, or by being subject to

the constraints entailed by the character and distribution of these views of appropriate normative behaviour;

3. as a result of being facilitated or constrained by the *interpretative schemes* of the agents within the relevant structural context.

Given what we have seen of Giddens's account of external constraints, of the relation between constraints and structures in his theoretical framework, and of the broader logical implications of his position, it would be absurd to continue to insist that there is no place, and can be no place, in structuration theory for external structures that either pre-exist agency or have a causal influence on the outcome of agent's practices.[10] The same is true for the issue of the 'autonomy' of external structures in Giddens's work, as is shown by the clear possibility of distinguishing between external structures and the agent-in-focus. It is quite as possible in structuration theory as it is in realist social theory to distinguish between structure and agency.

The upshot of this is that structuration theory, contrary to Archer's argument, does have a notion of dualism that is perfectly compatible with Archer's notion of a dualism between structure and agency. To remind ourselves, Archer argues that social realism and its methodological component, morphogenesis:

> need a means of identifying structure(s) independently of their occupants and incumbents, yet of showing its effects upon them (establishing the reality of structures via the causal criterion), whilst coping with the intervention of other contingent relations, and accounting for the eventual outcome which either reproduces or transforms the original structure ... this is predicated upon the non-conflation of structure and agency and their analytical separation on a temporal basis (Archer, 1995, pp. 167–8).

Cohen and Shilling on Position-Practices and their Relations

There is one final issue, related to the quotation from Archer just cited, that it is necessary to confront before we can move on. This is the issue of whether, and/or to what extent, one can identify structures independently of their occupants. I want to argue that Archer is wrong about structuration theory when she claims that it 'disallows the pre-existence of structures (roles, positions, relations) which are ... made both *co-existent* and also *co-terminous* with agency. Structures then become the responsibility of agents in the present tense which leaves behind a final splatter of question marks' (Archer, 1995, p 99; cf. p. 95). Archer goes on to provide the splatter of questions which are so fundamental to social theory that structuration theory's putative inability to confront them would, if it were true, render it preposterous. It is worthwhile, in the face of such an assault, taking a few more lines to consolidate the defence so far made of structuration theory.

Firstly, I want to further undermine the possibility of agreeing too easily with Archer by noting that one of the main authorities for her argument that structuration cannot disentangle the agent from external structures, John B. Thompson, doesn't himself hold to such a position. He believes, on the contrary, that on the basis of the general ontology of structuration one would have no difficulty in acknowledging that:

> institutions, conceived of as regularized practices which are 'deeply layered' in time and space, both pre-exist and post-date the lives of the individuals who reproduce them, and thus may be resistant to manipulation or change by any particular agent (Thompson, 1989, pp. 72–3).

Secondly, and more substantively, I want to stress that along with its insistence upon the pre-existence of structures in general, structuration theory also has no problem in finding a place for both the pre-existence and the emergent qualities[11] of roles and positions as significant aspects of the constitution of those structures. This can be seen, for example, in Ira J. Cohen's use and elaboration of a combination of Giddens's notion of 'social positions' and Roy Bhaskar's notion of 'position-practices' (which he prefers to the overly passive concept of 'role' although there are clearly some inheritances from Merton's notion of role-set, see chapter 1) in chapter 6 of *Structuration Theory* (Cohen, 1989, pp. 207–13; also cf. Bhaskar, 1979, pp. 48–51; Giddens,1984, pp. 83–4 and pp. 282–3). Cohen specifies and details a whole series of properties possessed by, or impinging upon, position-practices and what he calls *position-practice relations*, properties that include:

- positional identities defined in terms of identifying criteria such as documented qualifications and observable attributes
- clusters of practices through which identifying criteria, prerogatives and obligations are made manifest in ways that are generally acknowledged by others
- the range of other positions-practices that must be, or can be, interrelated with a given position-practice
- a range of institutionalised reciprocities, including asymmetrical power relations, through which position-practice relations occur (p. 210).

Whilst more detailed Cohen's use of this notion has striking similarities with Archer's own adoption and adaptation of Bhaskar's earlier conceptualisation (cf. Archer, 1995, pp. 152–3). Whilst Cohen wishes to modify Bhaskar's sense that there are structural ' slots into which active subjects must slip in order to reproduce structure' (Cohen, 1989, p. 209) this is only to the extent that Bhaskar under-emphasises the point that such 'slots' need themselves to be continually sustained through practices or active 'position-taking'. Cohen believes this is important in order to avoid the reification of structures and, instead, to retain the ontological emphasis on praxis within processes of structuration.

Institutionalised positions, positional identities, the sense of prerogatives and obligations, and so on, can all be seen as the emergent properties of past practices and as the pre-existent conditions for subsequent actions. Such a conception is clear in Cohen's example of the 'vertical' position-practice relations between workers on the shop floor of a car factory and upper-level administrators of the plant. These 'positions', and the relational practices they presuppose, once established, will pre-exist the particular human agents that subsequently inhabit, reproduce or transform those position-practices. The same can be said of Cohen's notion of 'horizontal' position-practice relations which:

> exist between the assembly-line workers, and workers who extract raw materials and build component parts through labour transacted in a variety of remote work sites. In addition, following the insight into social relations which underlies Marx's analysis of the 'fetishism of commodities', position-practice relations may also be identified between the workers who produce automobiles and the agents who purchase and use these automobiles during the course of their daily lives. Even this, however, may not exhaust all possibilities. By virtue of the fact that taxes or social insurance fees are withheld from their paychecks, as well as by virtue of legal rights which may be invoked to forestall certain unsafe or 'unfair' managerial procedures, the position-practice of workers may also be related to position-practices in various 'branches' or bureaucracies of the state (i.e. position-practices in the relevant reproduction circuits of the state system) (Cohen, 1989, p. 212).

There is, therefore, a very real sense in which key dimensions of these position-practice 'slots' can be identified independently of their incumbents. It must be remembered, however, that their reproduction is contingent, *inter alia*, on the activity of position-taking and making and is by no means automatic. For Cohen these positions and the practices and relations that underpin them endure as structured clusters of institutions to the extent that successive generations of agents participate in their reproduction (Cohen, 1989, p. 210). Nevertheless, whatever changes are brought about at times 2 to 4, there will be a range of emergent characteristics of positions and position-practice relations that have more or less consistently crystallised at time 1 and which can be identified independently of the character of particular incumbents.[12]

Similar and complementary points to those made by Cohen are put forward by Chris Shilling in the context of arguing for the ability of structuration theory to provide a bridge between macro and micro studies in the sociology of education (Shilling, 1997/1992, pp. 355–6). Shilling argues that the idea of social positions allows one to separate the bundle of practices associated with the job of a particular kind of teacher at a given time from the way that any one incumbent performs that role. After the 1988 Education Reform Act in Britain this bundle of practices included, amongst other things, 'implementing a highly bureaucratised national curriculum, with its attendant assessment requirements, and responding to the demands of school governing committees and the local management of schools' (Shilling, 1997/1992, p. 356). Expectations will not be exhaustive of a social position, they may well be contested, and any given teacher, for a number of reasons, may or may not carry out the corresponding range of expected practices. On the other hand, it is likely that if a certain threshold of performance is not reached with respect to many of these expectations then punitive sanctions would be likely to follow over time. It is, in any case, possible to identify bundles of practices associated with social positions at any one time, and to do so at time 1, before the incumbent begins her job, or her day. As Archer well understands, one advantage of emphasising the *sui generis* nature of external structures at time 1 is that there may well be a disjuncture between the requirements loaded onto a position and the ability of an incumbent agent to carry out such expectations. This may be due to lack of training or to personal inadequacy, but it may also be due to an overload of expectations, and this, in turn, will often reflect a mismatch between the bundle of expectations and the resources made available to the incumbent of a position. This would place the onus of change on one or the other of these external structural dimensions rather than on the agent valiantly struggling to do the impossible. Thus, for example, writing in 1991/92 Shilling noted that:

> there is mounting evidence that the social position of teacher is not equipping individuals with the capacity to carry out the expected practices attached to this identity as a result of the 1988 Education Reform Act (Shilling, 1997/1992, p. 356).

In addition to the emphasis on the pre-existence and autonomy of position-practice relations, one can also draw from the above examples taken from adherents of structuration theory a commitment to *emergent properties* of the kind outlined by Archer in *Realist Social Theory* (p. 14). An essential aspect of the definition of emergence that Archer provides there – in combination with other aspects such as the autonomy of different strata and their possession of independent causal powers – is that the properties and powers of some strata of social existents and practices are anterior to those of others, 'precisely because the latter emerge from the former over time, for emergence takes time since it derives from interaction and its consequences which necessarily occur in time' (Archer, 1995, p. 14). For example, one can extract from Cohen's example the fact that the company's ability to continue to employ workers at time 4 would, all things being equal, have emerged from its ability to make a profit in the previous time cycle which, in turn, must have emerged from the workers' capacity to assemble automobiles and the consumers' actions in purchasing them. The capacity of assembly, in turn, will have been emergent from the combination of previously learned skills, the factory infrastructure and the component parts. The component parts themselves will be emergent from the processes of the extraction of raw materials and the labour applied to their manufacture. The subsequent acquisition of these components by the assembly factory is itself an emergent product of organisation, finance, transportation and the infrastructure the latter relies upon. The taxes taken from their paychecks emerge from all these factors combined and these, in turn, contribute to the emergence of the federal and state budgets, and so on.

It is worth pausing here to ask whether Cohen's account of position-practice relations, meeting as it does Archer's objections to what she felt structuration theory to be, does not in so doing fall into the same trap as Giddens's 'structural sets' (such as that representing Marx's account of the key structural relations involved in the capitalist system of production – see p. 49) that were criticised by Thompson. Is Cohen not in fact similarly falling back upon a more conventional notion of structure whilst, like Giddens, failing to account for and to justify its continued putative identification with structuration's emphasis on agents drawing upon rules and resources? This is not the case as long as we understand the elaborate conceptual framework of position-practice relations as being pitched at the level of ontology-in-general, and the particular illustrative examples offered by Cohen as providing only an initial frame or set of markers, informed by the ontology-in-general, for the subsequent hermeneutically-informed investigation of particular agents drawing on particular combinations of structures. The illustrative examples are not yet examples, in and of themselves, of structuration-*in-situ*, but the degree of detail Cohen provides at the conceptual level means that it is far more apparent how one would begin to investigate particular research questions paying attention to hermeneutic-structural issues than it is for Giddens's much emptier, more abstractly systemic, notions of structural principles, structural sets and structural axes.

Moreover, the complex apparatus of position-practice relations provides a useful meso-level bridge by means of which conceptions of larger historical forces and more conventional, broader, notions of structure can potentially be brought into contact with studies based on strong structuration. For whilst Cohen's meso-level conceptual framework has a key role to play, there is a sense in which the very need to incorporate such a relational framework reinforces Thompson's central point that a meaningful investigation of agents drawing on rules and resources seems also to require wider frames of analysis. The argument here is that a strong structuration synthesis requires us to add to Thompson's emphasis on institutional and systemic-structural levels of analysis a further level that emphasises the immediate *in situ* relational configuration of forces that constitutes the horizon of action for particular agents. The points against Archer, however, also remain valid –

notwithstanding what has been gained from her emphasis on external structures – in that it is wrong to suggest that structuration theory's particular emphasis on the inter-relationship between structure and agency means that structures (whether external structures or internal structures) cannot be emergent, autonomous, pre-existent or causally influential.

Mouzelis on Modifiable and Intractable External Structures

The work of Nicos Mouzelis again provides an interesting contrast to Archer's in that he has no problem accepting that there is a notion of external structures, of dualism, within structuration theory. At the same time aspects of his work can be seen as complementary to Archer's position in that they provide further refinements to the conceptualisation of dualism, of the relation between situated agents and the external constraints they face. Both Archer and Mouzelis take things further than Giddens in this respect. Mouzelis's concepts are developed at the level of ontology-in-general but they are sensitive from the start to questions of ontology-*in-situ*. Whilst in discussing the relations between internal structures and agency he drew on the structuralist and post-structuralist notion of the 'paradigmatic', he now uses the notion of the 'syntagmatic' from the same tradition. The syntagmatic in linguistics refers to the surface patterning of language as it is spoken or written, as it manifests itself in time and space once it has been produced, in contrast to a focus on the grammar, mechanics and sources of its actual production. In the context of social relations Mouzelis means the syntagmatic to refer likewise to the moments at which actions and interactions unfold in time and space. Such unfolding necessarily involves 'the relationship between situated actors and what Giddens calls the structural properties of a social system (or what to conventional sociologists are social structures)' (Mouzelis, 1991, p. 37). It refers to the unfolding relations between situated actors and the patterned social relations of the external structures as they exist in time and space.

Mouzelis creates another continuum here, at one end of which are those external structures that an agent can significantly affect, structures that the individual agent is able to change. Mouzelis labels this 'syntagmatic dualism' and I will sometimes use this term, although I will usually refer to the notion with the phrases *modifiable dualism* or *malleable dualism* to indicate more obviously the ability of the agent to have some sort of impact on the external structures.[13] At the other end are those external structures that are relatively intractable to the agent's (or a given plurality of agents') actions that act as constraints, that place limits upon the options open to her. Mouzelis labels this 'syntagmatic duality' which is potentially very confusing given the meanings that other authors attribute to duality. Consequently, I will label this concept of Mouzelis's, *intractable dualism*, drawing attention both to external structures (dualism) and to the inability of agents to affect or change those external structures.

As we shall see in the next chapter Mouzelis links these concepts very effectively to notions of social hierarchies and he is clear that what might be an intractable external constraint to one agent wouldn't be so to another agent differentially situated in terms of positions higher up the scale of a social hierarchy of one kind or another. The latter are what he calls 'macro-actors' – for which he gives the examples from the field of education of college directors, university vice-chancellors, and ministers of education; this concept overlaps with, but is not identical to, his use of the notion of collective actors mentioned above (see p. 57) – whose location enables them to take decisions which extend more widely in time and space, whose power base gives them a capability such that the consequences of their decisions and actions affect the situations of many people (Mouzelis, 1991, pp. 39 and 107). Mouzelis manages, amongst other things, to provide concepts that can provide a useful counter to what he calls the 'the populistic obsession of micro-sociologists' with treating all 'laypersons' or members of society as somehow equal in terms of their social effects. The subtle separating out of different types of relations between actors and the external structures that confront them serves quite effectively to 'underline the highly unequal contribution of actors to the creation and recreation of social orders' (Mouzelis, 1991, p. 108).

William H. Sewell Jr's Reformulation of Structures

In an article published in the *American Journal of Sociology* in July 1992 and much cited subsequently, William H. Sewell Jr argues that there are serious unresolved problems with Giddens's claim that both of the rules and resources elements of his conception of structures should be seen as virtual. He argues that only the former – structures as rules – should be thought of as virtual, whilst the latter – structures as resources – are better thought of as actual. A qualification he adds to the conceptualisation of the 'rules' structures as virtual is that he prefers to replace the overly rigid and potentially misleading terminology of 'rules' with the notion of cultural 'schemas'. He argues that the terminology of 'cultural schemas' is more flexible and encompassing, and thus better able to signal the many different possible aspects of meaning and meaningful action (Sewell, 1992, pp. 7–8). I agree with Sewell, and for the reasons he gives, that the use of the term 'schemas' is preferable to the notion of rules, which imposes a false sense of homogeneity on a complex and varied range of phenomena. I prefer 'schemas', however, to 'cultural schemas' as the generic term to use for this, retaining the possibility of attaching one from a range of adjectives to the term depending upon the particular instance at hand. It is also unclear to me why Sewell wouldn't want to include formal, codified, cultural schemas in addition to more informal schemas.[14] Having said this, he explains with clarity and force why he takes the various schemas that make up this aspect of structures to be generalisable. They provide agents with cultural knowledge of 'how to go on' in a range of different circumstances. Such schemas, he says:

> can be used not only in the situation in which they are first learned or most conventionally applied. They can be generalized – that is, transposed or extended – to new situations when the opportunity arises. This *generalizability* or *transposability* of schemas is the reason they must be understood as virtual. To say that schemas are virtual is to say that they cannot be reduced to their existence in any particular practice or any particular location in space and time: they can be actualized in a potentially broad and unpredetermined range of situations (Sewell, 1992, p. 8, original emphasis).

Sewell wishes to include within such generalisable and transposable schemas not only the 'deep' binary oppositions that structuralists and post-structuralists emphasise; although he certainly would want to include these. He also wants to include 'the various conventions, recipes, scenarios, principles of action, and habits of speech and gesture built up with these fundamental tools' (Sewell, 1992, pp. 7–8). This understanding of Giddens's notion of virtual 'rules', under the new label of cultural schemas, is highly reminiscent of Bourdieu's notion of habitus, and indeed, later on in the article, Sewell acknowledges his debt to the French theorist, noting that the term 'generalisable' in the formulation quoted above is taken from Giddens whilst the term 'transposable' is from Bourdieu. Sewell is particularly attracted to the latter term due to its implication that the cultural knowledge, skill or disposition will not only be applied differently in different circumstances but will also itself undergo subtle transformations in form and content in the process of such concrete application (Sewell, 1992, p. 17 and n. 9). In this context he approvingly quotes Bourdieu's definition of habitus as:

> a system of lasting transposable dispositions which, integrating past experiences, functions at every moment as a *matrix of perceptions, appreciations, and actions* and makes possible the achievement of infinitely diversified tasks, thanks to analogical transfers of schemes permitting the solution of similarly shaped problems (Bourdieu, 1977, p. 83, emphasis in original; quoted in Sewell, 1992, p. 17).

Sewell argues that resources are not virtual in the same way as are such cultural schemas. Giddens classifies resources into two types, authoritative and allocative. The first of these involves control over people, the second control over things, and so Sewell translates these in terms of the human and non-human. Both are media of power and having control over either of these two kinds of resources can increase an agent's 'transformative capacity' or ability to bring things about (Sewell, 1992, pp. 9–10). Sewell argues that it is 'particularly doubtful' that non-human resources such as factories, weapons, land and blankets, and so on, used in a variety of social situations are virtual rather than actual 'since material things by definition exist in space and time. It is, moreover, only in particular times, places, and quantities that such material objects can serve as resources' (Sewell, 1992, p. 10).[15]

More than this, however, Sewell argues that it is also difficult to accept that authoritative or human resources – power or command over persons – are virtual rather than actual. Examples he gives of the power one person has over the actions of others include the power of a Roman Catholic priest to hear confession, the obligation that children feel towards their mothers, and the fear and reverence subjects feel towards their king. He argues that such resources exist in time-space: 'they are observable characteristics of real people who live in particular times and congregate in particular places. And it is their actualization in people's minds and bodies that makes them resources' (Sewell, 1992, p. 10).

Sewell concludes that the structures at the heart of Giddens's notion of the duality of structure need to be conceived as having a dual character, with rules or schemas (meanings and norms) being seen as virtual, and resources as actual. As he puts it: 'Structure, then, should be defined as composed simultaneously of schemas, which are virtual, and of resources, which are actual' (Sewell, 1992, p. 13). He goes on to say that if we think in this way of there being two kinds of structures then we can also think of the two kinds as sustaining and affecting each other:

> If resources are effects of schemas, it is also true that schemas are effects of resources. If schemas are to be sustained or reproduced over time – and without sustained reproduction they could hardly be counted as structural – they must be validated by the accumulation of resources that their enactment engenders. Schemas not empowered or regenerated by resources would eventually be abandoned and forgotten, just as resources without cultural schemas to direct their use would eventually dissipate and decay. Sets of schemas and resources may properly be said to constitute *structures* only when they mutually imply and sustain each other over time (Sewell, 1992, p. 13, original emphasis)

Despite the service that Sewell provides in drawing attention to the under-elaborated tension between resources and rules, and between the virtual and the actual in Giddens's writings, the conclusions he has drawn are flawed and confusing. Firstly, with respect to the above quotation, Margaret Archer has convincingly argued against Sewell that there is no reason whatsoever why we should expect rules and resources – schemas and resources – to be so closely wedded to each other. She is quite right to insist that the 'relation between "rules and resources" is a matter of contingency not necessity' (Archer, 1995, p. 112). I would add that there is also no reason to restrict the notion of structure to entities whose reproduction is sustained over time. One of the most important dimensions of the duality of structure is that structures have inherent qualities that can be drawn upon by agents at time 2. In order to have these qualities they need only exist in the moment (time 1) immediately prior to their being drawn upon. There is no need for them to have existed for any longer than this in order to qualify as structures that provide such conditions of possibility.

Secondly, and more importantly in the present context, Sewell takes a wrong turning in moving from his insightful observations about the tensions between the actual and the virtual in Giddens's conception of material resources (see chapter 1, p. 18) to the conclusion that schemas are virtual and all aspects of resource are actual. Thus, for example, when writing of the power resources or capabilities of the priest, the mother and the king, Sewell is mistaken to reduce these to the actual. For the whole cycle of structuration in which power is drawn upon as medium and emerges as outcome is not captured by a simple observation of the characteristics of real people, living in particular times and congregating in particular places. In arguing that it is the 'actualisation' of such things as authority and obligations 'in people's minds and bodies that makes them resources' (Sewell, 1992, p. 10) Sewell is in fact no longer talking of just the actual but also of the virtual. Once one begins to speak of what happens in people's minds and bodies in relation to their orientation to social context, then one necessarily involves the realm of the virtual. No doubt part of the problem is the under-developed and under-explicated nature of Giddens's own writing on these concepts. In any case, Sewell's mistake is the result of an over-simplified model of what is involved in the structuration process. He underestimates what is logically involved in Giddens's notion of the virtual, reducing it to only one of two key dimensions of the concept that have not thus far been introduced.[16] I want to argue that it is as a result of this 'flattening out' of these two aspects of the virtual that he fails to see the role that resources play within this realm. On the basis of this formulation I will argue that resources have a fourfold existence in the structuration cycle, and that Sewell's limited conceptualisation of the virtual prevents him from being able to capture this. I will first explain what I mean by there being two relevant aspects to Giddens's virtual (internal) structures, only one of which is grasped by Sewell, and then I will go on to show how Sewell's limited conception leads him to neglect the role played by resources within the virtual.

We have already seen that Sewell includes in his understanding of the virtual only the idea of the generalisability and transposability of cultural schemas (i.e. the generalisability and transposability of internal structures). These, we can recall, include the various conventions, recipes, scenarios, principles of action, habits of speech and gesture and the discursive binary oppositions by which the world is perceived and/or practically apprehended. Agents can and do draw upon these schemas in a plurality of new contexts, as in the case of the complex repertoires of skills employed by agents in the interaction rituals analysed by Goffman, and implicit in such use is the ability of agents to act creatively (Sewell, 1992, pp. 8 and 20). I agree with Sewell that Giddens does include this dimension within his notion of the agent, evident not least in the influence of Schutz, ethnomethodology, Goffman and Wittgenstein upon his work and in his related emphasis on agents' practical consciousness, and that it contains many elements that are identical to Bourdieu's notion of habitus. I feel that Bourdieu's treatment of this conceptual space is more fully developed, however, and that it provides a greater sense of inherited substance and weight than Giddens's treatment. I will return to this point in the next chapter.

On the other hand, an important dimension of internal or virtual structures is neglected when Sewell identifies them solely with the realm of the transposable and the generalisable. The neglected dimension is what I will call the 'conjuncturally specific' aspects of internal or virtual structures. For Giddens's emphasis on knowledgeability and stocks of knowledge is linked not only to agents' transposable and generalisable knowledge but also to the specific 'circumstances of their action and that of others' (Giddens, 1984, p. 375), and also to questions concerning the 'bounds of agents' knowledge-ability in the shifting contexts of time and space' (Giddens, 1984, p. 328). Giddens emphasises, for example, that any study of the unintended consequences and unacknowledged conditions of action would require reference to the knowledgeability of the relevant agents. Such knowledge-ability would, of course, involve knowledge of generalisable procedure and mastery of generalisable techniques (cf. Giddens, 1984, p. 22), but it would also involve specific knowledge of the specific circumstances of particular, shifting, contexts of time and space. Whilst the analytical distinction between the two forms of virtual (internal) structures is not one that Giddens has himself made explicit, a strong case can be made that it is their implicit combination that makes his structuration approach distinctive. Much of what Giddens has written about agents drawing upon the social structures of legitimation, domination and signification would make no sense unless both dimensions were included. Again, more will be said on this in chapter 3.

Having established Sewell's limited conception of the virtual we can now go on to show how this leads him to neglect the role played by resources within it. For on the basis of the more elaborated notion of the virtual one can now distinguish between four different moments of the structuration cycle, each with a particular relation to resources. These four 'moments' of structures within the cycle are:

1. as external, latent or potential, material and ideational conditions of action, including resources that may be directly controlled by oneself, although conceptualised as external, and those that are in various ways dependent upon the compliance of others;

2. as an agent's virtual internal structures with the character of *generalisable* stocks, schemas and skills that provide the transposable basis of 'how to go on';
3. as an agent's virtual internal structures with the character of *conjuncturally specific* knowledge of the norms, interpretative schemes and power resources of the relevant agents within context;
4. as the medium of the exercise of power at the point of interaction.

Each one of these moments would be involved in the range of processes by which:

- an agent benefits from her 'power' to use, in action, a 'material' weapon or a blanket;
- a priest or confessor engages in the joint actions of giving and hearing a confession, thus benefiting from the 'non-material' power of the priest's authority;
- a sequence of joint actions is produced such that a king manages to effect the compliance of his subjects or a mother that of her children.

Sewell identifies only the second of the four moments as virtual which, given that the virtual quality of *resources* is most evident at the third moment relating to the specific conjuncture, means that it is now more understandable how he comes to altogether overlook the role that resources play within the virtual. Whilst one can, in fact, see many of the aspects of the second moment as resources (the ability to use language or skills, for example), it is more immediately obvious that social practices involving the kinds of resources that Sewell focuses upon – for example, the material resources of blankets, land, factories and weapons – would be informed by a relationship between these external things and an agent's conjuncturally specific perception or knowledge of these. Agents would thus be engaged in *a phenomenology of resources*. They wouldn't just use them in some sort of mechanical or behaviourist fashion such that their only existence was at the point of use. The same considerations apply with respect to the king, priest or mother's conjuncturally specific perceptions of the humans whom they wish to comply with their wants (human resources). In other words, if the third moment had been recognised then it would have been difficult for Sewell to overlook the importance of the virtual quality and role of resources. The overall hermeneutic frame of an agent will contain within it both rules *and* resources, to use Giddens's terms. If we were to adopt Sewell's preferred label of 'cultural schemas' then this too would need to acknowledge a space within such schemas for a phenomenology of resources. Resources would, indeed, have an external, actual, basis, but they would also have an internal, hermeneutic, basis. Thus, for example, the overall cultural schema would *contain within it* conceptions and perceptions of a range of authoritative and allocative power resources relevant to the various horizons of action that emerge as an agent engages in this or that activity. In other words, it is not only schemas that are virtual. Resources as perceived within these schemas should also be conceived of in virtual terms.

A logical implication of this is that non-human objects (land, weapons, food, and so on) will, on the one hand, be part of the external structural context (and so will have an actual existence in Sewell's terms), but they can also, just as clearly, play a part – more or less accurately, and inflected by the particular phenomenological perspective or cultural schema of the agent(s) in focus – in the internal structures (the virtual) that can be drawn upon by the agent. The distinction between external and internal structures is essential to this observation. It is only once the resources of external structures (say weapons, or food) have been perceived (often in a pre-reflective, taken-for-granted manner) as internal structures by agents who then act on their basis (they wield and fire the weapons, they cook and eat the food) that those external structural resources will become a tangible, actual, part of the action produced. They will, at such moments, provide what Giddens calls the 'material levers' for the action (Giddens, 1979, p. 104).

It is necessary to add another layer of complexity to this picture. Informed action with respect to, say, material resources would draw from conjuncturally specific internal structures that indicated whether one owned or had proximate control of those resources. More than this, it would often also include conjuncturally specific perceptions of the norms, interpretative schemes and overall power (including other resources) of the actors within the context who in fact did have proximate control of those resources, or who had the ability to place obstacles in the way of your acquiring them. The perception of one's own ability to acquire the use of those 'actual' material resources would depend, therefore, upon an internal knowledge of human agents within the relevant external structural context. This shows, amongst other things, just how much care needs to be taken when working with either Giddens' or Sewell's very simple analytical separation of forms of power into:

- command over persons (authoritative power) and command over objects and other material phenomena (allocative power) in Giddens's case;
- human and non-human resources in Sewell's case.

Both types of power are quickly involved in close inter-dependence with each other in most actual social uses of material resources such as land, weapons, food, or factories. In societies with complex divisions of labour, power over the constitution of one's own capabilities (resources) will typically be highly circumscribed. Much will depend upon others within the external structures, their resources, practices, and the virtual schemas they draw from in allocating and authorising. Exercises of power will usually involve a range of configurations of both human and non-human resources in their production.

The divide into authoritative and allocative resources can only ever be a short-hand means of suggesting a relative emphasis within a much more complex process.

Such exercises of power will also typically involve structurally situated actors in chains of what symbolic interactionists call 'joint actions' (for example, Plummer, 1991; and 1995, pp. 18–31). With respect to one of Sewell's examples, the mother's ability to get the daughter to comply with her own wants would be one link in such a chain. The emergent result of the child acting out an obligation towards her mother at the level of the actual would necessarily have involved both the mother and the daughter in processes of drawing upon internal structures, upon their virtual perceptions/cultural schemas in relation to this power relation. The mother's capability to successfully command her daughter to do what she wants her to do (actualising the mother's authoritative resource) will involve both her and her daughter drawing upon mutually understood, often tacit, meanings ('what do I want my daughter to do?', 'what does my mother want me to do?'), and on normative obligations ('she should/will feel obliged to obey me', 'am I obliged to comply with my mother's wishes?'). There may also be a perception of the potential power sanctions involved in not complying, or the daughter's loyalty and commitment to her mother may be so unquestioned that this never becomes an issue. Once the daughter acts, drawing on her internal perception of structures to produce a social practice of compliance with her mother's wishes, then she does 'actualise' her mother's authoritative power. But this is only the end product, the outcome, of a structuration process in which both mother's and daughter's perceptions of authority relations – their perceptions of these resources as an element of internal structures – played a central role. Similar things could be said about the king's relations with his subjects or the priest's relations with his confessors. There would inevitably also be material factors involved in this process, whether this was the use of a church building for confession or of an army's weapons by a king in search of his subjects' compliance. For most purposes it is better to conceptualise *both* allocative and authoritative forms of power as involving the ability to harness varying composites of material and non-material, human and non-human resources. In turn, each of these forms of power will be produced in cycles of structuration in which the virtual structures of the participating actors will be as important as the dimensions of resources and of people that can be said to be actual.

In the course of evaluating Sewell Jr's contribution, and the contribution of the other writers discussed above, to the critique of structuration theory I have tried to draw lessons for a revised and stronger theory of structuration. The next chapter provides a more detailed, extended and systematic exploration of this stronger, reinvigorated, conception of structuration

3

Strong Structuration 1: Ontology

In this chapter I again take up the themes of strong structuration, ontology-*in-situ* and empirical analysis, themes that, in chapter 1, were contrasted briefly with Giddens's version of structuration theory which restricts itself more to the abstract, philosophical level of ontology-in-general. Here I expand upon and clarify this distinction; outline what I see to be the relation between ontology-in-general and ontology-*in-situ*; and state what I believe the role of ontology in empirical research to be. I take up the abstract ontological concepts associated with position-practices and their relations, which were introduced in the last chapter, and argue that these and the associated ideas of other authors can provide an invaluable meso-framework within which to situate individual concrete level studies of structuration. Within this framework I go on to draw from the range of critical contributions to structuration theory reviewed in chapter 2 in order to consolidate the lessons from these debates into a more developed ontological synthesis containing both in-general and *in-situ* dimensions.

In order to highlight the refinements produced by this synthesis I intend to develop in more detail points that were broached sideways on in the previous chapter by expressly breaking down the notion of the duality of structure into four analytically separate components. I do this in order to clarify the characteristics of each component and the role that each of the four play within the cycle of structuration. For ease of reference I will label this four-dimensional nature of the duality of structure as the 'quadripartite nature of structuration'. Finally, I argue that this model allows us to advance our thinking about the power of external social forces to limit an agent's 'ability to do otherwise'.

Many of the criticisms aimed at structuration theory were themselves pitched at the abstract, philosophical level of what I have called ontology-in-general. But we have seen that an equal concern of critics of structuration has been the lack of guidance as to how structuration theory could be applied at the substantive level, how it could inform empirical analysis. These critics have been concerned with questions of the '*who* did what, and *when*' variety (Parker, 2000, p. 84, original emphasis). They have felt that issues of '*which* structures, *what* agencies, in what sort of *sequences*' (McLennan, 1984, p. 125, original emphasis) have been neglected, as have those of 'how' these agents and structures combined when and where they did so. The reason, for example, for differentiating between different kinds of duality within the agent, as in Mouzelis's distinction between a taken-for-granted duality and a more critically reflective duality, is in order to distinguish between different kinds of duality within particular agents in substantive, *in-situ*, cases. One can see immediately that these concepts are geared less to what all agents at all times have in common, and more towards identifying the degrees of difference between agents in their relationship to the specific internal structures that inhabit them. It seems to me that this orientation of theory towards the situated, empirical, level is a positive one, and one that structuration theory needs to develop in order to maximise its potential.

As we have seen, Giddens's version of structuration theory is pitched almost entirely at an abstract, philosophical, level. It concentrates on the creation of concepts about entities that exist in the social world, that apply at all times and in all places. These concepts are systematic in the sense that they are logically consistent with each other. They are said to be relevant to empirical research, but not in any way that can be spelt out in any detail. The abstract concepts are said to be tools to sensitise the researcher in a general, unspecified, way to the kinds of things she might find in the social world.

I wish to retain the value that Giddens gives to abstract ontology-in-general, but things must not be left there. The full potential of structuration theory cannot be fulfilled whilst it remains only in the clouds, content just to sprinkle a few magnanimous drops of rain down onto the fields below in whimsical, haphazard gestures designed more to draw attention to the abstract ontology than to nurture a greater understanding of particular times and places. What I call 'strong structuration' encompasses ontology-in-general,[1] and remains concerned to develop structuration theory at this level, but it also brings in an emphasis on what I have referred to as ontology-*in-situ*. This entails taking ontology-in-general and pointing it towards the ontic, towards the realm of particular concrete and/or situated entities in the world with their particular qualities, relations, shapes, tone, texture, colour and so on (see Dreyfus, 1991, pp. 19–21 and 89; and Thrift, 1996, pp. 11–12 and 17). The ontic is the level at which empirical evidence can be sought, and the purpose behind pointing the abstract ontology towards the ontic is, precisely, in order to encourage it to do more work at this substantive and empirical level.

The Role of Ontology in Empirical Analysis

In making explicit the role of ontology at the empirical level it is useful to distinguish between three different aspects of this role (see figure 3.1). The

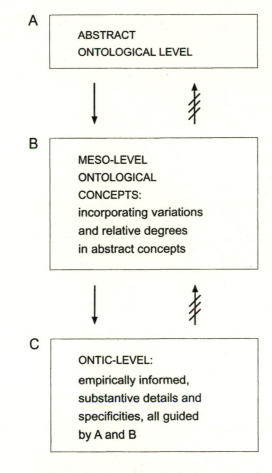

A ABSTRACT
ONTOLOGICAL LEVEL

B MESO-LEVEL
ONTOLOGICAL
CONCEPTS:
incorporating variations
and relative degrees
in abstract concepts

C ONTIC-LEVEL:
empirically informed,
substantive details and
specificities, all guided
by A and B

⟶ guiding influence of ontological concepts on empirical research

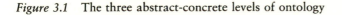 influence of empirical research on the modification and elaboration
of ontological concepts

Figure 3.1 The three abstract-concrete levels of ontology

first is the shape or form that ontology at its most abstract and generalised
level provides as a guide to empirical researchers. The second is the ontic level
of particular concrete and/or situated entities in the world just described; the
way that the abstract ontology looks when it is filled out and shaded in by the
details and empirical evidence of actual social relations in particular times
and places. The third aspect traverses the other two. This meso-level of
ontology concerns the way in which it is possible to talk about at least some
abstract ontological concepts in terms of scales or relative degrees. Thus, it is
possible to talk about:

- more or less knowledgeability, about a range of different objects of knowledge;
- more or less critical reflection by an agent upon her internal structures;
- motivations or desires that have a greater or lesser degree of intensity;
- a fewer or a greater number of choices available to an agent-*in-situ*;
- specific clusters of external structures that are more or less durable or modifiable by one or a number of agents-*in-situ*;
- fewer or greater numbers of consequences of particular actions that are unintended;
- a number of unintended consequences of which some will be more or less important to specified agents;
- modifiable external structures that would be likely to take more or less time to change.

The list could be extended in many directions[2] (see figure 3.2, page 80) but the most important point is that if one is in the business of building bridges between abstract ontology-in-general and substantive, empirically informed, studies then such sliding ontological-ontic scales can be extremely useful. They enable one to identify relative variations in the ontic manifestations of general ontological concepts without losing sight of the necessary logical relationships between the two levels of analysis. By so doing these junction concepts can provide additional form, ballast and stability to the enterprise of making explicit the relationship between what one looks for as empirical evidence, on the one hand, and an ontological conception of the kinds of entities that exist in the social world, on the other.

Thus, for example, a researcher drawing on Giddens's abstract stratification model of the agent but directing it towards 'finding out' about something at the *in-situ* ontic level, might be guided by it towards looking for evidence for the 'unintended consequences' of a particular agent's action. The kinds of evidence that would be admissible and relevant would, in turn, be shaped by the related abstract notion that agents are both knowledgeable and purposive entities. What is *unintended* would therefore depend upon what purpose was *intended* by the agent when she performed the action that led to the said consequences. The fact that the consequences that ensued were not the intended ones, were unexpected ones, is most likely to indicate that the agent was not knowledgeable enough about her circumstances to understand the likely effect of her actions. In doing empirical work the sociological researcher would draw on the basic shape of the abstract ontological categories and attempt to discern exactly what the agent intended and the extent of her knowledgeability about the circumstances in which she acted. Perhaps in the first instance one could do this by interviewing her (or him), and allowing her to recount her story.

Such a case is described by Travis Kong in a study, informed in key respects by structuration theory, of the self-identities of Hong Kong gay men within the global cultural constellation (Kong, 2000). One of Kong's respondents, whom he calls Norman, had made a clear decision not to come out as gay. However, a gay class mate who was attracted to him began to phone his house, and did so frequently enough for Norman's aunt to understand what the phone calls indicated about her nephew's sexuality. She, in turn, told Norman's father. Norman recounts the subsequent conversation with his father as follows:

> he knows how to make you tell the truth. He asked me in a very nice way if I was gay. It seemed that being gay didn't bother him. He seldom talked to me in this nice way. But after I admitted it, he changed his face completely. He said, 'I won't give you any money anymore and please leave this house.' He talked in a very unusual, quiet and calm way: 'Do you know how other relatives will think about me if they know you are like that? ... If I'd known before, I would have killed you at birth (Kong, 2000, p. 127).

Leaving aside the more complex possibilities of psychological self-deception or wishful thinking – this would seem to be a case of unintended consequences. We can judge that this is so by directing the concepts of unacknowledged conditions of action, knowledgeability and purposiveness at the evidence available for this particular case. It seems clear that Norman had allowed himself to hope that his father would accept his sexuality. Telling his father was meant to invoke this hoped-for response. With echoes of Mouzelis's points about critical reflection, Kong relates how coming out to the family usually involves young gay men from traditional backgrounds in much serious thought and calculation about: their material and financial situation; about what he calls the 'disciplinary Chinese values' of filial piety, in which a good son is defined as an obedient son; about the implications of the 'iron law' of marriage, 'the regulatory obligation for a son to continue the family's blood'; and about the shame that could be brought upon a family by the son's perceived abnormality and deviance (Kong, 2000, p. 129). In Norman's case the moment of telling had not been chosen by him, it was forced upon him by confrontation following the aunt's disclosure to his father. The knowledgeability he brought to the interaction and his purposive conduct was probably, as a consequence, more intuitive than calculative, more a response developed within the flow of a process from which he had little chance to step back, consider tactics and weigh up the circumstances and the probabilities. In any event, after the telling Norman was stunned by his father's reaction: 'I couldn't understand how he could say those kind of things to me' (Kong, 2000, p. 128). The unintended consequences were plural and of varying types, intensities and significance, including:

- the emotional rift between father and son;
- Norman leaving the house to stay with a friend;
- the borrowing of money from a relative to pay his tuition fees;

- a constant underlying fear that his father would report him to the police as he was still a minor, and the consequences this might have for his friend;
- and, finally, a real fear that his father could, in fact, kill him, a conviction that was symbolised for him by the rekindled distant memory of seeing his father 'open a monkey's head by hitting it with a stick and then eat its brain' (Kong, 2000, p. 127).

The inter-related ontological concepts of unintended consequences, purposive action and knowledgeability provide the impetus to look for certain things within the interactional sequence. On their own they are

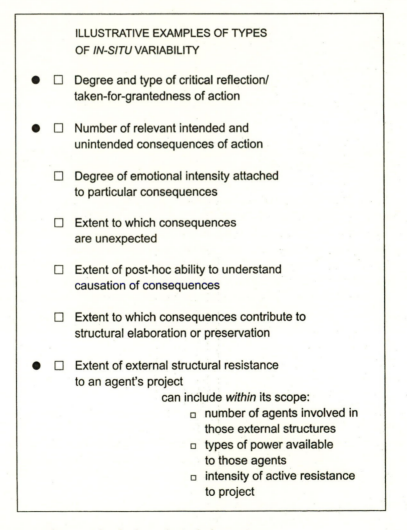

Figure 3.2 The meso-level of ontological abstraction

relatively empty. Once they are directed towards a situated set of practices, brought to the level of the ontic, to a case such as Norman's, each of the concepts takes on content and detail, they take on numbers of instances, factors and so on, and they also take on relative degrees. Knowledgeability is knowledge, or lack of knowledge, of something or some things. It is also more or less knowledge of that something or things. Making explicit the meso-level of ontology means that *in-situ* variability is introduced in a manner that remains systematic (see figure 3.2). Purposive action has an object and degree of intensity attached to it. Consequences that are unintended can be distinguished from intended consequences. Consequences, whether few or many, are identifiable and particular, with more or less significance to specified agents, and so on. The move from structuration in the abstract to structuration *in situ* is thus aided and abetted by a combination of all three of the levels identified with the role of ontology in empirical analysis.

Situating Agents Within The Intermediate Zone of Position-Practices

The central significance I have placed on the abstract ontological notion of the duality of structure has strong implications for the kind of work in which structuration theory is able to engage at the substantive level. The duality of structure and agency within the agent that is central both to structure as the *medium* of practices, and to the production of structure as the *outcome* of practices, entails a combination of the ontological categories of hermeneutics and structures within both key moments in the structuration cycle. In terms of epistemology and methodology this means that any adequate attempt to investigate the process of structuration at the substantive level will have to engage, at least at a minimal level, with a combination of hermeneutics and structural diagnostics. It seems entirely apparent to me that empirical studies that don't do this are simply not structuration studies. A pragmatic implication of needing to combine an investigation both of structures and of hermeneutics is that the detail implied by this will necessarily limit the scope and scale of studies that can be given the structuration treatment. It is this consideration, more than Giddens's contingent use of the bracket of institutional analysis, that means I am sceptical of the claim that structuration could ever be used, in any non-platitudinous sense, to investigate large sweeps of history. Thus, notwithstanding my clear sense that John Parker greatly underestimates the importance of the duality of structure, I feel that he puts his finger on something essential when he argues that the proper domain of study for students of the interplay between structure and agency is what he calls the 'intermediate temporality' of historical processes. This is a scale of temporality within which one could specify both relations between specific events and agency, and relations between events themselves. He argues for the investigation of an intermediate depth of historical time which would enable one to identify:

> [the specific] processes which can produce durable structures, regular patterns of interaction and developmental tendencies with relatively high predictability on the one hand, and volatile, unstable, randomized, quick-changing unpredictability on the other (Parker, 2000, p. 107).

Such investigations, I would insist again, should involve both hermeneutic and structural analysis if they are to qualify as studies of structuration. I would also want to enter the necessary caveat that one could imagine focusing in detail on two events separated by: (i) a long period of time; or (ii) large tracts of space, that can then be demonstrated to have a relation one to the other which is identifiably a relation of structuration. An example of the former, of which there are many examples, could involve the events around a colonial power's establishment of particular borders or political arrangements and divisions and, many years later, the outbreak of conflict and violence that is directly influenced by the former processes and the outcome they produced. An example of the latter could involve direct relations between physically separated agents, by means of technologically-aided communicative interaction. It could also involve the effects of the decisions or actions of one global agent on another global agent or on a local agent, whether the actions be that of a trans-national business executive, a player on the international financial markets, a high-ranking official of a state or non-state military organisation, or an inspirational cultural or sporting personality whose performances are beamed by satellite to the four corners of the world. For these reasons the idea of an intermediate zone should not be taken overly literally, but the essential point remains. It will simply not be possible to investigate the interplay of structure and agency in any meaningful sense without a sufficiently discriminating, austerely delimiting, focus of attention on a restricted number of germane points on the historical and geographical landscape.

The processes that produce the kinds of regular and durable, or unpredictable and unstable, patterns that Parker talks about with respect to an intermediate zone of temporality suggest to me the kind of terrain of investigation that is marked out by Cohen's elaboration of position-practices and their relations (see chapter 2). The cluster of interdependent concepts produced by Cohen here are pitched at the abstract level of ontology-in-general but it is difficult to imagine them being pointed towards large continuous historical sweeps of the ontic level. They would lose too much detail to still be recognisable as dealing with the phenomena designated by Cohen's categories. Likewise, it would be impossible to investigate the kinds of clusters of position-practice relations set out by Cohen whilst restricting oneself to the present moment or to action conceptualised only as individual action. Position-practices and their relations direct one necessarily towards a meso or intermediate zone, that – as indicated by my caveats above – can stretch out this and that way in time and space, but, to the extent that an intermediate analysis does this, it cannot cover every nook and structuration process in between, or even within, the points it focuses upon.

Thus, we return to a point already presaged in the previous chapter. At the level of ontology-in-general, the concepts involved in position practices and their relations can provide not only a guide for substantive *in-situ* studies, but also a contextualising frame for them. This overlaps with Thompson's points about providing broader institutional and systemic-structural frames for specifically focused studies. However, it differs in that the focus here is much more limited as it centres on the manifestations of these wider forces within the practical action horizon of particular agents. The emphasis is on this action horizon, as perceived by the agent and/or the social researcher. Also, the concepts associated with position-practices can themselves only provide a frame in a limited manner, in the way that can be done by an abstract set of concepts as opposed to the kind of frame that can be provided by a substantive account of particular social structures. The extent to which, and the ways in which, the abstract ontological concepts of position-practices and their relations can tell one about an actual historical process of structuration will, of course, depend upon more than the abstract concepts. This will depend in the first instance upon how the concepts are directed towards the ontic, how they are translated into *in-situ* categories. From here it will depend upon the adequacy of the empirical evidence with respect to the objects of study adumbrated by these categories.

The conceptual cluster of position-practices and their relations direct one to similar sorts of entities and relationships – compatible and overlapping ones – as those picked out by a number of other authors engaging with structuration theory. Such a case is that of Bourdieu, as outlined in the introductory chapter, when he talks of the *networks of relevant relationships* – 'such as the family structure, which is tied to the job market, itself tied to governmental hiring policies, and so on' – that make an event, such as an outbreak of violence in a high school in the case cited, really understandable (Bourdieu, 1996/1998, pp. 6–7). I am also thinking of Mouzelis's emphasis on vertical and horizontal social hierarchies and the way that these are implicated in differential power relations, and of Zygmunt Bauman's and Richard Kilminster's arguments for the value of Norbert Elias's notion of figuration (Bauman, 1989; Kilminster, 1991). Kilminster, for example, argues for an approach that thinks in terms of 'a plurality of people in webs of interdependencies' (Kilminster, 1991, p. 98; quoted in Thrift, 1996, p. 54). Whilst not rejecting the basic ontological tenets that *are* developed in structuration theory,[3] Kilminster argues convincingly for an extended ontology of structuration processes. He argues for a notion of 'combined relatedness', for an approach that can grasp the mutual influencing, buffeting and simple affecting of some people within a social web or a 'functional nexus' by others whom they may or may not know or be aware of, but with whom they are interdependent (Kilminster, 1991, p. 99; cf. Thrift, 1996, pp. 54–5). Such a frame has immediate implications for any *in-situ* study, in that it would lead one to look for, and to expect to find, signs that any one agent was already embroiled in a social web of direct and indirect influences and buffetings. One would expect these to take on particular ontic shapes and forms in and through routine and intermittent reciprocal practices, through obligations and prerogatives, all carried out on the basis of a range of situated and differentially empowering identifying criteria (for example, of qualifications, wealth, titles and other signs of office or institutional power, observable attributes and so on). In confronting a whole range of structuration type questions, from the identification of constraints and opportunities, or of strategic possibilities and obstacles, through to the nature and consequences of unquestioned, taken-for-granted, praxis, it would almost inevitably be the case that the substantive characteristics of such a configuration would have a significant causal impact on the *in-situ* process of structuration.

The Quadripartite Nature of Structuration

A combination of the defence made in chapter 2 of the central tenets of structuration theory, together with the amendments and refinements that have developed out of the critical literature, leaves us with a somewhat altered view of a tradition that is still, nevertheless, distinctively structurationist. To consolidate what has emerged I will analytically distinguish between four separate but inter-linked aspects of the duality of structure (see figure 3.3). The four aspects are:

1. *External structures as conditions of action*, which have an existence that is autonomous from the agent-in-focus, and which within structuration are conceived in terms of the structural context of action faced by that agent-in-focus at time 1. They can be thought of at the abstract ontological level, as with thinking of the notion of relevant networked position-practices at the abstract level, or they can be considered at the *in-situ*, conjunctural level of particular agents and structures against a substantively more concrete framework of position-practices. In either case, they should be distinguished from the more systemic level conception of conventional social structure that Thompson identifies. The emphasis, to repeat, is on the action-horizon of *in-situ* agents as perceived by that agent and/or by the social researcher;

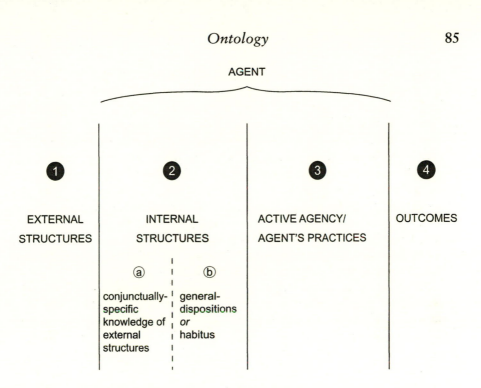

Figure 3.3 The quadripartite nature of structuration

2. *Internal structures* within the agent, which themselves can be divided analytically into two components, namely, conjuncturally specific internal structures and general-dispositional structures or, following Bourdieu, habitus;[4]
3. *Active agency*, including the ways in which the agent either routinely and pre-reflectively, or strategically and critically, draws upon her internal structures;
4. *Outcomes (as external and internal structures and as events)* which, given the emphasis on clearly distinguishing between internal and external structures, will also need to include the overlapping but differential effects of actions and interactions on both external and internal structures, as well as all other kinds of outcomes. The effects of agents' practices on extant structures can involve change and elaboration or reproduction and preservation. Under other kinds of outcomes can be included the success or otherwise of agents' purposes irrespective of their effect upon structures. The structural context can serve to either facilitate or frustrate agents' purposes. The impact on internal structures can be thought of as part of the overall effect of structuration on agents, which is something that Archer has clarified with her emphasis on the properties of agents that are emergent from interaction (Archer, 1996, 2000, *passim*).

In terms of the duality of structure, it should be clear that the internal structures within the second of these different parts are drawn upon as the 'medium' of agent's conduct, whilst the internal and external structural outcomes within the fourth part represent structure as 'outcome' of conduct. The latter will, in turn, constitute the internal and external structures at time 1 for the next round of structuration. The third part of active agency constitutes the active, dynamic moment of structuration, but this is a moment that can never float free or .be uprooted from the other parts of the structuration cycle. Even when people have been uprooted from their familiar surroundings by migration due to war, famine, economic hardship or some other reason they will still embody their learned habitus and bring it to bear, more or less effectively, on the exigencies of particular social relations in a definite time and a new and unfamiliar place.

I will say more about the detailed nature of each of these four parts of the structuration cycle, and about the inter-relations between the parts. Instead of simply going through each of the parts one by one, I will approach this task by way of a number of different roads and pathways, each of them, I hope, revealing an aspect of the added subtlety, power and potential of strong structuration. In the process I will try to clarify further the epistemological relationship between the quadripartite cycle as ontology-in-general and its role in empirical analysis at the level of ontology-*in-situ*. To help with this clarification I will illustrate a number of points by reference to Richard Whittington's analysis of managerial agency and to my own substantive analysis of Government-finance relations in Britain, 1964–7 (Whittington, 1992; Stones, 1988, and 1990, pp. 32–55). For the latter, the article I will primarily draw from was published in 1990 and, whilst heavily informed by structuration theory, it does not exhibit the more refined strong synthesis that it will be here adapted to illustrate. Nevertheless, the fact that it can be used to illustrate a good many aspects of this synthesis, and at the level of ontology-*in-situ*, should reinforce the case I have made thus far that Giddens's version of structuration can be adapted so as to be put to systematic empirical use. This case study also consolidates the case for an easy consistency between the structuration approach and notions of external structures.

For ease of exposition I will begin the more detailed account of the nature of the four parts in the middle of the cycle, with parts two and three, internal structures and agent's conduct. The difference between these second and third parts will probably, in any case, require spelling out in somewhat more detail, as will the difference between the two components of the internal structures: the conjuncturally-specific and the general-dispositional or habitus. Both kinds of internal structures have distinct relationships to external structures, and I will indicate what these are. These latter relationships are very under-developed in Giddens's work due, not least, to the relative lack of attention paid to external structures.

Two Kinds of Internal Structures: The Conjuncturally-Specific and the General-Dispositional

It will be recalled that the distinction between conjuncturally-specific internal structures and more transposable and generalisable schemas emerged in chapter 2 out of the discussion of the work of William Sewell Jr. It was concluded that both kinds of internal structure are virtual. Whilst Giddens's work implicitly recognises both aspects there is no clear distinction between the two and they are often conflated. The same is true of Bourdieu, although he has done the most amongst social theorists to consolidate the importance of 'the system of transposable dispositions' drawn upon by agents in producing performances across an infinite range of diversified tasks. Both theorists are heavily influenced in their respective emphases by the phenomenological tradition: the insights of theorists such as Schutz, Merleau-Ponty, Garfinkel and Goffman are plain to see, explicitly or implicitly in their formulations.

There are four reasons why I have given the label of 'general-dispositional' to the second dimension of internal structure, a term meant to be used interchangeably with the notion of habitus. The first and second reasons explain why I don't just rely on the notion of habitus and leave it at that, given that I will use the two terms interchangeably. One is that I want to distance myself from the overly deterministic connotations that some commentators see in Bourdieu's use of habitus. And secondly, I have a somewhat impressionistic sense that Bourdieu's notion, evocative as it is in many ways, is perhaps too much associated with practical action to be able also to signify enough of the feeling of a general world-view incorporating dimensions of culture as discourse. The third reason is that the 'general' in general-dispositional serves as a clearly labelled contrast with the more contextualised knowledge of particular conditions of action indicated by conjuncturally-'specific' structures. And the fourth is as a reference to the way in which Sewell's observations on transposable dispositions correspond with Mouzelis's adoption of the term 'dispositional', referring to the emphasis of Bourdieu and G. H. Mead on adaptable dispositions, orientations and social skills. Mouzelis incisively distinguishes between this dimension of social life and two others, the positional and the situational. Aspects of the positional are very close to what I mean by conjuncturally-specific structures. As I outline the general-dispositional and the conjuncturally-specific I will also discuss each of Mouzelis's terms in order to draw from them and to bring out their relevance to, and compatibility with, each of the parts of the quadripartite cycle.

The General-Dispositional/Habitus

The dispositional is said by Mouzelis to refer, as indicated above, to the spheres delineated by Mead's emphasis on skills and Bourdieu's notion of habitus. I will concentrate on the latter here. We can envisage this, along the same lines as in chapter 2, as encompassing transposable skills and dispositions, including generalised world-views and cultural schemas, classifications, typifications of things, people and networks, principles of action, typified recipes of action, deep binary frameworks of signification, associative chains and connotations of discourse, habits of speech and gesture, and methodologies for adapting this generalised knowledge to a range of particular practices in particular locations in time and space (cf. Bourdieu, 1972/1977, pp. 78–87 and 159–71, and 1998; Bourdieu and Wacquant, 1992; Sewell, 1992, pp. 7–8; Crossley, 2001, pp. 91–119). This realm is embedded in corporeal schemas and memory traces and is best conceptualised as existing, for the most part, in a taken-for-granted and unnoticed state, part of what Bourdieu calls the *doxa*, the universe of the undiscussed and undisputed (Bourdieu, 1977, pp. 167–9). It is drawn on 'naturally', without thinking, in the majority of the actions that agents engage in. In this mode, it doesn't occur to us to question the dispositional – habitus – we don't even notice that we are basing our actions upon it, it is that close to us. In this sense it has the same status and enigmatic character that Habermas attributes to the lifeworld, a realm that often conveys the feeling of absolute certainty only because we do not know *about* it; its paradoxical character is due to the fact that the knowledge of what one can count on and how one does something is still connected with – undifferentiated from – what one prereflectively *knows* (Habermas, 1987, p. 135, original emphasis).

On the other hand, the relation between habitus and external conditions can become a dissonant one. One's taken-for-granted mode of being can be subverted and unsettled, making one suddenly conscious of that which previously was pre-reflective. Even in relatively undifferentiated and culturally solidaristic societies of the kind that were traditionally studied by anthropologists one would not expect lives so smooth and harmonious as to prompt no questioning at all of the dispositions and discourses inherited from prior socialisation and past practices. This is ever the more so in the plural and differentiated conditions of late modernity. It is therefore important, as Nick Crossley notes, not to draw a line at the level of ontology between habitus and what is noticed and reflected upon. Habitus should be seen as able to include the latter. The line that does exist between the unquestioned habitus of *doxa* and the universe of discourse and argument (the *orthodox* and the *heterodox*), is a contingent and shifting line between an unquestioned habitus, on the one hand, and the part of habitus that is open to critical reflection and discussion, on the other. It is not the case, as Bourdieu *sometimes* claims, that when what is taken for granted becomes questioned and a point for debate then it is suddenly no longer part of habitus. Rather, habitus itself can be the object of reflective and reflexive attention, it can be questioned as the 'natural attitude' is seen, noticed and made explicit (Crossley, 2001, pp. 136–8; cf. Bourdieu, 1977, pp. 159–71). On a wider note,

Crossley also criticises Bourdieu for under-estimating, in his conceptualisation of habitus, the extent to which 'rational and conscious calculation' enter into everyday life as a matter of course (Crossley, 2001, p. 117).[5] These critical points are consistent with Giddens's belief that there is no bar to the discursive penetration of practical consciousness, and with Mouzelis's conceptualisation of the varying degrees of critical reflection and distance that can be adopted towards internal structures (see above, chapters 1 and 2).

The Conjuncturally-Specific and the Positional

The positional refers to the notion of a role or position which has embedded within it various rules and normative expectations. Different roles or positions will have particular kinds of 'games' that they are oriented towards. As examples of such roles/positions Mouzelis mentions his own position as a university teacher and also clusterings of inter-related roles such as manager, foreman and worker (Mouzelis, 1991, pp. 52 and 199).[6] These notions of position and clusterings of positions have a clear fit with Cohen's position-practices and their relations. Mouzelis' emphasis, however, when sketching out the differences and relations between his three concepts, is more on the way that position-practices and their relations look from the perspective of the situated agent as she engages with her context. One could say that he is looking at position-practices and their relations from the perspectives of particular situated agents within a given nexus of such practices. In fact, the explicit emphasis is on, firstly, the situated agent's sense of the normative expectations that come with the position. Secondly, it is on the capacities, or what Steven Lukes (1974) and Giddens would call the 'power to', embodied within the position. Mouzelis actually refers to these powers as 'normatively-generated capacities embodied in the actors' social roles/positions', and as 'normatively-regulated capacities for mobilising role relevant resources' (Mouzelis, 1991, p. 51). He thus draws attention to the inter-connection between the normative orientations of the various agents within context and the power capacities that will be available to the incumbent of a particular role.

From the viewpoint of the positioned agent this is very similar to what Giddens is saying when he talks of the virtual structures of legitimation/norms and domination/power within the agent. Only the structure of signification is missing from the discussion. Indeed, Mouzelis goes on to compare both the role/positional and dispositional aspects of social life with 'what Saussure called *langue* (that is, a *virtual* order of rules conceived in a contextless manner)' (Mouzelis, 1991, p. 199, original emphasis). Both the normative expectations associated with positions and an agent's dispositions should, says Mouzelis, be conceived as 'memory traces' in that actor's mind. The difference here between Giddens and Mouzelis lies in the fact that the latter makes a distinction between two kinds of internal structures – to use the terminology we have been employing – the positional and the dispositional. Strictly speaking, the conjuncturally-specific dimension of the internal structures is only one aspect of a role or a position, but it is clear that Mouzelis would have to build some such conception of internal structures into his concept of position. Also, whilst he leaves much to be done in terms of conceptual elaboration and development, Mouzelis is also clearly differentiating this aspect from what I have called the general-dispositional, or habitus.

It seems to me that a good deal of critical purchase can be gained at the substantive level by insisting upon and developing this notion of conjuncturally-specific internal structures. These are directed outwards towards the external structures at time 1, and they involve an agent's knowledge of the specific context of action. Whilst such knowledge will be perceived, made sense of, categorised, ordered and reacted to, on the basis of the general-dispositional, it is still analytically and causally distinguishable from these more transposable dimensions. Thus, although transposable capacities and dispositions will be involved in apprehending and reacting to conjunctural specificities, the details of the latter are not themselves transposable and generalised. They have contours, shapes and textures whose specificity within time and place is of great import to the agent facing those external structures. These are aspects whose clear delineation is of limited consequence to a structuration theory preoccupied with ontology-in-general, but whose conceptualisation is indispensable for a structuration theory dealing with ontology-*in-situ*, directed at the ontic and at questions of 'which' structures and 'what' agencies, questions of who, what, where, when and how.

This is to focus on the particular details and idiosyncratic exigencies of, and hence the specific knowledge required to deal with, this building, this lecture theatre, this city, these organisational routines and these particular people, as distinct from a focus only on the generalisable, transposable dispositions one brings to dealing with any building, any lecture theatre, any city, any organisational routines, all people. Even with McDonald's, that symbol of late modern standardisation and predictability,[7] the spatial positioning of the door, the bathrooms and the children's area still varies from restaurant to restaurant and the menu changes from time to time and from country to country. The latent, virtual, capacities that are drawn upon by an agent as a particular horizon of relevance is thrown up by a given activity will depend, *inter alia*, upon how that agent perceives the context of action. To know how to behave in this room with these people, how to stay in business in these external circumstances, or whether it is safe here and now to exercise one's formal right to freedom of speech, will all involve some sort of appreciation and perception of external structures. It is the part of these perceptions that refers to the particular content of this time-place situated context that I want to capture through the notion of conjuncturally-specific internal structures. The notion provides a feasible and useful means of distinguishing between the perceived substantive content of contemporary external structures and the other existents within the agent. Finally, the distinction between the two kinds of internal structures also draws attention to the fact that there are likely to be significant differences, despite overlaps, between the ways in which these two types of structures come to be initially constituted, in the histories of how they came to be the internal structures they are.

It is important to understand that conjuncturally-specific knowledge is not reducible to knowledge gained within the immanent interaction. It may be relatively enduring knowledge, for knowledge of relatively enduring external structures may have been built up over a period of time. These internal structures may well have been formed long before they are drawn upon in any particular sequence of interaction or, alternatively, aspects of them may indeed be gleaned in the course of an unfolding interaction. They needn't always have a past, but they can have a past, can have been formed *a tergo*, to use Habermas's term (Habermas, 1987, p. 135). This might seem more apparently self-evident for habitus than for the conjuncturally-specific. But, to appreciate that this is also the case for the latter, one only has to recognise that one didn't build in a day the particular *mixture* of general-dispositional capacities and the more specific knowledge that enters into the ultimately habitual negotiation of the very particular routines, procedures, characters, resources, and spatial and other forms of organisation of one's workplace or place of study. Remember the first day, changes in procedure, a new colleague. Conjuncturally-specific knowledge is acquired and embodied over time (the left hand swerve at the end of 'that' corridor, the poetic pass to 'that' player predicted to be in the right place at the right time, the trust in 'that' person not to let you down emotionally or organisationally).

The knowledge that constitutes the conjuncturally-specific internal structures can be analytically divided up into knowledge of the three ontologically inter-related aspects of structures picked out by Giddens. That is, knowledge of the interpretative schemes, power capacities, and normative expectations and principles of the agents within context. In talking of the knowledge of agents in context we are talking now of the relations between internal structures and external structures. More specifically, we are talking of the relations between the conjunctural internal structures of the agent-in-focus and the overall hermeneutic schemas of relevant agents within the external structures. Along the three axes mentioned the agent-in-focus would have more or less knowledge, of greater or lesser quality, of the following aspects of agents-within-context. Firstly, (*of interpretative schemes*) there would be conjunctural knowledge of how particular positioned agents within context would interpret the actions and utterances of others. The knowledge that is ultimately relevant to the agent-in-focus may well be her sense of what the interpretative *conclusions* of the agents-in-context are likely to be (what I will call their *action-informing* interpretations). However, in order to have a reasonable sense of what these are likely to be she would also have to understand much more about the processes of interpretation within those agents, including the ways they tend to draw on their own general-dispositional and conjuncturally-specific structures. It should be noted here that there is an inner temporality within the agent-in-focus's 'knowing' about what the agent-in-context is likely to do. This temporality involves her in, from the vantage point of the unfolding present, taking a position on what the agent-in-context might be expected to do in a situated future based on what can be interpreted about what she has been and what she has done in various situated pasts (cf. Urry, 1996 and 2000, pp. 114–16). The agent-in-focus looks both backwards and forwards at the same time in making judgements about acting, often routine taken-for-granted judgements, that unavoidably involve the hazy, precarious, assessment of what these actions' unacknowledged conditions and unintended consequences might be.

Secondly, (*of power*) the agent-in-focus would have more or less conjunctural knowledge of how agents within context see their own conjuncturally-specific power capacities. The agents-in-focus will typically consider this relationally with respect both to who they themselves rely on for power resources, and how much and what kind of power other goal-relevant actors can command. The agents-in-context would, of course, grasp these power relations within the horizon of their own interpretative schemes. Again, the knowledge that is ultimately relevant to the agents-in-focus may well be others' final conclusions about their probable use of power in a particular circumstance (these others' *action-informing* assessments of power relations). But, again, for the agents-in-focus, a confident *verstehende* grasp of what these conclusions of external agents are likely to be would require a deep hermeneutic grasp of their perspectives on relational power capacities and expected outcomes.

Thirdly, (*of norms*) the agent-in-focus would have more or less conjunctural knowledge of how the agents within context would be likely to decide to behave, gleaned from their perception of the fit or tension between: i) those agents' ideal normative beliefs (from within the general-dispositional) about how they should act *and* ii) how they may be pressured to act in the immediate conjuncture. A central factor in the relationship between the ideal normative dispositions of the agent in context and her likely actual actions will be her conjuncturally-specific sense of the distribution of power. She may not like what the agent-in-focus is about to do, but given her desire to continue trading with or working for that agent, together with her relative lack of power, she may have to act according to pragmatic schemas that embody pragmatic norms rather than the normative ideals that will, thus, remain hidden from view. As with the other two categories the agent-in-focus will require an appreciation of the hermeneutic processes of the agent-in-context that has quite some depth and quite some detail in order to be at all confident of the conclusions the agent-in-context will draw upon in the production of her conduct (her *action-informing* assessment of relational norms). When the agent-in-focus draws upon her conjuncturally-specific internal structures she is drawing upon the above knowledge. It may be useful, at some times, to think of this in terms of her drawing upon her knowledge of the combined *action-informing conclusions* of relevant networked agents-in-context. At other times it may be more useful to think of her drawing upon the more encompassing, deeper and more detailed, appreciation of the *hermeneutic-structural processes* of those agents-in-context.

There is more, it seems, to drawing on virtual structures than a reading of Giddens or his strongest critics might have led us to believe. By focusing on the conjuncturally-specific aspect of virtual structures we have been able to begin to bridge the theoretical gap within Giddens's version of structuration between the structures within the agent that are the 'medium' of structuration, on the one hand, and the external structures, on the other. Nigel Thrift makes a complementary and reinforcing point linking what I have labelled as 'conjuncturally-specific' internal structures to an elaborated notion of external structuration processes compatible with the above discussion of networks of position-practices. In an evocative and telling phrase Thrift writes that Giddens's ontology: 'over-emphasises action as individual and never fully considers the ghost of networked others that continually informs that action' (Thrift, 1996, p. 54). It would be difficult to exaggerate the importance of this insight. The lesson I draw from it is that the agent(s)-in-focus should always be conceptualised from the start as being in the midst of, as already being caught up in the flow of, position-practices and their relations (see figure 3.4). Thrift frames this in terms of an over-emphasis by Giddens on socio-spatial 'presence'. I would add that this is also palpably bound up with the level of abstraction, of ontology-in-general, at which Giddens typically operates. Thus, Thrift insists on the need for a much greater sense of the force of what is absent on the constitution and presencing of actions and interactions. In effect, Thrift conceives the agent-in-focus's apprehension of the conditions of action as being informed by conjuncturally-specific knowledge of networked others who may well not be involved in the interactional conduct which they so inform. These others can be absent from the face-to-face or mediated interaction between particular agents even whilst they affect that interaction. Like Kilminster, Thrift sees the agent's view of her conditions of action as one in which they stretch away in time and space, and in which they do so in all sorts of networked directions, each with their own sets of relationality and varieties of reciprocity, inter-dependencies and infrastructures. Some of what an agent's conjuncturally-specific knowledge of these 'ghosts of networked others' will involve, including a sense of their action-informing schemas, can be illustrated by reference to the case study of Government-finance relations in Britain mentioned earlier.[8] This is also an example of what Thrift elsewhere has asked from structuration theory; an example of how structuration theory can be used empirically, in the arena of a particular place in a particular historical period of time, to challenge existing interpretations of events by contextualising in context (Thrift, 1985, p. 621).

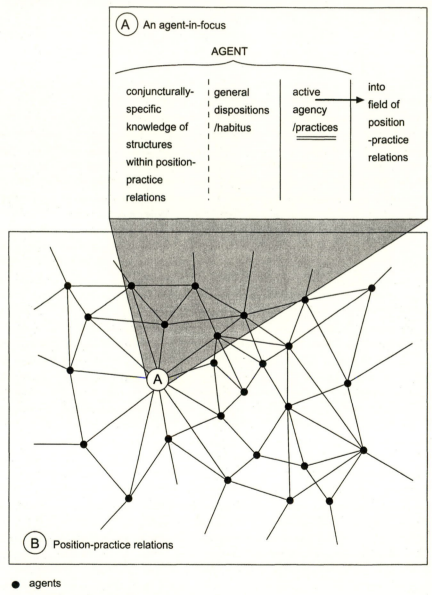

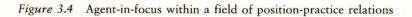

Figure 3.4   Agent-in-focus within a field of position-practice relations

A Case Study in the Positional, General-Dispositional and Conjuncturally-Specific: City Interests and the Wilson Government 1964–70

The general-dispositional frame of the Labour Governments of 1964 and 1966 was, as one would expect, a combination of principles and recipes for practical action, on the one hand, and ideal discursive schemas, most significantly a particular variant of Keynesian welfare state social democracy, on the other. The frame was influenced by the revisionism of Tony Crosland and others, and can be characterised by a principled commitment to full employment, higher living standards, and an expansion of social welfare services such as health and education. These commitments, in turn, were envisaged to rely upon an economic surplus resulting from a planned expansion of the economy in which high levels of demand and investment would feed off each other. In terms of macro-economic strategy it was believed that an increase in demand would produce a high level of pressure on capacity which would, in turn, stimulate new investment. Such investment would then add to capacity, raise productivity per person and increase the rate of growth (Stones, 1991, p. 37; cf. Opie, 1972, pp. 157–77). Broad planning controls would also be introduced in a complementary industrial policy that would be instituted in a corporatist partnership between the state and both sides of industry (Coates, 1975, p. 92). Macro-economic demand management, however, was at the heart of all this, as without a consistently high level of demand in the economy none of this would be possible. There was a need to avoid at all costs a return to the stop-go policies of the Tories, in which deflation in a crisis was followed by a short boom and then retrenchment, all without any rational connection to the national economic cycle. The reason for the periodic deflationary exercises had been the equally periodic runs on sterling which the Government had attempted to stem by increasing interest rates, cutting public expenditure and all the other associated measures that were traditionally required to regain the confidence of the foreign exchange markets.

Influential explanations amongst academics as to why successive Governments seemed to defend sterling even at the expense of domestic economic growth were either that there was a hegemony within the state of what Geoffrey Ingham has called the City–Bank(of England)–Treasury[9] nexus (Ingham, 1984; see also Longstreth, 1979) or, in a variation of this, that there was a powerful 'overseas' or sterling lobby dominant within the Government and the administration which saw the value of sterling as an indispensable pillar underpinning Britain's international standing in a post-imperial age (Blank, 1978, pp. 120–1; Grant, 1987, p. 81). These explanations seemed to be confirmed when the new Labour Government proceeded to defend sterling at what was widely accepted to be an overvalued rate of sterling from the point of view of export competitiveness. This was especially so as the Government, despite what they had promised and their overt commitments to the contrary, had employed the usual techniques of sterling defence: trimming public expenditure plans, increasing interest rates, and introducing incomes policies that threatened the harmonious corporatism of the National Plan. The City–Bank–Treasury and the 'overseas lobby' arguments, however, don't offer any remotely convincing hermeneutic-structural arguments to convince us either that the Government's apparent ideal dispositional frame had, in fact, never been sincere from the beginning, or that, somehow, the general-dispositional frame was altered in office after persuasive ideological-normative lobbying by the said groups.

Such arguments, in fact, typically abstracted from the *in-situ* conditions of action within which British Governments found themselves positioned in the post-war years with respect to the international financial system. It wasn't that the ideal normative commitment[10] within the general-dispositional frame should be placed in doubt but, rather, that the perceived specifics of the immediate conjuncture within which the Government had to act were distinctly unfavourable to the realisation of those ideals. In short, the use of the pound as an international investment and trading currency meant that Britain was tied into a network of vertical interdependence[11] with overseas investors in sterling. The type of power-dependent external constraint Britain was tied into here was of the kind that only a country with an international currency experiences. As Benjamin Cohen puts it:

> [w]hilst 'every country is subject to an independent balance of payments constraint on its domestic policies. . .only a country issuing an international currency is subject to the *additional constraint* which results from the threat of reduction or withdrawal of past foreign accumulations of its money. This is the threat of the so-called overhang or liabilities (Cohen, 1971, p. 39, original emphasis; quoted in Stones, 1991, p. 36).

The internal structures of core actors within the Government, including Harold Wilson the Prime Minister, and James Callaghan, the Chancellor of the Exchequer, contained a quite specific perception of the power possessed by these holders of sterling to withdraw their investments and cause a run on the pound. Knowledge and interpretation of this power was based, not least, upon a conjuncturally-specific apprehension of Britain's liquidity position. In 1964 total sterling liabilities to foreigners amounted to approximately £3895 million and they remained well over £3000 million up to the end of the Wilson Government's time in office (Cohen, 1971, pp. 92–3, 102–3, tables 5.3 and 5.4; source: Bank of England Quarterly Bulletin (BEQB)). In 1964–5 Wilson, Callaghan and others close to them understood that the £3895 million was a power resource available for the foreign holders of sterling – the relevant agents-in-context or networked others – to draw upon; they perceived this figure as a capability those actors possessed on the basis of the particular network of position-practices based on the use of sterling as an international investment currency.

In the event of the sterling holdings being removed or significantly depleted by withdrawals of foreign holdings, the Labour Government would have been faced with a run on the foreign exchange reserves of gold and dollars. If there was a danger of the reserves not being adequate to cover the demands made upon them then, in the absence of alternative sources of foreign exchange, the Government would be forced to choose *between* a decisive deflation of the domestic economy with the aim of cutting the consumption of imports and thus reassuring the overseas sterling holders, or 'freezing' the sterling balances *and* risking international retaliation on a massive scale (Stones, 1988 and 1991, pp. 36–7). Both of these scenarios, as we have noted, represented everything that the Government wanted to avoid; either would have meant the end to any hope of putting into practice the political and economic strategy embodied in its ideal general-dispositional commitments and orientations. These commitments meant that the vertical power relationship with the foreign holders of sterling was a crucial one. The asymmetry of the power relationship was all the more severe given that Britain's autonomous foreign exchange reserves (that is, those that weren't borrowed from overseas) were extremely low; they were approximately £121 million in 1964–5 (Hirsch, 1965, p. 449; also see *The Banker*, July 1965, p. 437). These autonomous reserves were supplemented by foreign exchange borrowing from the United States, the European Central Banks and the International Monetary Fund (who we can refer to collectively as the 'underwriters' of sterling). However, this just served to make the Labour Government vertically dependent upon an additional cluster of position-practice relations.

Such relations were the object of the conjuncturally specific internal structures of actors in the Government and the Bank of England who were aware that by 1964 the British state had sterling liabilities of £991 million to international organisations including the IMF, and of £523 million to officials of non-sterling countries (Cohen, 1971, pp. 92–3, table 5.3; source BEQB). These sums were to increase relentlessly during the next few years as the Government drew on its reserves in order to defend sterling's exchange rate. By the end of 1969 the two figures were £2123 million and £1517 million respectively (Cohen, 1971, pp. 92–3; source BEQB). Such borrowing was, for the most part, on a short-term basis. Thus, what Giddens would call 'allocative power' over the UK's extant exchange reserves regularly reverted to the underwriters. And key Government actors were well aware of many of these specifics. As in the case of the sterling holders, Wilson, Callaghan and others within their 'non-devaluation' camp understood very well that the underwriters too held the power to withdraw the resources that provided the external structural conditions of possibility for Labour's high-demand strategy. They were also made well aware of the conservative and orthodox dispositions of the underwriters and their consequent requirement that the

Government adhere to 'sound money' principles as a condition of continued borrowing. This meant stable internal prices, a disciplined underlying balance in external payments, cuts in public spending and a passion for incomes policies (Stones, 1991, pp. 40–1; see also Brandon, 1966, p. 86 and pp. 93–4; Cooper, 1968, p. 46 and p. 89; Cairncross and Eichengreen, 1983, p. 177). This knowledge placed the Government in a dilemma as the deflationary conditions that were required by the international financiers in order that they should continue to support sterling were in direct conflict with the policy of sustained reflation that was at the heart of Labour's general-dispositional ideals.

Many commentators both at the time and since argued that a Government genuinely committed to its putative ideals, and not in thrall to a hegemony of any combination taken from the City–Bank–Treasury axis or sterling lobby, would have released itself from this dilemma at a stroke by simply devaluing sterling. This, it was argued, would, at one and the same time, have improved Britain's manufacturing competitiveness and erased the threat of the sterling overhang. This, in turn, would have provided the Government with the freedom to pursue its high-demand, high-growth strategy without the pressures towards deflation imposed by the various actors within the international financial system. However, this simply ignores the question of what would have happened to the 'banking' or liquidity aspects specific to sterling after a devaluation.

These were questions which had to be taken into account by the major decision-makers, as is made clear not only by academic commentators on international finance but also by the correspondence, memoirs, diaries and recorded interviews of these actors and their policy-advisors, and by the analyses and narratives of financial journalists (cf. Brandon, 1966; Wilson, 1971; Callaghan, 1987; Stones, 1988). Firstly, there was a real danger that a devaluation would provoke sterling holders into withdrawing their funds from sterling *en masse* and thus demanding, in return, foreign exchange that Britain did not have. Secondly, there was a wider danger that a devaluation of the pound could bring the dollar down with it and 'damagingly disrupt' the whole basis of the present international monetary system' (Hirsch, 1965, p. 87; also see, for example, Tugendhat, 1965, p. 226; Cairncross and Eichengreen, 1983, p. 213). Thirdly, there was a technical conjunctural reason against devaluation that straddles the first two. In order to try and persuade foreign holders of sterling not to undertake a wholesale withdrawal of their sterling investments in the event of a devaluation, then that devaluation would have had to be in the region of 30 per cent. This would hopefully have convinced holders of sterling that their losses from the devaluation were already water under the bridge, and that the best way of recouping some of their losses was to keep their money in sterling because, after such an excessive devaluation, their investments could now only increase in value. This would have been the lowest risk strategy for the British (although it would have raised its own problems to do with the immediate rise in the domestic cost of imports) but it carried a sting in its tail for the USA:

> If, as the British authorities would ... have to contrive, the devaluation was to a level at which sterling was clearly likely to float upwards again under natural market pressure, this would be likely to provoke not a withdrawal of funds from London but a massive inflow, not only from the Continent but mainly and perhaps devastatingly from New York, pulling the rug from under the dollar (Hirsch, 1965, pp. 90–1; quoted in Stones, 1990, p. 39).

As the journalist Henry Brandon put it, 'a mild drop [in the sterling exchange rate] would not have discouraged speculators and a sharp one would have brought everybody's house down' (Brandon, 1966, p. 98).

Labour's response to its positional dilemma was the kind of strategic response suggested by Mouzelis's notion of a critical duality. In its policies it attempted to steer as close to its strategic ideals as possible without causing too damaging a break with the 'ghosts' of the absent international financiers who were underwriting sterling. Thus, the Government's fear of the sanctions embedded in the position-practice liquidity networks meant it did, to a certain extent, attempt to respond to and assuage what it perceived as the overall hermeneutic orientations of the international financiers. In this way it hoped that the underwriters' action-informing decisions would not be as damagingly punitive as they would otherwise have been. On the other hand, it is important to understand that the assuaging was only partial – in the sense that Labour maintained levels of demand as high as it believed it could get away with – and tactical, rather than the result of an ideal normative commitment to the underwriters' schemas. In speeches and public pronouncements directed at the financial community the Government made a virtue out of financial rectitude and presented its policies as restraint incarnate. The tenor of Government calculation in this respect is graphically captured by a private comment made by Harold Wilson in July 1967 and recorded by a colleague in the Cabinet, Barbara Castle:

> On Monday ... the Chancellor [James Callaghan] will make a speech of impeccable virtue in the economic debate. Like the parson, he will preach on Sunday and start fornicating for the rest of the week. Economic righteousness on Monday next, and then the economic fornication will start (Castle, 1984, p. 281; quoted in Stones, 1991, pp. 41–2).

There is much more that could be said about these networked conditions of action, and how they were perceived by key state actors in terms of both constraints and, to a lesser, tactical degree, as providing opportunities. Not least, one could say more, in principle, about the duality of structure and agency within the hermeneutic frame of the sterling holders and the various underwriters. One could say more, also, about the nature of their action-informing 'conclusions' in a range of micro-conjunctures between 1964 and the devaluation of sterling in 1967. One could also say more about the varying degrees to which the key state actors grasped both this duality within the hermeneutic schemas of these variously situated 'ghosts' of networked others and the various shifts in their action-informing conclusions through the months and years. Investigating the latter would mean investigating the quality of the more specific internal structures that Wilson, Callaghan and others drew upon in their actions as they adhered partially and tactically to the demands of those involved in the various sterling position-practice relations: the United States, the various European Central Banks, the International Monetary Fund, and official and private market holders of sterling.

Pursuing the latter possibility either in this case or in a similar one would surely lead one to revise the sense of the high degree and quality of conscious penetration of the conditions of action – conditions of action that have several different sets of position-practice clusters stretching away from the agent-in-focus in all sorts of networked directions, each with their own *in-situ* dualities of structure and agency – that is sometimes thought to be suggested by Giddens's notion of knowledgeability. Against the background of this example, it is easy to see why Thrift, drawing on a combination of Heidegger and Wittgenstein, insists that the orientation of agents to the external structuration processes is best conceptualised from the outset as something that is often indefinite and indistinct. Whilst it is important to note that some agents will, at times, employ a greater degree of critical reflection towards their conditions of action than at others (cf. Mouzelis, 1991, pp. 27–31), and that such a strategic consciousness might lead to a greater appreciation than otherwise of relevant features of their conditions of action, these will very often be relative differences in capabilities to be measured against the grounds of an altogether hazier, less transparent starting point. This, of course, has direct implications for the weight we should expect to be given to unacknowledged conditions and unintended consequences in the structuring of social life. The conduct of agents, for Thrift, is best seen as the creative coping of practically oriented, all too finite, creatures situated in conditions of limited clarity; conditions that are massively irreducible to the moment of action (Thrift, 1996, p. 60).

Active Agency, Agent's Conduct and the Situational

What Mouzelis calls the 'situational' – the situational-interactional conduct of the agent – involves a combination of the two kinds of internal structure. They combine either in the process of an agent consciously and/or strategically deciding or choosing to act, or in the process of an agent just simply acting and reacting, doing it, without any conscious decision to do so.

It should always be remembered that the 'doing' of action or interaction in a particular time and place is not reducible to the virtual, latent, perspectives, conjunctural-knowledge, dispositions and capabilities of the internal structures. As Mouzelis puts it: 'although the meanings of particular actions are quite obviously related to social positions and dispositions, they are not moulded by them entirely. They take their final shape in the process of interaction itself' (Mouzelis, 1991, p. 198).

In addition to internal structures *per se*, I want to pick out five aspects of active agency (see figure 3.5) that are important to consider in investigating the character of, and the dynamism within, agent's conduct. Each of these aspects are consistent with Giddens's stratification model of the agent (chapter 1, pp. 24–6), some of them directly reproduce his categories whilst others cross-cut them in varying but self-evident ways:

1. The *horizon of action* arising from the motivated, purposive action in hand. This horizon is of central significance as its designation of the 'contexts of relevance' will influence which particular aspects of the virtual, latent, structures will be animated (cf. Schutz, 1962; and Habermas, 1987, pp. 122–3).

2. One should also be alert to the possibility of creativity, improvisation and innovation within an agent's conduct. This is 'not ... to imply mysterious creative urges and forces' (Crossley, 2001, p. 116) voluntaristically free, somehow, from context and past determinations. Rather, they will be a response or reply to the exigencies of the situation on the basis of a *combination* of the orientations, principles, habits and skills sedimented within habitus (what Bourdieu refers to as the mastery of one's

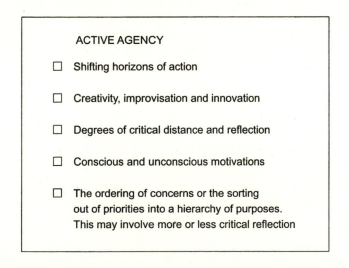

ACTIVE AGENCY

☐ Shifting horizons of action

☐ Creativity, improvisation and innovation

☐ Degrees of critical distance and reflection

☐ Conscious and unconscious motivations

☐ The ordering of concerns or the sorting
out of priorities into a hierarchy of purposes.
This may involve more or less critical reflection

Figure 3.5 Some analytically distinguishable elements of active agency

inheritance and acquisitions, as in the mastery of an art whereby freedom is given the only durable form it can have (Bourdieu, 1999, p. 340)) *and* the perceived demands of the conjuncture. The reference to 'situational exigencies' refers not only to specific conjunctural knowledge but also to the way in which the 'very process of interaction *is* the process of making action and situation understandable and accountable' (Fuchs, 1989, p. 123, original emphasis; quoted in Mouzelis, 1991, p. 198). Following the traditions of ethnomethodology and of Goffman, Mouzelis draws attention to the fact that the interaction process itself requires both effort and the accomplished deployment of skills, method and knowledge in an unfolding process. He insists upon the moments of openness, indeterminacy and uncertainty that can never be eliminated by pre-given conceptions about what is supposed to happen, or of what should happen. Within a particular classroom with particular students, he says,

> specific cleavages between class members, say, or specific teacher-student interchanges, can enhance or sabotage my teaching performance in ways that cannot be primarily derived from or understood by mere reference to role expectations or social dispositions (Mouzelis, 1991, p. 199).

3. In considering active agency it is important to include Mouzelis's points about the varying levels of critical distance that agents bring to the internal structures that are the medium of their actions.

4. Whilst I will say relatively little in substantive terms about psychoanalysis in this book, partly because I believe that structuration theory is potentially compatible with a number of different conceptions of the unconscious, it does seem fairly self-evident and uncontentious that the unconscious can play a relatively autonomous and dynamic role in agent's conduct. It has the potential to be an influencing dimension with a degree of autonomy from both types of internal structure, even if it will often also have a causal influence on the emergent character of those structures. It is important in this respect, as Ian Craib has forcefully argued against Giddens and other social theorists' overly simplified, and overly social, conception of the psychological, to acknowledge the depth, complexity and internally conflictual nature of the agent (see, for example, Craib, 1989; and 1992, pp. 166–77). Craib argues that agent's conduct will often be characterised at its core by a lack of conceptual clarity and even by flat contradictions:

> Deciding is not a simple matter and is often surrounded by internal conflicts, and it is quite conceivable that we might feel that one part of ourselves has decided something and that another part is fighting on the side of different decisions. I have heard it described as having a committee meeting going on in one's head. We can become aware of having decided something without being conscious of taking the decision, of having forgotten something, perhaps conveniently, without being aware of doing the forgetting (Craib, 1992, p. 172).

Speaking more broadly, it is clearly the case that both conscious and unconscious emotions can have an autonomous affect on the way that both general-dispositional and conjuncturally-specific internal structures are, first, mediated and perceived, and, then, are drawn upon by agents in the production of practices. This can take many forms, from projection and introjection through a range of kinds of attraction, attachment, distaste, repulsion, anxiety and fear, through to many group and individual forms of identification, misapprehension and denial (see Craib, 1989; Bendelow and Williams, 1998).

5. Finally, one would look for a central component of 'the rationalization of action against the background of the agents' reflexive monitoring of their conduct' (Giddens, 1993/1976, p. 90). The aspect of rationalisation referred to here involves sorting out priorities mentioned in chapter 1 (p. 26) such that different projects in the same or distinct spheres of life are integrated with each other into what Giddens calls a 'hierarchy of purposes' and with close parallels to what Archer has recently discussed at length in terms of an 'ordering of concerns' (2000, pp. 230–41; 2004, *passim*). The rationalisation of action thus draws attention to the existence of plurality. It acknowledges a plurality of possible projects attached to various status and role positions. The 'ordering' that this makes necessary will, as Craib's points on the unconscious make clear, often be other than entirely coherent and 'rational'. Also, the terminology of 'integration' used here doesn't necessarily imply harmony and the lack of tension between roles, concerns or projects. There may or may not be inner conflict of varying degrees of intensity and with varying degrees of potential for compromise. In line with the third point above, the ordering of concerns will also be more or less pre-reflective and taken-for-granted or critically reflective (see Giddens, 1993/1976, pp. 89–91).

Recognising the two different dimensions of internal structures that are drawn upon in the integration and ordering of projects can provide this aspect of structuration with greater critical purchase. Dealing with plurality in relation to conjuncturally-specific structures will involve agents in a sorting and ordering of projects, and will be informed by habitus, as always. However, the distinctiveness of plurality at the conjuncturally-specific level is that it refers to a sense of the immanent conditions of action. The ordering into a hierarchy of projects, here, will be greatly affected by what the perceptions of the empirical and substantive terrain of action appear to indicate about the chances of success, and about the probable attendant costs, associated with particular projected projects, together with a sense of which of these projects are judged as either mutually exclusive or mutually attainable.

On the other hand, plurality within the general-dispositional structures, or habitus, could include a range of elements from moral, religious, political, economic, professional, organisational discourses and principles, through all kinds of general-dispositional practical skills, to cultural, aesthetic and other tastes and habituated desires. How an agent draws upon this pluralistically composed habitus in practice will depend partly upon how, and the extent to which, the various elements have affected each other in the process of cohabitation. As an agent engages in a range of specific practices, these engagements will themselves make up part of the process of cohabitation and will constitute an important aspect of the dynamism within whatever re-configuration and hybridisation of elements takes place. The form that any dynamism and hybridisation will take with respect to each practice will depend upon the particular horizon of action. For just as such horizons bring into play conjuncturally-specific contexts of relevance, they will also bring into play certain combinations of elements from the general-dispositional domain, leaving others in the background, dormant. In what follows I will try to provide a more concrete sense of the process by which choices are made between a plurality of possible practices as a result of prioritising some concerns over others. I will first address the role of the general-dispositional and then go on to look at that of the specific-conjunctural.

Plurality within the General-Dispositional

In an important article on structuration theory and management, 'Putting Giddens into Action: Social Systems and Managerial Agency' (1997/1992), Richard Whittington makes some useful points in thinking through the phenomenological or general-dispositional internal structures that are drawn upon in the agent's ordering of purposes. These are internal structures that provide sets of competing pressures and/or opportunities at the same time as they provide a certain latitude to the agent. Whittington uses Giddens's terminology and where necessary I will interpret and translate the terms of his argument in the light of the points I have made about strong structuration. I will do this, I hope, without doing any injustice to the thrust and integrity of his argument. He attempts to draw out some of the implications of Giddens's commitment to 'multidimensional social systems' for the analysis of management and organisations. By 'multidimensional social systems' Whittington is referring to those aspects of Giddens's work that I have discussed in terms of his commitment to pluralistic non-reductionism (see chapter 1, pp. 40–4). However, Whittington builds more of a bridge than Giddens does between this latter style of theorising, which I have argued should not itself be thought of as structuration theory, and structuration theory *per se*. The aspects of articulation identified by Whittington are those at which the broader 'plural social structures' (Bryant and Jary, 1997, p. 156) are brought together within the hermeneutics of the agent. He speaks in terms of 'structural diversity' or 'cross-cutting systems of activity' and their implications for agent's conduct (Whittington, 1997/1992, p. 377).

In the part of his argument that I will focus upon Whittington concentrates on the influence of these plural structures on what is, in effect, the formation of agents' habitus in the differentiated conditions of late modernity. His primary argument is that it is useful to see the general-dispositional as being made up of a range or plurality of discursive schemas, orientations and principles for action. He argues that the increasing complexity and diversity of contemporary social organisation means there will very often be tensions between different principles and orientations and that these tensions can be divided into two types.

The first set of tensions – reminiscent in some ways of Merton's notion of role-sets, but here with a discursive and dispositional twist – results from the different and/or conflicting discourses, principles and orientations directly relevant to position-practices or roles within a particular institutional domain. Thus, for example, 'as the modern nation-state has expanded into the spheres of economic and social policy, its structures have splintered into a plurality of "sub-systems"' (Whittington, 1997/1992, p. 378; cf. Rhodes, 1988; and Smith, 1993 and 1999), each with 'objectives and modes of operation' that are remote from what Whittington sees as the previous overarching hermeneutic schema of patriotic adhesion to 'unity, order, nationalism and success' (Winkler, 1976, quoted in Whittington, 1997/1992, p. 378). Similarly, with the emergence of the large, diversified and managerially-controlled firm, its complexities have fragmented the simple hermeneutic schema 'of the profit-maximizing rule into a plethora of competing managerial "logics of action"' that are irreducible to a simple contradiction between capital and labour (Whittington, 1997/1992, p. 378).[12] Both politicians and managers, says Whittington, within their own situated positions are faced by a variety of conflicting possibilities for conduct. The discourses, interpretative schemas, principles of action, modes of operation, and so on, that they draw from are increasingly characterised by 'ambiguity and plurality', with no one set of 'rules' able to claim sole right to legitimacy and plausibility: '[c]hoice is possible, even mandatory, because more than one course of action has systemic legitimacy' (Whittington, 1997/1992, p. 378).

The second set of tensions, providing agents with even more latitude for agency, results from plural social identities (of the kind Merton illuminated with the notion of status-sets, see chapter 1, p. 26) that don't just arise from their role as manager, politician, carer, accountant or police officer but from the fact that they 'are also people, who, as full members of society, operate in a diversity of systems' (Whittington, 1997/1992, p. 379) and are therefore able to draw upon stocks of socio-cultural schemas and dispositions drawn from a multiplicity of sources. Whittington imposes some sort of analytical order on this multiplicity by specifying five ideal-types of relatively autonomous social spheres that each have their own typical forms of organisational position-practices and sets of schemas and resources.[13] These are not meant to be exhaustive but are meant to reflect a degree of empirical significance that has already been identified in the institutionalist literature. If identified by what Whittington calls their 'dominant structure' and 'organisations' (using structure in the conventional sense) these are:

- ethnic and religious (clubs and churches);
- capitalist (firms);
- familial (households);
- state/political (executive, legislative and judicial);
- professional and academic (professional bodies and universities).

On the basis of this non-reductionist diversity of systems Whittington goes on to give a number of examples of how a cross-cutting overlap between such spheres could play a significant role in the structuring of the habitus within agents: of male managers who, within the workplace, control female labour as both sets of agents routinely and pre-reflectively draw on the habitus of patriarchy derived from practices within the household; of large firms 'who define themselves as 'national champions' to enlist the support of their nation-states against overseas competition'; and accountants and engineers who 'deploy their professional expertise and legitimacy as they compete for managerial supremacy' (Whittington, 1997/1992, p. 379).

These examples could be thought of in terms of their relationship to the specific-conjunctural in that they are clearly speaking about position-practices. However, although Whittington's points here are made at a less abstract level than those of Giddens's ontology – all time and all places – in that they are periodised within late modernity and make substantive references to differentiated sectors of that social world, they are still pitched at a relatively abstract and generalised level. This type of analysis, as it is generalising in its very orientation, is much better equipped to bring out plurality within the general, transposable, characteristics of habitus than it is for the analysis of the conjuncturally-specific characteristics of internal structures.

It is worth mentioning a final example with this in mind. This is an example of ethnic minority entrepreneurs who draw on their community networks to gain protected sources of custom and finance. Whilst Whittington clearly means to include some reference to position-practice relations he only does so in a relatively abstract and generalised way. The main effect of the examples, again, is to bring to the fore the character of the general-dispositional. The constitution of such ethnically-based community networks – as we shall see in chapter 5 when looking at Ewa Morawska's study of a Jewish immigrant community in Johnstown, Pennsylvania – involve, in a quite profound way, the participants' transposable spheres of virtual schemas and skills. Such networks routinely rely upon a *mutuality* of world-views, cultural schemas, typifications, ethical precepts, principles of solidarity, and so on, that define the general-dispositional. In this and his other examples Whittington alerts us:

- to the plural and diverse nature of general-dispositional structures in contemporary society;
- to how this provides agents with a great degree of potential latitude for choice and selectivity amongst and between schemas, principles and orientations (including orientations towards different sources of power/ resources);
- to how resulting schemas, principles and orientations can affect the perception of the immediate structural terrain.

Plurality within the Conjuncturally-Specific

These points made by Whittington need to be complemented by a parallel recognition of the role of plurality in 'conjuncturally-specific' internal structures. As we have noted, although the general-dispositional will affect the phenomenological appreciation of the conjuncture, it is equally the case that the resulting (phenomenologically mediated) appreciation of the specifics of the conjuncture will have its own powerful impact – through a sense of opportunities, constraints, potential sanctions, costs and satisfactions – on an agent's 'ordering of concerns', and hence upon the configuration of the overall, emergent, hermeneutic frame.

These specifics will potentially be as *plural*, in their own way, as the general-dispositional is in its own way. This has already been brought out to a great extent in the case study of the foreign exchange, 'sterling', policies of the British Labour Government in the period of 1964–7. Here it was seen that with respect to the foreign exchange component of macro-economic policy the Government possessed sets of role-relationships, or sets of position-practice relations, with a plurality of different actors, national and international. The status of each of these different sets of actors as a specific part of the structural context, with interests, demands and power potentials of their own, needed to be considered by the Government in formulating policy (see above, pp. 95–100). The researcher-observer also needs to consider the actors in this way in order to understand the terrain. Explicitly recognising such a plurality allows one to focus on the status and the micro-specifics related to any one of these actors-within-context without losing a sense of their overall place within the relational nexus. Attention to such micro-specifics should include the hermeneutic-structural frames of whichever actors are brought into focus. In the present context we can focus in this way on the relations between the Government and the City–Bank–Treasury actors. In order for these relations-in-focus to be truly under-standable the grasp of the Government's position-practice relations with the international financiers must be sustained in the background as part of the overall relevant configuration. On this basis it becomes possible to substantiate the argument that the policy orientations of the Labour Government were not driven by the City–Bank–Treasury nexus. Rather, they were driven by the desire to sustain as high a level of macro-economic demand as possible, a goal that required the appeasement, to a certain degree, of the normative expectations of the international financiers with whom the Government had a quite distinct set of position-practice relations.

Investigating the hermeneutic-structural frames specifically within the actors within the City–Bank nexus allows one to see that these actors had a plurality of objectives and commitments related not only to sterling but to a range of conjunctural position-practices. One soon sees that many of these other objectives and commitments were not supported by the Government's policies. That is, the Government did not appease the normative ideals and expectations of the City–Bank nexus in many policy areas. More than this, the Government applied sanctions to many key City–Bank practices, no matter how important they were to perceived City interests. This bolsters the thesis concerning the Government's strategic commitment to a sustained level of macro-economic demand management, irrespective of the City's interests *per se*.

It can be shown that the opposing thesis that the driving force behind the non-devaluation of sterling was the Government's desire to serve City interests is a misleading and simplistic 'surface appearance'. When treasured City position-practices were not relevant to the Government's wider macro-economic demand objectives they were easily and wilfully sacrificed. Rather, the Government had a stable hierarchy of policy priorities within their financial strategy in which the defence of sterling was at the top, and whose understood but unintended consequence was the serving of those City interests that were dependent upon the maintenance of a strong currency. Other areas of policy, aimed at different conjunctural clusters of position-practice relations involving the City, were much lower down in the Government's hierarchy of priorities, or didn't figure at all within the entire range of Government purposes, or were even favoured targets for negative sanctions. This was apparent in the Government's pragmatic reaction to the conjuncture as it:

- refused to heed the demands of the City–Bank axis for cuts in public expenditure;
- ignored the resulting burden of restraint placed on monetary policy;
- imposed additional restrictions on the export of direct and portfolio capital (whilst the administrative costs of these controls were made the responsibility of the banks);
- ignored City–Bank demands to cut Government spending overseas, especially in relation to defence and foreign aid;

• visited significant penalties upon the financial community by means of the Selective Employment Tax, the Corporation Tax and the Capital Gains Tax (Stones, 1990, pp. 42ff).

City interests were protected in the 'sterling' policy area where the City's strategic wants coincided with those of the international financiers, but in the policy decisions directed to other sets of position-practice relations City interests were 'cheerfully subordinated to Government interests in the confident knowledge that liquidity was not directly implicated' (Stones, 1990, p. 42).

External Structures: Conditions, Outcomes and Irresistible Causal Forces

Many aspects of external structures and their relation to the quadripartite character of structuration have already been broached. In discussing, for example, conjuncturally-specific internal structures one soon begins to deal with the external structures that these internal structures purport to grasp. That is, one is soon dealing with conceptions of external structures whose existence is autonomous from the agent-in-focus, which face that agent at time 1, which can constrain that agent as well as providing her with possibilities and capacities, and which can constitute unacknowledged conditions of action and be the basis for unintended consequences of action. We have already seen, also, that external structures involve position-practices and their networked relations, that the agents-within the external structural conditions are *in situ* just like the agent-in-focus, and that these networked others are themselves involved in a duality of structure and all that this entails. In this section I will look at external structures as independent forces and pressuring conditions that limit the freedom of agents to do otherwise. I will show how the quadripartite conceptualisation of structuration allows us to retain Giddens's emphasis on the skilled, knowledgeable and active character of agents whilst also being much more realistic about the extent to which external social pressures constrain the actor.

Structuration's emphasis on the agent's own hermeneutic frame, and also on the ability of agents 'to do otherwise', tends to open it to suspicion from those who sense the power of systemic forces to push agents around either against their will or without them really understanding what is going on. Such sceptics believe that these two particular emphases of structuration necessarily lead to an under-estimation of the ability of social structures to impose themselves upon agents, moulding, constraining and pressuring their lives in a way that radically circumscribes their freedom. At an extreme there seems to be a sense that structuration harbours an idealistic view of agents as all-capable, all-knowledgeable, and continuously reflective in a questioning manner. Less extreme critics make concessions to one or other of these dimensions, or to some degree with each. Nevertheless, the general, damning, suspicion remains. In what follows I present the beginnings of an attempt to place these problematics at the heart of structuration theory's concerns.

As has been noted several times, Margaret Archer, in her critique of structuration in *Realist Social Theory* rightly calls attention to the properties of what I have called external structures, and to Giddens's neglect (I would say 'relative' neglect) of these. In doing so, it will be remembered, she emphasised the independent causal influence and the autonomy of these structures (see chapter 2, and cf. Archer, 1995, pp. 97–9). Archer spends more time elaborating the latter notion than the former, but the notion of independent causal influences is an intriguing and provocative one for structuration, for reasons to do with the problematic just mentioned. The challenge is increased given the way that strong structuration has, in turn, pointed to a number of shortcomings in Archer's own conception of external structures. The issue at the centre of this problematic is ultimately that of how to retain the integrity of strong structuration theory's emphasis on:

1. the relative autonomy of the agent from external structures at time 1;
2. the duality of structure and agency;
3. the active dimension of agent's conduct;

and the role of hermeneutics within each of these, whilst also finding an appropriate space for structural causal influences on that agent's life that are beyond her ability to control. In order to pursue this challenge it is necessary to look more closely at what it might mean for structures external to a given agent-in-focus to have both 'autonomy' from, and 'independent causal influence' on, that agent (or a given group of agents).

Ian Craib has argued that Archer's treatment of these sorts of issues allows her to look at 'degrees of freedom and restraint' in a way that Giddens cannot (Craib, 1992, p. 151). I think this is right to the extent that the under-developed nature of Giddens's conceptualisation of external structures does hamper attempts to consider the various degrees of freedom and choice available to agents. On the other hand, we have already noted that Archer's conceptualisation of external structures is also under-developed in identifiable ways. Her understanding of the autonomous and causally influential nature of external structures needs to be imbued with a greater explicit sense of the role of agents and duality *within* the external structures. However, Archer's conception of structures as in some senses separate from agents, as autonomous, does help us to think about questions of external constraint. In discussing external social structures as the emergent properties of previous interplays between structure and action, Archer writes, *inter alia*,[14] of their relative endurance and possession of causal powers (Archer, 1995, p. 167). As we have seen in chapter 2 it is possible, according to Archer, to identify 'structures independently of their occupants and incumbents' (pp. 167–8). This is what Archer means when she uses the short-hand notion of separating the structural 'parts' from the 'people'. Logically, this means that it is possible, to some degree, to identify the *causal powers* of the external structures that constitute a role/position independently of their occupants and incumbents. In chapter 2 it was noted that this is a position shared with proponents of structuration such as Cohen and Shilling. Because Archer believes that it is only by separating the parts from the people, the external structures from the agents-in-focus,[15] that one can then go on to identify the interplay between the powers of the two, she also believes that this is how one can clear a space within which to determine the effect of the causal powers of the structures on the agents. Archer believes that such structures can, in fact, 'exert systematic causal effects on subsequent action' (Archer, 1995, p. 167). She is keen, in this respect, to stress that there are often 'situational tendencies' within societies that will give a certain general direction and dynamic to the kind of interplay that one might expect between structure and agency. This point is provocative in thinking about the effects of wider 'conventional' structures on specific processes of structuration.

To engage with questions of freedom, choice and determination with a greater degree of precision we need, however, to build on Archer's insights and be more explicit and careful about the nature of the autonomy of external structures, and about the ways in which it is possible for them to exert an independent causal influence on outcomes. It is worth setting this out in some detail. I want to argue that in order to fully counter the suspicion that structuration theory is condemned to be overly voluntaristic, and also to be consistent with strong structuration theory the conceptualisation of external causal influences on agents must be able to encompass two types of occurrence.

The first, to which I believe the label of *independent causal influences* is appropriate, is when the external structures have complete autonomy from the agents whom they affect. They affect the social conditions within which these agents otherwise do manage to 'make history', but they affect these conditions in a way that is entirely independent of those incumbent agents' wants, desires and conduct. This involves external structures that are constituted, reproduced or changed entirely independently of the agent-in-focus, without her compliance, irrespective of her wants, and even when they directly affect her life. One can think of the ways that the structures of employment, health care, pensions, the housing market, military escalation and so on, will, at a given time 1, be entirely independent of a plurality of identifiable agents.

The second type of occurrence is when agents do have the physical capacity to resist an external influence – to do otherwise – but in phenomenological terms *feel that* they do not have the ability to resist. In such cases the label of *irresistible causal forces* is more accurate than 'independent causal influences'. This allows space to recognise both that the relevant external structures have their own *sui generis* autonomy from the agent-in-focus, and that their powerful influence on the agent is not independent of that agent's phenomenology. The agent's feeling of being powerless to resist combines both external structures and all the components of agency.

Thus, by 'independent causal influence' I mean that the external structures have the kind of causal influence on agents' lives that those agents do not have the physical capacity to control or resist. In such cases it is immediately clear that the causal influence of the external structures is labelled as 'independent' precisely because its efficacy is completely independent of the control of the agents-in-focus. With 'irresistible external forces' the causal influence is more qualified in that the feeling of the relevant agents that they cannot control or resist a particular causal influence is dependent upon their hermeneutic frame of meaning with all of its wants, dispositions and ordering of concerns. Once this frame is introduced and taken seriously however, and this is a point made forcefully by John B. Thompson (1989), structural influences *are* often experienced as not only intractable but also as irresistible with respect to the claims of compliance they make on given agents. Moreover, this is most often not just a subjective misrecognition of external conditions. It is often, rather, a realistic enough appraisal of the independent external conditions and the matrix of sanctions and rewards they promise to flesh and blood agents with a depth of values and commitments. It is true, on the one hand, that many of the external conditions that we experience as independent, as imposing their own *force majeure*, would not be experienced as such without this hierarchy of values and concerns, of things that are held precious. But without such commitments human beings would be hardly recognisable. Real people are less free to 'do otherwise' than abstract agents. Whilst there may be many conceivable options open to an agent when the circumstances are abstracted from that agent's 'every want and desire', such a conception of 'pure and rarefied' agents is 'for all practical purposes, irrelevant' (Thompson, 1989, p. 74).

Thompson's point is that very often situated agents will only have one 'feasible option' for the reasons outlined. The external structures have causal efficacy in these cases not because they are independent of the subjectivity of the agents, but precisely because an existing subjectivity is influenced (in a duality of structure and agency) by independently existing external structural constraints and pressures. The notion of 'irresistible causal forces' captures this sort of value-dependent influence, and so is able to encompass a major set of processes by which external causal influences encounter the wants, desires and principles of agents, resulting in a pragmatic 'trimming' of the latter. The 'trimming' means that agents compromise their ideal set of wants, desires and principles in order to be realistic; they sacrifice some things in order to safeguard others. Given that we are talking about circumstances in which the agent does have the physical capacity to resist the external forces, the invocation of 'irresistibility', with its implication of an overpowering force working through subjectivity, is both fitting and evocative.

Just because an agent actively complies with the exigencies of external structures this does not necessarily entail the absence of a sense of imposition or duress. *In situ* agents are always already in the midst of sets of position-practices and status-sets with all their attendant commitments and obligations, and they are also already inhabited by a phenomenological frame of meaning including all kinds of general-dispositions, psychological and emotional attachments, and wants and desires, by means of which, *inter alia*, they apprehend and relate to those everyday practices and obligations. At various times in the life of an individual – more in some lives than others – there may be choices to begin large projects, to begin to pursue long-term goals. At other times fulfilling the obligations of the positions taken up by these past choices, and by the many aspects of life's eventualities that seem never to have been chosen at all, means that there is more application, routine skill, limited improvisation, negotiation, compromise and muddling through to the tasks of agency than there is major decision-making. In these cases, any 'choosing to do otherwise', to use the phrase that Giddens identifies with agency, is of a low key and partial nature. There are cases when whole ways of life are changed, but these are extreme cases. Many of the things an agent does will be experienced, more or less tacitly, as things that are required of them by their embeddedness in a particular range of position-practices. As incumbents of those positions they will have imposed upon them, independently of what they currently would ideally like to do, a certain range of things that have to be done, with more or less willingness, alacrity, flair, doggedness or resignation. They will very often experience these demands as irresistible causal forces precisely because their overall ordering of concerns – involving their various wants, desires, attachments, dispositions, orientations, and bonds – make responding to such external structural influences the only 'feasible option'.

Even at the level of ontology-in-general Giddens gives too much weight to the ability to choose to do otherwise in his conception of agency. It is often just as important to respect agents' other qualities. To acknowledge, for example, that there can be just as much dignity in an agent's ability and choice to just 'carry on' instead of doing otherwise, to find value in the life they are already living. These are issues that are much in debate in the fields of political and moral philosophy and it would be unwise to give too much weight *a priori*, without argument, to one particular human capability. And at the concrete, *in situ*, level it is important to develop means of examining in greater detail the variety of ways in which flesh and blood, situated agents with particular frames of meaning feel both able and unable to resist, regulate or control the putative causal impositions of external structures. This would allow us to examine the quantity and the quality of feasible options available to specific situated agents, and also to look at the micro variations in agents' ability to resist and regulate external influences – and thus to affect the boundaries of the feasible – within the external context that confronts them.

The breadth and depth of irresistible causal influences on agents can be highlighted by making explicit some counter-factual conditions; conditions that would have to be met for agents to be able to resist external pressures. We can identify three types of properties an agent must possess if she is to be able to resist the pressures of particular external forces:

- The first of these properties is that of *perceived power* or *capability*. One can easily see that the majority of agents, most of the time, will feel the need to comply with the demands of particular external structures in order to procure anything from basic needs and requirements to the routine fulfilment of positional obligations. Such agents will usually feel compelled to comply with many external pressures due to their limited capability to create any realistic, feasible, alternative sources of meeting their various needs.

The other two properties required for an agent to feel able to resist are:

- that of *adequate knowledge* of relevant external structures, including alternative avenues of possibility, that would enable the agent-in-focus to do otherwise in the specific micro respect designated
- the agents' ability to gain a *requisite reflective distance* from their conditions of action.

Deficits in these last two factors clearly often work hand in hand, and also together with a perceived deficit in the power required to resist or transform *in-situ* external structures, or to alter one's position in relation to such structures. Together, and to their different degrees, they would limit the *in-situ* ability of the agent to do other than she does. Such is the case, for example, with Paula Spencer, the narrator of Roddy Doyle's *The Woman who Walked into Doors*, who doesn't leave her abusive husband because she doesn't know who would help, where to go, how they would help, whether she would be invisible to them, whether they would just treat her as an 'alco', how she would get money, how she would bear the shame and the disgrace, how she could stop Charlo coming after her and killing her, and the kids (Doyle, 1998, p. 209). Paula's case is self-evidently close to that of Giddens's limit-case of coercion, but it is still also an important distance from it. And in that distance we would want to acknowledge the quality of autonomy in Paula's agency and the emotional and psychological bonds with her children and with unnamed others that limit what it seems feasible for her to do. Equally, however, one can see the sense of speaking of the irresistible causal force of external structures in her life, of pointing to the set of social conditions of existence she inhabits as playing an unwanted and powerful role in a life she would like to be different but which she continues to live.

The agent who might resist would require all three properties of:

1. *adequate power* to resist *without* endangering the conditions of possibility for the realisation of core commitments;
2. *adequate knowledge* of alternative possible courses of action and their probable consequences;
3. *adequate critical distance* in order to take up a strategic stance in relation to a particular external structure and its 'situational pressures'.

All things being equal, the greater the possession of these properties the greater the agent's ability to regulate, modulate, deflect or erase specific aspects of such external demands and pressures. Adopting such categories in case study research one would be likely to find a differential ability to resist the independent influence of external structures, depending upon positions within organisational hierarchies and horizontal position-practice relations and also according to other positional social categories such as class, age, cultural capital, sexuality, gender, race, ethnicity, and so on. The absence of any one of the three properties would make it difficult for the agent to resist the external structures, and this means that the external structures would continue to pressure the agent in the usual ways, would sometimes perhaps overwhelm the agent. The absences might well, in part, be due to insufficiencies within the agent, but it is often precisely these and other paucities that allow the external structures to exert their influence irrespective of what the agent would actually want, *counter-factually*, if she had more knowledge, power and critical awareness. Conversely, it is easy to see, and important to see, that at the other extreme from a case such as Paula Spencer's, agents could have, and often do have, all three necessary pre-requisites for possible non-compliance. Social elites often have more resources to find ways not to comply and to do so with impunity, but many less well positioned agents will often have at least some of this same capacity. Others will still comply anyway simply because they positively want these particular aspects of the life they are living. In such cases external structures still influence the lives of these agents, there is no retreat into voluntarism, but we have reached that end of the continuum at which the causal influence of these structures are resistable; they are not experienced with any sense of *force majeure*. The agents in these moments *could* resist the influence of particular structures without jeopardising the conditions of possibility for the realisation of core commitments, but they don't resist because they have no desire to.

To begin to explore the properties of particular agents in particular circumstances, to investigate the in-situ level of social relations, we need to move beyond ontology-in-general and into the area of methodology and empirical research. This is a major focus of the next chapter.

4

Strong Structuration 2:
The Research Focus and
the Wider Picture

I have emphasised the centrality of the duality of structure and the quadripartite nature of the structuration cycle to structuration theory. Their centrality is, in turn, closely linked to the specific range of questions and problems (explananda) that structuration theory is most suited – in some cases uniquely suited – to address. There is a deepening of the differences between the strong project of structuration and Giddens's restricted concern with ontology-in-general when the former's more developed, refined and ontically directed ontology is also used systematically as a guide to empirical evidence. Thus, not only does strong structuration insist upon a more developed ontology in the area around the duality of structure, it also insists upon a closely related concern with epistemological and methodological issues. The research strategy of strong structuration is characterised by a closely attentive reflexivity with respect to the logical and methodological consistency of relations between ontology at the abstract level (ontology-in-general) and this ontology as it looks at the substantive, ontic level (ontology-*in-situ*), and with respect to the traces of empirical evidence that are called on to substantiate claims about the latter.

Systematic research relations between these levels are necessarily heavily dependent upon precise definitions of the specific objects of empirical study. The definitions of these objects, in turn, are typically dependent upon the specific problems, questions and question-types that are to be investigated and addressed. These points cannot be emphasised too strongly. They arise for all social theoretical traditions. I have argued that the ontological concepts at the heart of structuration theory have a distinctive capacity to be linked to an investigation of a certain, significant but limited, range of question types and issues. Framed and located within the parameters of position-practices and their relations (see chapter 3), strong structuration's objects of study are by definition those that involve *in-situ* questions about the hermeneutics of agents in combination with structural diagnostics. The questions can be aimed at any or all of the four parts of the quadripartite nature of structuration, as each of these involves both hermeneutics and social structures.

Often an initial focus on one aspect of the cycle will lead, logically and systematically, to other specific aspects of the cycle relevant to the depth exploration of the question(s)-at-hand. For example, with respect to the two types of internal structures that make up the second aspect of the quadripartite cycle one can soon see that a particular focus on one or the other of these would be particularly appropriate for certain kinds of questions. Thus, a focus on conjuncturally-specific internal structures would allow one to begin to gain critical purchase on strategic, practical, political (in the widest sense), *in-situ*, questions and issues regarding the range of possibilities for action and the potential consequences of such action. Such a focus would allow one to look at conjunctural constraints, probable sanctions, opportunities, impossibilities and possibilities. What is it possible to do? What might it be possible to do if...? What, and who, are the obstacles? How intractable are these obstacles? There would be a clear path between an initial focus on the conjuncturally-specific internal structures relevant to such questions and a concern with the nature of the external structures and likely outcomes that they attempted to grasp (the first and fourth parts of the quadripartite cycle).

A focus on general-dispositional internal structures, on the other hand, would allow one to understand more about the particular character of certain agents' more or less taken-for-granted world view, with all of its practical and broader socio-cultural and discursive elements. By looking at this one could gain a critical purchase on such things as:

- how these agents perceive the world (including their phenomenological approach to conjuncturally-specific aspects of that world);
- what the internal relationships are between different aspects of that world-view;
- how intensely attached the agents are to particular elements of their overall vision;
- how they came to have particular elements of such a vision in the first place;
- what would have to change for them to see the world differently.

The link to conjuncturally-specific internal structures is clear in that the latter are always perceived from the perspective of the general-dispositional. There will also be a general-dispositional element within each of the agents within the external structures relevant to any of the questions associated with the conjuncturally-specific internal structures. It was Giddens's seeming impatience with these kinds of *in-situ* concerns that so disappointed some supporters (for example, Thrift, 1985, pp. 620–1) and perplexed many others. Once driven by these and other in-range substantive questions, and refined by the variable meso-level ontological concepts characterised in chapter 3 (pp. 76–84), one can see that a whole assembly of abstract and generalising concepts associated with Giddens's version of structuration theory all take on a very different complexion. They take on more dynamic and critical power once marshalled by the demands and rigours of addressing questions about particular processes in particular times and places.

Against this background I will now address two major aspects of the research process in the present chapter. The first deals with epistemology and the use of methodological brackets as a guiding tool in research directly informed by the ontology of structuration. I argue that the methodological brackets of agent's conduct analysis and agent's context analysis are the two forms of bracketing appropriate to structuration theory. To reinforce the emphasis on methodological reflexivity and precision I outline a number of different methodological steps that can be involved in the research process, underlining the varying specific foci of these steps and their variable relationship to the guiding frames of methodological brackets. Finally, I indicate that most actual substantive cases, especially those that are complex in terms of numbers of agents and extensions in time and space, require the combination of several such research steps into what I call a 'composite study'. I draw out some aspects of such studies and end with a formal characterisation of four types of 'composite' research project, differentiating them one from the other by means of their specific question-type (or explanandum) and hence the different objects of study to which they are directed.

The second major aspect of the research process that I intend to look at in this chapter deals less with structuration *per se* and more with, firstly, how one is to provide both a wider historical and spatial frame for structuration studies, and secondly, with how one can find points of articulation between such an orienting frame and the structuration studies themselves. This aspect can be thought of in terms of the points mentioned in the introduction with respect to C. Wright Mills's *The Sociological Imagination*. It is an attempt to add, to the intersection of agents and external structures in the form of position-practice relations, a sense of further intersections with broader frames and dynamics of historical and social trajectories. I will move on to the first theme in a moment but I first want to say a few more words of introduction about what to expect from the broader themes of the second part of the chapter.

I noted in the introduction and in chapter 1 my view that Giddens's project of structuration, somewhat ironically given its abstract orientation, entertained too broad a sense of the appropriate scope of structuration theory, of the range of issues or question-types for which it is an appropriate tool. In particular, there was a confusion between pluralistic, non-reductionist approaches to social causality associated with historical sociology, state theory and other aspects of social theory, on the one hand, and structuration theory, on the other. Such non-reductionist pluralism is not, in and of itself, structuration theory. This is particularly the case in Giddens's hands as he erases from his presentation of substantive analyses in these areas almost all trace of the hermeneutic-structural processes that give the duality of structure its distinguishing character. Consequently, in the second, longer, part of this chapter I will outline what I see to be the proper role for such pluralistic, non-reductionist, approaches with respect to empirical studies of structuration.

I begin that section by drawing on the theoretical approach of Michael Mann's *The Sources of Social Power* as an example, together with a closer focus on his particular analysis of the French Revolution. My argument is that this kind of comparative historical sociology, with an emphasis on broad social developments, can be used to great effect as a means of locating and framing the more specific substantive studies of structuration within the context of the broader, more conventional, structures that John Thompson discusses in his critique of Giddens (see chapter 2).[1] Indeed, I argue that Mann's work is of more immediate use than Giddens's historical sociology in this respect because of features related to its more detailed and substantive quality. The discussion of Mann's work, and of the work of others in this section, is also part of an attempt to demonstrate the advantages of eschewing theoretical partisanship for its own sake, and moving towards a practice of combining different theories in order to produce more powerful critical frameworks for addressing particular questions. The nature of substantive structuration studies means that they are naturally located at the meso and micro levels (with the caveats expressed earlier, see p. 82), and there are many theoretical approaches with a more macro and/or otherwise complementary emphasis that could often be most fruitfully combined with structuration theory. The gain, it seems to me, would be two-way. In order to demonstrate this I will, in addition to Mann's historical sociology, also look at: Joan Scott's post-structuralist discourse analysis of the struggles of Parisian female garment workers in 1848; Eamonn Carrabine's study of Her Majesty's Prison, Manchester (Strangeways) between 1965 and 1990 using a combination of the Foucaultian discourse/governmentality approach and aspects of structuration theory; and further aspects of my own study of the 1964–70 Labour Government's defence of sterling, this time focusing on the wider locating and framing features of the international financial system, including the role of the IMF and the US Government.

Epistemological and Methodological Considerations in the Research Process

Giddens's self-conscious preoccupation with ontology and the concomitant lack of attention to epistemology has been incisively analysed by Bryant (1992). The lack of concern shown by Giddens with respect to the bridge between ontology and empirical evidence means that the complex specificity of issues concerned with establishing the validity of research accounts (Bryant, 1992, pp. 143–4) and, I would add, to do with the variety of question-types and knowledge claims, have been left almost completely unremarked. I would also argue that in the one key aspect of knowledge claims with which Giddens did concern himself he made a damaging mistake. This concerned the appropriate forms of *methodological bracketing* necessary to apply the ontology of structuration theory at the concrete, substantive, level. I will clarify the nature of methodological brackets below but essentially they guide a focus on certain aspects of the substantive level rather than others. Which is the most appropriate bracket will follow logically from a combination of the ontological concepts employed and the precise question about the substantive issue to be addressed. All of the questions or question-types falling within the remit of structuration theory require one or both of two forms of methodological bracketing:[2] *agent's conduct analysis* and *agent's context analysis*. Giddens identified the former but unwittingly paired it with a form of bracketing (*institutional analysis*, see chapter 1, pp. 43–4) appropriate for certain types of non-reductionist analysis but not for analysis employing the notion of the duality of structure and the other associated concepts at the core of structuration.

It is implicit in what I have just said, however, that I do want to defend the notion of methodological bracketing itself. This conceptual-practical tool, formulated by Giddens, can be developed, elaborated and used to significant effect. As noted, brackets provide sets of regulative and selective guidelines that can direct the researcher to some dimensions of a social object rather than others. They thus act as a means of increasing reflexivity about what precisely is involved in a particular knowledge claim. Bracketing allows one to focus more sharply on the issue of which abstract and meso-level ontological concepts are 'relevant' to a piece of research. Which concepts and, more precisely, which parts of these concepts, will be relevant to a particular research question will vary. The chosen brackets will purposefully leave the objects of study denoted by some concepts in the shadows. Alternatively, they might leave just parts of a concept's concern's in the shadows. Thus, if the ontological concept involves agents' perceptions, then some aspects of an agent's perceptions might be thought to be important within a given form of bracketing but not others.

This purposeful selection and limiting of focus allows one to be clearer about the significance of any piece of *empirical evidence* cited in support of a claim about the object of study. The evidence may be seen to be just a shard, a fragment, when placed against the whole area of all the relevant aspects of the abstract and meso-level concepts. The combination of relevant concepts seen in the round, and the specific question, brought together within a form of bracketing, provide a benchmark against which such evidence can be assessed in terms of its detail and coverage. Moreover, such broad notions of bracketing provide only the initial orienting framework in addressing questions appropriate to structuration. From within this ontological-methodological framework, we shall see that it is useful to go on to distinguish between a series of further research steps in which the selectivity and focus is even more subtly differentiated and refined.

Methodological Brackets: Agent's Conduct and Context Analysis

Before proceeding to look at these further distinctions, however, I also want to note a number of decisive limitations with Giddens's own handling of the notion of methodological bracketing. I have already discussed some of the deficiencies of institutional analysis in chapter 1, and the point I want to make here is that he simply makes a mistake in choosing 'institutional analysis' as the appropriate form of bracketing to complement and support 'agent's conduct analysis' in putting structuration theory to substantive, empirical, use. It was a mistake because whilst institutional analysis may be useful for developing certain aspects of pluralistic, non-reductionist accounts of social processes, it does not have the ability to address the processes of structuration.

It will be remembered that institutional analysis 'places in suspension the skills and awareness of actors, treating institutions as chronically reproduced rules and resources' (Giddens, 1984, p. 375), whereas agent's conduct analysis 'places in suspension institutions as socially reproduced, concentrating upon how actors reflexively monitor what they do; how they draw upon rules and resources in the constitution of interaction (Giddens, 1984, p. 378).[3] I want to argue that what I label agent's *context* analysis, rather than institutional analysis, is the appropriate form of methodological bracketing to support agent's conduct analysis, that is, to cover the aspects of the dialectical process of structuration that are not covered by agent's conduct analysis. Explaining what I mean by agent's context analysis is most easily achieved by contrasting it with agent's conduct analysis and with institutional analysis, respectively.

Agent's *conduct* analysis draws upon the ontological category of knowledgeability (as part of an agent's internal structures) in a way that leads us back to the agent herself, her reflexive monitoring, her ordering of concerns into a hierarchy of purposes, her motives, her desires, and the way she carries out the work of action and interaction within an unfolding sequence. Attention becomes focused on the agent's critically reflective and pre-reflective processes of sifting and sieving at the point where the conjuncturally-specific internal structures relevant to the context of immediate action forge a reconciliation of sorts with the active agency and the general-dispositional frame of meaning of the agent. It is this process of negotiation and reconciliation – pragmatic or otherwise – that produces the conduct of the agent and that can, in a range of circumstances, lead to an attenuation of the agent's general-dispositional frame.

By way of contrast, *agent's context* analysis draws on the notion of knowledgeability, in the sense of conjuncturally-specific internal structures, in order to lead us more clearly outwards into the social nexus of interdependencies, rights and obligations, asymmetries of power and the social conditions and consequences of action (see Stones, 1991, and 1996, p. 98; also see Bryant and Jary, 2001a, p. 17, and 2002, p. 258). It leads us, through the agent, out into the conjunctural terrain of action. It takes us on a journey from the agent and her hermeneutic frame of meaning, with a particular focus on the perceptions of conjuncturally-specific internal structures, out towards the external processes of structuration whose relations with those internal structures we have said have previously been too little explicated in structuration theory.

Agent's context analysis can be used to analyse the terrain that faces an agent, the terrain that constitutes the range of possibilities and limits to the possible. Amongst other things such knowledge is necessary for the agent if she is to think counterfactually about strategic possibilities. Just as it allows an explicit emphasis on the *agent-in-focus*'s awareness of potential courses of action, agent's context analysis also allows the *social researcher* a perspective from which to identify and assess the range of relevant causal influences, the potential courses of action, and the probable consequences of both, and to judge these assessments against those of the agent (see Stones, 1996, pp. 98–100). The researcher's perspective within agent's context analysis is, for example, able to respect the hermeneutics of the lay actors relevant to an explanandum at the same time as it is able (in principle) to acknowledge the kinds of independent causal powers and influences discussed in chapter 3 that may have by-passed the participating agent.[4] Agent's context analysis can 'round off' the accounts that can, in principle if not always in fact, be given by agent's conduct analysis. It covers parts of the structuration cycle that the latter does not reach. Without agent's context analysis the researched agent would be deracinated and condemned to be turned inwards upon herself, cut off from any account of her hermeneutic and practical engagement with external structures. It follows that structuration theory cannot do without agent's context analysis if it is to be applied systematically in empirical research. It simply cannot be operationalised adequately without it. The two forms of bracketing working together are required to release the substantive potential of structuration theory. At the same time, in contrast to institutional analysis, agent's context analysis does not treat institutions as chronically reproduced rules and resources. It doesn't assume the institutional properties of the settings of interaction to be methodologically 'given'. It treats the immediate meso-relational configuration of institutional position-practices as significant objects of investigation. In doing so it also recognises the need to investigate 'the skills and awareness of actors within this institutional context of action'.

The bracketings of agent's conduct and agent's context analysis provide means whereby particular questions, or objects of investigation, and the more or less discrete ontological insights of structuration are brought together and considered in relation to questions of empirical evidence. Knowledge of the analytical procedures specific to the different forms of bracketing help the investigator to decide on the types of evidence and substantiation required for any particular question. For many questions there will be a need to use aspects of both conduct and context analysis. One reason for this is that the concept of conjuncturally-specific internal structures often acts as a kind of hinge between external structures, on the one hand, and general-dispositional frames and agent's practices, on the other. Conjuncturally-specific internal structures point both outwards and inwards, and because of this they play a role in both agent's conduct and context analysis.

Question-Types, Research Steps and Objects of Study

This will be apparent as I describe some of the typical, recurrent, steps that provide more subtle and differentiated distinctions within the initial orienting framework of the broad notions of bracketing. Within the research process these steps will be combined in a variety of ways depending upon the specific question-at-hand. This means that the relevance of, and the importance of, any one of the following to any particular piece of research will also depend upon the specific problem or question-at-hand. The *recurrent steps* include the following:

1. Within the bracket of agent's conduct analysis, the ontological concepts can be drawn upon to *identify* the general-dispositional frames of meaning of an agent-in-focus. Such identification can include the further specification of some or all of the plural or diverse structures, indicated by Whittington, that help to structure the general dispositions/habitus of agents (*object of study*: general-dispositional frames).
2. Working from within an identified general-dispositional frame one can go on to focus specifically on the conjuncturally-specific internal structures

of the agent-in-focus, that is on the ways that the agent *perceives* her immediate external structural terrain from the perspective of her own projects, whether in terms of helplessness or empowerment, or a complex combination of the two. Again, such identification can include the further specification of a number of *diverse* structural clusters of position-practices, as in the example of the Government perception of the diverse structural clusters relevant to the interests of British financial institutions (see chapter 3, pp. 107–9). It is quite possible for both participant agents and researchers to overlook one or more structural clusters of great significance to the explanandum (problem-to-be-explained, or question) at hand. Attempts to falsify or to strengthen confidence in an explanation often therefore involve the search for relevant clusters whose causal contribution to the explanandum has been missed.[5]

Analysis of the conjuncturally-specific structures of the agent-in-focus may involve both:

> identifying relatively discrete conjuncturally-specific internal structural clusters (*object of study*: the – often plural – conjuncturally-specific internal structures that inhabit an overall frame of meaning, and the agent-in-focus's perception of the possibilities allowed by, and the constraints and influences imposed by, these perceptions of the external structures);

but then also:

> looking at the relationship *between* these clusters in terms of how they are perceived to impinge upon the particular projects of an agent-in-focus (*object of study*: the agent-in-focus's practical integration and/or hierarchical ordering of her various projects on the basis, *inter alia*,[6] of her perceptions of various conjunctural structures (above); that is, the possibilities allowed by, and the constraints and influences imposed by, her perception of the overall conjuncture).

The latter is placed squarely within agent's conduct analysis as it involves all those issues, including the ordering and integration of concerns, regarding the ways in which the agent reconciles herself to the exigencies thrown up by the various 'ghosts of networked others'. The former is more Janus-faced as the conjuncturally-specific internal structures at one and the same time point *outwards* into the agent's context and the terrain in which her projects will be pursued, and also *inwards* towards the rapprochement of the internal structures with what her projects are or will be.

3. Within agent's context analysis, one can *identify*, as a researcher: relevant external structural clusters; the position-practice relations that routinely constitute them; the authority relations within these and the material resources at the disposal of these hierarchically situated agents. However,

as achieving any depth in such analyses will involve looking, *inter alia*, at the general-dispositional frames of the agents within these structural clusters one also needs to draw upon agent's conduct analysis within the wider context bracketing. Following this, from the perspective of these general-dispositional frames, one will most likely need to investigate the conjuncturally-specific internal structures perceived from within them. Again, this is Janus-faced in terms of the two major forms of bracketing. From here, to the extent that the actions and potential actions of these *agents-within-structures* are relevant to the question at hand (to do, perhaps, with a causal sequence), one would need to look at the relationship of *their* conjuncturally-specific internal structures to *their* practical projects and purposes. This, again, is within the realm of agent's conduct analysis, within the frame of context analysis (*object of study*: the identification of relevant external structural clusters, including the overall frames of the agents within them).

4. On the basis of the identified external structures one can attempt – as a researcher – to specify the 'objective' possibilities open to, and the constraints upon, the agent(s)-in-focus. As regards methodological brackets, the same points apply as for the identification of external structures (step 3). However, it is still worth differentiating this fourth step from the previous step as, strictly speaking, one could focus on external structures without approaching them in terms of possibilities and constraints. With small changes in emphasis and focus different considerations of ontology and empirical evidence come into view. With both of points three and four, the *researcher's* specification can be compared to the parallel conception of the *agent-in-focus's* conception of the external structures within her conjuncturally-specific internal structures. Conceptions of the possibilities and constraints facing the agent-in-focus will depend, amongst other things, upon judgements about the independent and irresistible causal influence[7] of the entities that make up the external structures. As with the agent-in-focus's analysis of external structures this will often involve looking at a range of external structural clusters and at their inter-relationships. In distinguishing abstract from strong structuration it is worth noting that the considera- tion of enablements and possibilities here, within the *in-situ* framework of strong structuration, is always with respect to particular, specified, agents and their relative actual or predicted impact upon outcomes. This is in keeping with those conceptual points elaborated by Mouzelis with respect to the syntagmatic level, pertaining to those elements of external structures that can be transformed by a particular agent, and those that cannot (for example, Mouzelis, 1991: 39). And it contrasts starkly with Giddens's blanket insistence, from the perspective of ontology-in-general, that structures are always both enabling and constraining. This is a perspective that is unable to differentiate between the variable degrees of

possibility and constraint confronting particular agents in specific circumstances (*objects of study*: the possibilities for action and for structural modification allowed by external structures, and the constraints and influences imposed upon particular agents by these external structures).

Complex Question-Types and Composite Research Strategies

It is clearly also possible to combine various aspects within all the above points in order to follow through, in relation to a given explanandum, particular processes of structuration involving a number of different actors over a relatively extended period of time within a stated conjuncture. In order to pursue this latter strategy (which for ease of reference I will refer to simply as the '*composite strategy*') the question addressed will by definition have to be broader than one that only addresses the relations between one agent and her external structural context. In such cases the quadripartite notion of structuration will still be at work and relevant, but it will be happening in many places at the same time, with agents differently situated in relation to the external structuration processes. These agents will also be differently situated with respect to the explanandum, and they will contribute in a variety of ways, and more or less, towards the production of this phenomenon. Respecting the web-like nature of interdependencies within the process of structuration also entails giving due recognition to the fact that any one agent can be seen as both first and third person depending upon whose position in the nexus is in focus at any one time. It will also be the case that, *ceteris paribus*, the broader the scope and scale of any one identifiable causal sequence, or set of sequences, the less any one of the agents-in-focus will have the power to know about or control the entirety of that sequence, either on their own or in alliance with others.

The composite strategy, embracing each of the steps outlined above, and others, would have to be drawn upon in order to address a range of specific types of research question central to structuration. The *types of questions* include those which demand a focus on aspects already mentioned but which do so in terms of wanting to know what has causally produced those phenomena over a particular time period. Their focus is close to what Archer calls 'analytical histories of emergence' (Archer, 1995, pp. 324–8),[8] which I think of as *the histories of causal processes of structuration* that have *produced*, for example:

1. a particular decision, interactional sequence, set of spatial of temporal arrangements,[9] or event (one or other of these as explanandum);
2. present designated external structural clusters (the emergence of external structures as explananda);

3. the agent's current general-dispositional frames, including their relatively enduring character traits, dispositions and discursive orientations (the emergence of general-dispositional frames as explananda);
4. the internal structures within the frame of meaning directly concerning the details of the immanent horizon of action (the emergence of conjuncturally-specific internal structures as explananda); or, finally,
5. all or any combination of the above as explananda.

Relations between Strong Structuration and Studies of Greater Scope

The emphasis of structuration theory on the internal and external relationships between social structures and the hermeneutics of agents means that structuration studies will typically lean towards the deft and careful brush strokes of an artist intent on capturing the details of her subject. This raises the question of how we are to think about the relationship of such studies to those whose creators employ much broader brush strokes on much larger canvases. The question of the relationship between these two types of study is one that impinges on structuration studies themselves, for most structuration studies will benefit from being placed and situated within a broader historical and geographical framework (see figure 4.1). In looking at the full sweep of Giddens's writings in chapter 1, we have already discussed the difference between pluralistic non-reductionism and structuration theory, and the reasons why non-reductionist categories *per se* are not necessarily categories of structuration. Here, and taking the above as given, I want simply to move on to make a number of points about the roles that can be played by broad categories, such as those produced by non-reductionist studies, in providing a wider situating context for structuration studies.

In my view, the pluralistic non-reductionist emphasis on distinct institutional clusters that have at least a degree of contingency in their relationship to each other is attractive as a starting point from which to map out, provisionally, the context in which particular processes of structuration take place. The sense of the provisional and the preliminary needs to be stressed. The mapping out would be a rough and imprecise one, locating the more detailed structuration study approximately within broad historical and social trends and parameters. Simply for practical reasons there would always be limits to how far a study that is historically or geographically expansive could embrace the tenets of strong structuration in the treatment it gave to each and every aspect of its subject matter. The most that one could generally hope for would be to establish points of connection between such broad trends and parameters and certain key aspects of the duality of structure and the quadripartite nature of the structuration cycle.

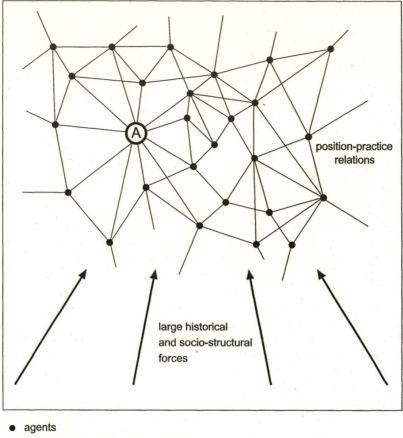

position-practice
relations

large historical
and socio-structural
forces

- **●** agents
- **—** networked links with other agents
- **↑** macro historical and socio-structural forces

Figure 4.1 The impact of large historical forces and conventional structures on agents and position-practice relations (also see figure 3.4, p. 94)

Pluralistic Non-Reductionism in Mann's 'Sources of Social Power'

To make these points more concretely I will focus here on Michael Mann's impressive first and second volumes of *The Sources of Social Power*, In some respects Mann's pluralist emphases are similar to those of Giddens. Both authors list several influential institutional domains each of which is said to have its own reality, efficacy and more or less relative autonomy. The major organising means and institutional networks of social power are said by Mann to lie in the different but overlapping spheres of Ideology,

Economy, Military, Political state (centralised-territorial) and Political states (geopolitical-diplomatic) (IEMP). There is a close parallel between Mann's IEMP categories and those presented by Giddens in *Central Problems*. A significant difference is that Mann does not have any pretensions to derive his categories from more fundamental ontological categories. They are grounded from the start at a more substantive, less abstract, level. Nevertheless, in the work of both authors a stress on non-reductionism and more or less contingent articulation is linked to a critique of 'unfolding models of social change'(cf. Giddens, 1979, pp. 222–5; Mann, 1986, pp. 531–2). For both authors it is the case that '[t]urning-points' in history could 'have led to quite other processes of social change' (Mann, 1986, p. 531). Mann, like Giddens, is clear that major historical and social outcomes have often been 'close-run' (Mann, 1986, pp. 30–2, 532). Having said this, it seems to me that in his repeated emphasis on 'might have beens' and 'almost weres' Mann achieves a healthier balance within his historical sociology between issues of contingency and open systems, on the one hand, and routines and determinations, on the other (Mann, 1986, p. 531). Mann is also far more explicit than Giddens in stating his belief that within the non-reductionist nexus he sketches out there also exist a whole variety of interconnections, interactions and causal sequences that are 'too complex to be theorised' (Mann, 1986, pp. 30–2, 532).

Mann is clear that the four IEMP sources of power 'are only ideal types; they do not exist in pure form' (Mann, 1993, p. 9). Actual power organisations, he says, 'mix them, as all four are necessary to social existence and to each other' (Mann, 1993, p. 9). This is, of course, consistent with what Giddens says about the ontological structural categories of legitimation, domination and signification, but because Mann's project involves detailed and intensive historical sequences and case studies he has more to say about the relationship between such general theoretical categories and the level of substantive historical detail. Mann writes that:

> My IEMP model is not one of a social system divided into four 'subsystems', 'levels', 'dimensions', or any other of the geometric terms favored by social theorists. Rather it forms an analytical point of entry for dealing with mess. The four power sources offer distinct, potentially powerful organizational means to humans pursuing their goals. But which means are chosen, and in which combinations, will depend on continuous interaction between what power configurations are historically given and what emerges within and among them. The sources of social power are impure and promiscuous. They weave in and out of one another in a complex interplay between institutionalized and emergent, interstitial forces (Mann, 1993, p. 10).

Thus, for example, in surveying the rise of classes and nation-states from 1760 to 1914 in the second volume of *The Sources of Social Power*, Mann employs his broad brush IEMP categories to 'refute single-factor theories' and to make 'broad suggestions about general patterns' (Mann, 1993, p. 87). He refers to the latter as rough and 'impure' generalisations concerning the primacy of power sources during periods within the analysed era (Mann, 1993, pp. 1–4). For example, he places 'final causal emphasis on military states and commercial capitalism' in his overall explanation of power developments within the period covering the American, French and Industrial Revolutions (Mann, 1993, pp. 4, 214–52). But generalisation is 'impure' because of:

- the inevitable complications caused both by the fact that the different forms of power inevitably entwine with each other and change each other's internal shapes and outward trajectories (Mann, 1993, p. 2);
- the existence of a series of other complicating factors within these institutional clusterings to do, for example, with forms of distributive and collective power, the entwining of classes and nation-states, and the existence of sectional and segmental, trans-national and local-regional actors and power organisations (Mann, 1993, pp. 1–21);
- the importance within the state of differing solutions to the 'representative' and 'national' issues (Mann, 1993, pp. 5 and 81–88);
- and the cumulative effect of all these interactions.

In short, the simple fact that, as we have seen, many aspects of the causal process are simply too complex to be theorised.

As Mann employs his theoretical categories to look at particular case studies, one cannot help but be aware, at one and the same time, both of the relatively imprecise, relatively under-theorised, manner of their application and of the clear analytical gain that derives from them in making sense of the 'patterned mess' (p. 4) of processes and events. From the perspective of strong structuration Mann's analysis provides a platform from which to make connections with questions directed to more subtle issues of hermeneutics, duality and the quadripartite nature of structuration. His narrative detailing of the historical scope, weight and dynamism of ideological, economic, military and political organisations and practices serve, from one angle, to highlight the immense and awesome force and *sui generis* nature of the sum of structuration processes external to any one actor. From another angle, they suggest points of likely or possible junction between such actors and particular clusters of practices. Because Mann's sense-making narratives are couched at a concrete historical level, they not only identify types of practices and contexts according to the IEMP model, but also particular people engaging in those practices at given times and places within those contexts. His case studies manage to combine a broad sense of the wider societal forces, networks and dynamics at work with markers as to the position and perspectives of particular agents within key conjunctural moments. The latter have their limitations, as I shall indicate, but the fact that Mann manages to include them at all within a project of such scope is valuable in thinking through the relationship between strong structuration studies and the wider networks and movements of history and society.

Mann's Case Study of the French Revolution

Let us take the case study of the French Revolution as an example in order to look more closely at what Mann's study achieves in these respects. This example can itself be framed by his more overarching argument. Couched in terms of the broadest categories in his 'rough' and 'impure' arsenal Mann argues that the two sources of social power that were dominant during the eighteenth century were the economic and the military. As we have seen, he wishes to place 'final causal emphasis' for the overall trajectory of power developments during this period on 'military states and commercial capitalism' (Mann, 1993, p. 4). He writes that by 1800 'the military revolution and rise of capitalism had transformed the West, the former providing predominantly authoritative power and the latter predominantly diffused power'. Because they were so closely entwined, neither can be accorded a singular ultimate primacy (p. 1). When he comes to speak of the particular case studies of the American, French and Industrial revolutions, however, the explanation is also linked to the other two sources of power. He sees transformations in the two power sources of capitalism and the military as having begun far earlier but, during the eighteenth century, as serving to foster 'ideological and political transformations, each with its own partly autonomous logic – the rise of discursive literacy and the rise of the modern state' (p. 4). His analyses of specific case studies, such as that of the French Revolution, take on more refined, specific and detailed features. Here, Mann devotes a good deal of attention to the fusion of three communication infrastructures that provided an ideological revolutionary elite – regime enlightenment, political rights lawyers and the diffusion of literacy among the petite bourgeoisie, the lower clergy and the upper peasantry – and to the rise and character of the French state – particularly its handling of its own finances – in providing an account of the immanent causes and trajectory of the revolution (pp. 167–87).

Mann argues that the French Revolution began because state militarism, and particularly reverberations from the Seven Years War and the American Wars of Independence, produced a fiscal crisis in which failure to institutionalise factionalism among the state elite around the Monarchy and various parties with entrenched privileges in society 'immobilized the entire old regime'. The resulting divisions, vacillations and sense of impotence within the state was exacerbated by 'unresolved factionalism' within both the army and the church (p. 207). In parallel with these developments rural class conflict was 'boiling up from its customary latent level' by the late 1780s.

Based on peasants with only local class organisations even the high levels of disquiet against proprietorial privilege apparent within this period should have been easily stilled, according to Mann, by the routinely enforced combination of political absolutism, militarism and Catholic ideology. However, he writes, 'it would be a dangerous time for monarchical elite, proprietary class, officers, and clerics to squabble' (p. 175). In the towns power was seized by an ideological elite with 'distinct Enlightenment preoccupations with moral principle' (p. 207). This elite could not be easily identified with the mainstream of either the bourgeoisie or the old regime, and Mann spends some time detailing the institutional and organisational bases for the *sui generis* nature and relatively autonomous bases and efficacy of these ideological practices (pp. 187–97). This ideological elite moved towards power and over five years from 1789 onwards attempted a precarious balance between the incompatible demands of king, court and foreign armies on the Right and a radical and vociferous but relatively vision-less urban petit bourgeois on the Left. Under the strain of having to steer between these forces the ideological elite 'discovered its basic power technique: moral persuasion to evoke a grand declaration of principle, which then proved coercive and self-fulfilling. Popular pressure ensured that later betrayal would risk dignity, position, even life' (p. 196). The National Assembly's almost unanimous vote on 4 August 1789 to 'destroy entirely the feudal regime' is a classic example of this ideological 'transcendence' at work, with noble after noble rising, 'amid great enthusiasm, to propose the abolition of yet more feudal dues and privileges. The scene has entranced historians' (p. 196). Although based on principled ideology the conjuncture was such that the practices based upon it, the sweeping away of many of the feudal and old regime privileges that had prevented solutions to the fiscal crisis and to the impoverished state of the peasantry, had powerful practical effects. These, in turn, had their own further influence on the redrawing of the boundaries of broad ideological and pragmatic alliances:

> Instead of all three estates [clergy, nobility and propertied commoners] being natural allies (with the king) against the propertyless, they had divided into the privileged versus the nation – with an ambiguous lower boundary. The principled nation had emerged interstitially (pp. 196–7).

Mann describes an accompanying process whose results were to emerge subsequently as the ideological elite engaged in specific interactions with the various classes. Many sections of the peasantry were ultimately alienated as the Revolution moved Leftward in 1792 and 1793 and moved towards price and quantity controls, backed by coercion, over rural produce (p. 200). From 1790 onwards, Mann argues, the Revolution centred on the relations between the ideological elite and the substantial bourgeoisie, on the one hand, and the petit bourgeoisie and artisans, on the other. The latter, the sans-culottes, dominated the national guard units and local government section committees. They mobilised crowds, especially around issues of unfair food distribution which from the start was seen to be the result of corruption and privileges claimed by the old regime. The popular crowd was important to pressure the king and the old elites but, says Mann, these groupings lacked 'coherent national organization' and so their realistic political ambitions were limited (p. 202). Between 1790 and 1794 the Jacobins established themselves at the core of the ideological elite. They developed an enormous network of clubs that rose in number from 24 in February 1790 to over 426 by March 1791 and over 6000 by early 1794. Mann notes that Jacobins came from all across the bourgeoisie and petit-bourgeoisie, with few nobles and virtually no peasants, labourers or servants: '[M]ost leaders remained substantial [*sic.*] bourgeois but, pressed by their galleries, moved to favor democracy' (p. 202). The combination of the ideological elite with what Mann calls the 'bourgeois and petit-bourgeois nation' ultimately led to the overthrow of the monarchy and the weakening and localisation of the power of the church. In the process, however, the unity of the ideological elite began to crumble leaving in its wake 'a more bourgeois class identity':

> Thus conflict *became* defined by both class and nation emerging interstitially entwined with ideological, military and political power relations. The final struggle between substantial bourgeois and petit-bourgeois class fractions displaced the ideological elite and allowed the victory of a national bourgeoisie and the end of the Revolution ... The link between old regime and postrevolutionary bourgeoisie was provided by the ideological elite. It solidified and then became bourgeois under the geopolitical pressure of old regimes (p. 208).

Locating External and Internal Structures within Mann's Historical Sociology

The scope and character of Mann's work taken together provide a framework through which it is possible to address a number of issues important to the structuration project. The emphasis in his work on the institutional clusterings of IEMP practices and on the weight and complexity of social processes draws attention to the immense pressure of structuration processes external to any one actor. Thinking in terms of 'composite' studies of structuration the work also draws explicit attention to particular examples of what Archer calls 'situational tendencies' within large processes of structuration. It also provides a framework in which one can situate questions about strong structuration processes in general; questions directed to issues of hermeneutics, duality and the quadripartite nature of structuration. More specifically, through its emphasis on the ways in which any one set of structural processes regularly escape the understanding and control of actors, this kind of work provides a broader, more holistic context, in which to think about the power of independent and irresistible causal influences on particular agents-in-focus.

Thus, for example, from Mann's discussion one can clearly discern some of the situational tendencies inherent in the fiscal crisis facing the French state in the 1780s, together with a 'rough' sense of their weight and relative intractability (Mouzelis's intractable dualism). Debt servicing had risen from 30 per cent of total revenue before the Seven Years War (1757–63) to more than 60 per cent after the war, whilst between 1776 and 1787 only 24 per cent of direct and indirect taxes raised reached the treasury, the rest either being used to pay off accumulated debt or finding its way into the pockets of the tax farmers (pp. 179–80). This picture is combined with mention of other structural clusterings that we have already encountered, to do with the impoverished peasantry and the impasse between different factions at the very heart of the state. These are clusterings within the 'open system' of eighteenth century French society that have a causal connection of one sort or another with the fiscal crisis and its relationship to the coming revolution. All of this is combined with a circumscribed but distinct series of hermeneutic claims about the ways in which key actors within this configuration perceived (conjunctural internal structures) the relevant external situation. Thus, we are told that '(m)inisters now realised that the peasants had been pushed dangerously near to subsistence' (p. 180). We learn both that Louis XVI, a potential macro-actor in Mouzelis's terms, 'dithered' and showed a lack of resolve:

> The king – and it must be counted as a necessary cause of the Revolution – dithered, caught between elite and party interests, an absolutist yet the protector of proprietorial rights. At each crisis he would first support reform and defy parlements, then bow to court intrigue, dismiss the reforming minister, and abort the reform plan (p. 180).

and that this agent's conduct should be placed in a meso-structural context of 'institutional incoherence' with almost every office of state suffering from factionalism within the proprietorial class, ministers who didn't control their own departments, legal officers belonging to autonomous corporate assemblies and an army and clergy who were internally divided (p. 181).

We also learn how Archbishop Lomenic de Brienne, Calonne's successor as finance minister, responded to the perceived pressure of shortage of funds by calling the Estates General. In the name of the crown he thus pursued divide and rule tactics, making a fatal move freighted with unintended consequences (p. 184).

With respect to questions of constraints and of what was and wasn't possible, Mann has clearly provided us with information on a number of structural clusters that would be relevant to any agent's analysis of context, albeit with broad brush strokes. He has also provided us with fleeting insights into ways in which agents experienced their relationship to structural forces and contexts. It is important to be clear about two points here. The first is that the scope and professed purpose of Mann's own study means that he rarely provides the degree of detail and careful discrimination between the concepts relevant to the quadripartite nature of structuration for his work to be placed squarely alongside studies which worked in a consistent, systematic and detailed way within the parameters of strong structuration. This would not be a surprise to Mann and neither should it surprise us. The second point is that notwithstanding what I have just said there are certainly many instances in Mann's work – such as the few examples in the last paragraph that were taken from a pool of many possible examples throughout his case studies – that either are already examples of strong structuration, albeit at a low level of contextualisation, or which are already specific enough in terms of 'where, when, who, how and which external structures?' for them to provide invaluable situating and framing starting points from which a strong structuration study could proceed.

Having said this, even with respect to the second point it is also the case that following up the references given to the scholarship involved in Mann's work – ultimately one of *comparative* historical sociology, after all – would lead us to more detailed, finer grained studies that may themselves allow us to marshal and answer more detailed strong structuration questions about constraints and opportunities. If we went to these sources for these purposes we would clearly have gone to them for a different reason than the one that led Mann to consult them. Answering strong structuration questions would entail careful attention to the guiding parameters of the quadripartite nature of structuration, especially to the combination of structural diagnostics and hermeneutics within the perspectives both of agents-in-focus and agents-within-context. Closer analysis of relevant agents' contexts would be needed, for example, to validate or falsify Mann's claims that things could possibly have turned out differently if the king and the privileged orders had 'known what lurked in the wings' (p. 170). He argues that with the aid of knowledge gained from hindsight – the kind of knowledge that was, in fact, to be available to counterparts in other countries at later dates with the example of the French Revolution before them – the king and the privileged orders 'would have acted differently', and also that the 'deep-rooted power processes of class, of geopolitics, and of ideology ... could have been stopped or redirected by power actors making different decisions' (p. 170).

Two different claims can be usefully distinguished here. The first is about conduct and the second is about whether that conduct would have been successful or not. Mann's implication with the first is pertinent to an agent's personal characteristics and conduct, and is that the king would have acted differently if his knowledgeability about the external structures had been different. The implication of the second point is about agent's context. It is now not simply that Louis XVI would have acted differently, but also that the external structural context was such that he would have had the capability or power to succeed in pursuing his revised goals. The combined argument is that what were overwhelming causal forces to Louis XVI in the events as they actually unfolded would not have been such to a differently informed monarch. This is because the issue, according to the logic of Mann's argument, may well have been less one of an absolute insufficiency of power and more a lack of the phenomenology, knowledge and skill necessary to take advantage of the possibilities for success that were in fact available. Mann ultimately acknowledges that Louis XVI was not 'in the class' of extraordinary chief executives of the period like Frederick William, Bonaparte or Bismarck, and satisfies himself with a counter-factual argument from his vantage point as an observer. This is the argument that 'if' the incumbent of Louis XVI's position had possessed different personal attributes and characteristics then he just 'might' have found a way to those solutions that Mann believes to have been objectively possible within the external structural context of the time (pp. 170 and 180).

More generally, Mann is keen to insist that he is not making universal claims in his work but claims related to structural configurations. Novel developments such as those we have seen at work in the French Revolution – involving not least the cementing and mobilising role of a transcendent principled ideology – emerge in 'interstitial power networks' (p. 170) beyond the boundaries of key actors' awareness, knowledgeability and, often, control. The issues of knowledgeability and control can, however, affect each other in that unacknowledged conditions within the agent's context mean, *inter alia*, that power actors are 'prone to miscalculate power possibilities' (p. 170).

Linking Ideology and Discourse with the General-Dispositional: Three Case Studies

The examples of entry points into strong structuration to be found in Mann's work explicitly considered above are those dealing either with structural clusters inhabiting an agent's context or with the conjuncturally-specific internal structures within agents. There is, however, another point of entry that we have not yet broached. This is to be found within the non-reductionist category of ideology which can provide a provisional sense of certain aspects of the general-dispositions of particular groups of actors. Broad accounts of ideological schemas can provide a starting point from which to look for more detailed evidence as to the cultural schemas inhabiting particular actors, and from which to investigate, for example, how such aspects of their schemas are combined with other relevant cultural, ideological and bodily dispositions and orientations. Thus, in his analysis of the revolutionary leaders in France up to 1794 Mann analytically singles out discursive elements of the Enlightenment within their general-dispositional schemas, as a prelude to arguing for the causal significance of these transcendent, principled ideological elements in crucial conjunctures.

Thus, he writes that 'Cobban was right: A Marxian-type bourgeoisie did not lead the Revolution' (Mann, 1993, p. 188). He notes that the leaders were not a cross section of the bourgeoisie, the petite bourgeoisie, or any class fraction. They were, in varying proportions as the revolution proceeded, crown officials, lawyers and other learned professions, including writers and clerics. Directly productive and commercial classes constituted only 15 per cent in the 1792 National Convention (pp. 186–9). He quotes Doyle (1980, p. 155) to emphasise this point: the Revolution had been 'a landslide victory for the noncommercial, professional and proprietary bourgeoisie.' Through an analysis of pre-1789 occupations amongst the revolutionaries from 1789 through to 1794, together with an emphasis on activism rather than simple participation, Mann argues, moreover, that within this configuration of revolutionaries the leadership gradually shifted from the legal officials ('the men of the conference room') to the writers and the clerics: the ideologists, the 'men of the podium' (Dawson, 1972, p. 125; quoted in Mann), as 'rhetorical persuasion replaced factional fighting among officials' (p. 189). In the course of his chapter on the Revolution, Mann presents, albeit briefly, the core principles of the *Encyclopedie*, the Enlightenment's manifesto (pp. 175–6), noting the significance given to the 'organized habit of criticism' and the antagonism accorded to superstition, particularism and privilege (p. 176). He also spends some time outlining the strikingly high numbers of members of the National Conventions, markedly so amongst activists, who 'participated in discursive Enlightenment networks of the printed word ... [publishing] scientific, cultural, or social works indicating intellectual interests similar in breadth to the concerns of the Enlightenment' (pp. 189–90). A page is devoted to the intellectual and cultural *curricula vitae* of the 'twelve who ruled', from Robespierre through Saint-Just and Carnot to Lindet, the core members of the Committee of Public Safety that ruled France from 1793 to 1794 (pp. 191–2). Mann draws on Weber to argue that these intellectual concerns of the elite embodied distinct 'ideal interests'. They were obsessed with *vertu*, political virtue, and 'they counterposed the rights of man and the citizen, justice, liberty, equality, fraternity, and citizenship for the "people" and "nation"' against the particularistic privilege represented by the old regime (p. 193).

It is important to be clear that in this account of Enlightenment elements within the general-dispositional frame of the revolutionary leaders, the same points apply as they did for Mann's treatment of conjuncturally-specific internal structures within agents. They are thinly detailed in themselves, but are bolstered by the scholarship he cites that could be interrogated further to test his claims. Further, more complex, questions could be asked, such as those discussed earlier (see the discussion in chapter 3, pp. 103–4) about the way that different aspects of the general-dispositional – of enlightenment values distinguished from those related to vested proprietorial interests, for example – are integrated together within the whole, and the extent to which they mutually influence one another. In other words, what do analytically separated aspects of the general-dispositional look like once they are re-embedded within the whole. One could also look in detail within various conjunctures at the relationship between aspects of the 'ideals' within the general-dispositions of the actors and the worldly exigencies impressed upon them by more immanently pressing internal structures. The evidence to answer such questions may or may not be available.

The formal analytical procedure by which Mann singles out discursive elements of the Enlightenment and relates them to the general-dispositional schemas of key actors is similar to that often implicit in studies influenced by Foucaultian notions of discourse and/or governmentality. As with Mann's comparative historical sociology, these studies can also provide useful framing devices by which to link strong structuration studies to wider societal processes. The type of frame provided and the character and extent of the links established varies between studies, and it will be useful to discuss two studies within this broad tradition that differ in some respects. Firstly, in the lack of an explicit analysis of the interplay between general-dispositions and conjuncturally-specific structures, there are noticeable parallels between Mann's work on ideology in the French Revolution – in the moments at which the focus is on the *sui generis* nature of the written or spoken texts in which ideology is expressed and on their implied role as part of the general-dispositions of identified agents – and Joan Scott's post-structuralist analysis of the discourses of the struggles of the female Parisian garment workers of 1848 in her seminal work *Gender and the Politics of History*. Her thematic emphasis, both in her more abstract chapters and in her empirically-based case studies, is on discursive elements that are theorised in abstraction from their relationship to the overall hermeneutic frame of concrete actors involved in practical action. For example, in the case study mentioned her focus is on the equivalencies, differences and oppositions within texts spoken, written and declaimed by seamstress leaders, whilst the relationship of these discursive configurations to the agents' perceptions of the variable specific circumstances in which they are enunciated remains unexplicated and untheorised (see Scott, 1988, pp. 19, 93–112). We learn that whilst in their political discourse the seamstress leaders, along with the male tailors and other workers, tied the redress of their economic grievances to reform of the political system, they based their demands not on craft solidarity, as the tailors did, but on the basis of fairness, economic justice and the special needs of women (Scott, 1988, p. 107). The latter are seen as central to the women's discourse as:

In democratic governments, they reasoned, all interests must be represented by those who knew and understood them. 'We ask not to be citizens,' they insisted, 'but citizenesses [*les citoyennes*]. If we demand our rights it is as women that we do so ... in the name of our sacred family obligations, of the tender servitudes of the mother.' Obviously mothers could not be subsumed in the category of the (male) citizen or worker (Scott, 1988, p. 106).[10]

Scott's thematic and theoretical focus is thus on discourse in terms of its emergent *sui generis* nature and, by implication its relationship to what we have called the general-dispositions or habitus of relevant agents. The focus is not on issues of agent's conduct whereby general-dispositional discursive commitments are stretched this way and that, re-tailored and trimmed, as they are brought into dialogue with the exigencies suggested to them by conjuncturally-specific structures. Much like Mann's focus on the ideological texts and/or on particular ideological aspects of the revolutionary leaders' general-dispositions, Scott's focus on discourse is not wedded closely to an analysis of the process of agent's conduct *in situ*. On the other hand, however, it does provide an initial framing perspective within which to locate a more dynamic strong structuration analysis involving other dimensions of the quadripartite cycle.[11]

The second study is a recent paper by Eamonn Carrabine published in *Theoretical Criminology* focusing on Strangeways (HM Prison, Manchester) between 1965 and 1990 and aimed at developing a social theory of imprisonment. There is an explicit combination here of the discourse/governmentality approach with certain aspects of structuration theory (Carrabine, 2000, pp. 309–31; see also Carrabine, 2004). In terms of a broad framing and locating device Carrabine recounts, for example, how the overarching discourse of prison governance at Strangeways moved from a 'bureaucratic-control' regime, which had been in place between 1972 and 1977, to an 'authoritarian-control' regime between 1977 and 1986 (itself a return to the *status quo ante* of 1965–72), and from there to a regime he characterises as 'professional-normalising' between 1986 and 1990. He understands the latter shift, which included the expansion of the prison system and increasingly punitive and repressive sentencing and parole policies, as in part a manifestation of the project of authoritarian populism that characterised the New Right's appeal to 'the people' over the heads of vested interest groups. But from the perspective of governmental techniques and the rationality of governance (political rationality) it is also seen:

in terms of a wider project of *new managerialism*, which was an attempt by the Conservative government to instil some of the private sector ethos into public policy concerns, in the interests of increased efficiency, less 'big government' in a bid to foster the enterprise culture. With specific reference to imprisonment, this has meant such things as privatization, agency status, key performance indicators and so forth (Carrabine, 2000, pp. 321–2, original emphasis).

Carrabine presents both the old (authoritarian-control) and the new (professional-normalising) discourses as containing combinations of means and ends components. In the 'authoritarian-control' discourse the ends component prioritises the maintenance of order and the imposition of conformity within the prison, with any disruptive behaviour being viewed as pathological. The desired smooth functioning of the institution is to be attained by means of military-style forms of regulation that can rely either on 'firm but fair' codes of conduct or on more divisive 'us versus them' rationalities (Carrabine, 2000, p. 318). By way of contrast, in the 'professional-normalising' discourse there is a clear objective to treat prisoners as far as possible according to the same standards that would be expected by 'normal' individuals in the community. The individuals would be seen as people who have been 'sent to prison *as* punishment, rather than *for* punishment or rehabilitation' (p. 318, original emphasis). Respect for the integrity of the individual prisoner places tighter limits on the measures that would be considered acceptable in enforcing conformity in pursuit of the prison's smooth functioning. The means of achieving normalisation, captured in the 'professional' discourse, are conceived as being centred on the judgement, responsibility and leadership qualities of the governor based on skills derived from years of practical routine experience (p. 318).

Carrabine sees the power of these two discourses to regulate as resting not only on the discourse considered in a 'pure' manner but also on the ways in which such discourses are 'translated' through actors, devices, strategies and networks of association into particular actions constituting regimes of regulation (pp. 318–19). At the level of the delineation of the broad historical categories of discourse we have no more and no less than broad frames that can provide points of possible entry into the analysis of these more conjunctural and specific moments of regime regulation. As with Mann's treatment of the non-reductionist category of ideology, Carrabine's discursive categories can provide, not least, a provisional guide to certain aspects of the general-dispositions of particular groups of actors. They cannot, in and of themselves, say very much beyond this. Even at the level of the specific general-dispositions of particular governors and prison officers it should be said that the broad discourses provide only a starting point from which to look for more evidence as to their more detailed manifestations. It is within the latter, for example, that one could investigate how such aspects of their schemas are combined with other aspects of their dispositions and orientations of the kind we discussed in relation to Whittington, plurality and the rationalisation of action in chapter 3.

Carrabine's study does, in fact, take things further to the extent of proceeding to combine a conception of discursive elements with a more *in-situ* sense of knowing 'how to go on' captured by Giddens's conception of practical consciousness. So, for example, Carrabine shows how the 'old school' prison officers, socialised during the period of a strict authoritarian regime of control in Strangeways, resisted the new regime that they experienced as a ' "softening" of approach, which did not correspond with their interpretation of how a prison should be run' (Carrabine, 2000, p. 323). In fact, his use of the notion of resistance via practical consciousness can be given added critical purchase, I would argue, if we divide it up into its general-dispositional, specific-conjunctural and practical 'agent's conduct' dimensions. Employing these concepts as analytical categories one can see that Carrabine is able to go further than Scott in that he provides both the wider discursive framework *and* a picture of the gap that can be created between an 'ideal' discourse and agent's conduct as a result of the resistance and trimming that can go on at the point of situated action. Such trimming, I should add, can be either because the pre-existing general-dispositions of particular actors are resistant to the pure or ideal discourse, or because the perceived (conjunctural-structural) exigencies of the situation press a degree of pragmatic trimming on an otherwise committed agent-in-focus.

For the old guard, the gap between the governmental discourse and situated action was due to the perceived incompatibility between the new discourse and the general-dispositions to which they were already committed. The general-dispositional 'preference for a firm, rigid, almost provocative style of interaction' with prisoners, a frame that was evident both in Carrabine's semi-structured interviews with prison officers and in their evidence to the Woolf inquiry, provided a set of inhospitable conditions of reception for the new professional discourse (Carrabine, 2000, pp. 322–3). For the new governor, however, positioned differently within the configuration of position-practices, the gap between governmental discourse and his situated action was not due to any tension between that discourse and his own general-dispositional orientations. Rather it was due to *in-situ* difficulties of power caused by the recalcitrance of the 'old school' officers. The external structures facing the governor, whilst not entirely intractable, were also not entirely amenable to his authoritative power.

In addition to the dimensions of framing already discussed it is also worth re-emphasising the epistemological distinction introduced earlier in the chapter between, on the one hand, a research question directed to the *identification* of aspects of the general-dispositional in itself and, on the other hand, one directed towards *the history of the causal process* that has produced, *a tergo*, that agent's current general-dispositional frame. In terms of Mann's account of the influence of Enlightenment principles into the French Revolution this could amount to a distinction between his accounts of crystallised aspects of the general-dispositional within a particular conjuncture, and the attention he devotes at other times to the *process* whereby these aspects were gradually taken on board and integrated into that general-dispositional frame. Within the latter category one can place Carrabine's passing allusion to the 'old school' officers' prior socialisation during the authoritarian and bureaucratic control era of prison governance (Carrabine,

2000, p. 323). Clearly such *a tergo* accounts can be more or less cursory, more or less detailed and systematic, and they can be more or less, consistently or variably, informed by strong structuration. Another more extended example of such framing is the account Mann gives of the development of the three communication infrastructures that contributed to the general-dispositions of the ideological revolutionary elite: those of regime enlightenment, political rights lawyers and the diffusion of literacy among the petite bourgeoisie, the lower clergy and the upper peasantry (pp. 175–9). More specific examples within the scope of this *explanandum* are the accounts given of: the activity of clerics, nobles and commoners in provincial literary academies and Masonic Lodges in the years preceding the revolution (p. 177); the church's role in the sponsorship of education, employing schoolmasters and increasing church attendance among the masses, and paradoxically beginning to secularise the morality they were teaching children and families (Mann, 1993, p. 175; Furet and Ozouf, 1982, p. 80); and the interaction between the sons of noblemen and tradesmen within the same classrooms as they underwent secondary education (Mann, 1993, p. 177; Palmer, 1985: 23).

A great deal of further detailed and careful work, combining hermeneutics with structural diagnostics, would be required for each of these examples to truly stamp them with the mark of strong structuration. Similar points apply to the particular example that I have pulled out from Carrabine's paper. The insights we get into the prior socialisation of the 'old school' officers is tangential to the main argument and substantiation of the article, and is consequently thin in terms of scope, detail and process. Nevertheless, again, both approaches are theoretical enough (delineating discernible ideological structural clusters) and concrete enough (identifying enough of who, where, when, how and which structures) to provide a situating frame and point of entry for this question-type appropriate to a deeper investigation on the basis of strong structuration.

Immutable Social Tendencies and Strong Structuration

It is essential to the general ontology of structuration that any point of the non-reductionist structural clusters identified as a contextual frame for a strong structuration case study can itself, in principle, be subjected to an analysis from the perspective of strong structuration. It is true that problems of scope and scale would certainly prevent very broad spatio-temporal frames from being translated *in toto* into the currency of strong structuration. Nevertheless, this would not prevent the researcher from selecting specific aspects of the context that provides the broader frame for one strong structuration study in order to subject it, in turn, to similar treatment. Keeping this possibility in mind is important in resisting the temptation to think too easily and prematurely of the broader frame as necessarily containing practices and situational logics that are somehow inevitable and immutable. This is the case whether one is talking of: the concrete logics of particular capitals, capitalist systems or capitalist states (see, for example, Jessop, 1982; 1990); of their articulation with the other non-reductionist clusters of practices singled out by authors such as Mann, Giddens, and the variety of neo-Marxists and pluralists mentioned in chapter 1; of the various forces of globalisation (see Giddens, 1990a, 1999; Held *et al.*, 1999; Tomlinson, 1999); of the logic of the various flows and fluids that are said to characterise the network society (see Castells, 2000/1996; Urry, 2000), and so on and so forth. All of these clusters of practices and their situational logics involve structures and agents in open systems engaged in quadripartite processes of structuration.

In any event, most 'situational logics'[12] are much more complex than they appear at first sight. An example of one kind of capitalist logic would be the pressures exerted by international finance on the policies of national governments. When looked at from afar the logic can seem straightforward and immutable. But when looked at in particular historical and social contexts whatever logic there is appears to be much more contingent, emergent from a number of specific relations between agents within networked clusters of structured practices. This contingency doesn't necessarily imply significant agency choice. The key social pressures may still be experienced as irresistible or have effects completely independently of a given agent-in-focus. It does imply, however, that the reproduction of a 'situational logic' has to be produced and reproduced again and again by a plurality of agents within a variety of structural clusters. To investigate how durable or fragile, mutable or immutable, a particular cluster of practices is will often require an analysis that is based to some degree on strong structuration. Another example from my research into the economic policies of the British Labour Government of 1964–70 may make this clearer. As we have seen, the research focused on the way this social democratic Government managed its economic policies in the context of the constraints and opportunities afforded by sterling's use as an international currency.

A key focus here was on what I would now call the general-dispositional frame of the Cabinet Ministers, their internal perceptions of their structural context, and the actions and interactions they carried out on the basis of their overall frame of meaning. I also analysed relevant aspects of the external structural context from a researcher's point of view. Some of this analysis of external structures was carried out on the basis of concepts consistent with strong structuration, for example the analysis of the general-dispositions and conjuncturally-specific structures of two distinct groups (the *sound money ideologues* and the *sound money pragmatists*) within the central bank, the Bank of England (Stones, 1988, pp. 205–34). However, other aspects of the analysis of the external structural context were more in the broad non-reductionist framing and locating style of Mann's work. Thus, there was an attempt to establish the frame of the international monetary system, and to search out any situational tendencies within it that might have imposed pressures on the policies of the Labour Government.

To this end, I identified a series of different groups who, each in their different ways, combined to produce the cluster of relational position-practices that composed sterling's use as an international currency (the sterling structure). Broad sets of general-dispositional motivations were attributed to the main groups of actors, but the level of hermeneutic analysis employed here was, on the whole, very low and the attributed frames of meaning were based more on supposition from afar than on the close analysis of agents *in* structured *situ*. I would label this kind of analysis as *theorist's conduct analysis*,[13] distinguishing it from the more authentic and detailed concern with the agent's own situated view of the world engaged with in agent's conduct analysis. The different groups identified were: actors engaged in private market relations on the basis of commercial criteria; actors from within the networks of the overseas sterling area, primarily governments who kept at least some of their foreign exchange reserves in sterling as a legacy of the British Empire, whose conduct was suggested to be based more on national political and economic interest than on solely commercial market criteria; and, finally, international official and governmental 'First World' actors such as the International Monetary Fund, the Bank for International settlements, the Finance Ministers of the EEC and the US Treasury, who were short-term and long-term 'underwriters' of sterling whose primary motivating interest was in the stability of the international monetary system.

There are many points within this structural context that could be selected as an object of study and analysed in more detail on the basis of some or all of the elements of the quadripartite cycle of structuration. At one level, not all questions about situational tendencies need to be answered by an in-depth hermeneutic analysis, and certain aspects of the contingency of the reproduction of the sterling structure can be seen fairly clearly without this. On the other hand, insights into the relative durability or relative fragility of particular resource structures almost always depend upon at least a minimal sense of the general-dispositional frames of key agents, and some kind of grasp of the points at which they would and could invoke sanctions when their internal structural sense of the appropriate behaviour of others is sufficiently transgressed. Thus, to take just one example, in looking at the international monetary system of the 1960s it is apparent to most observers, certainly with the benefit of hindsight and subsequent scholarship, that the power of the USA to support sterling on the basis of the strength of the dollar was waning with the weakening of the dollar itself. Thus, broad situational tendencies can be identified here but it is important to remember that structuration processes were involved in reproducing these, processes in which the practices of key actors were informed by structural-hermeneutic concerns. At the level of international monetary politics this involved issues of power, normative commitments and close attention to formal indicators and struggles over their meanings. Once these latter abstract concepts are applied as guides to the conjuncture of the late 1960s then it is soon apparent that there is much that we don't know about the implications of any long-term trend for the exigencies and outcomes of any one set of events. What are the implications of the dollar's secular decline for sterling's fortunes in the late 1960s? From within the relevant structural nexus how much power did key actors have to make a difference? A closer investigation, bridging the different scales of analysis, can show how it is possible to avoid the wilder excesses of both determinism and voluntarism.

US reserves of gold at this time had fallen below levels considered acceptable by surplus nations such as Germany, France and other members of the Group of Ten (G10) in relation to their own holdings of dollars (Brett, 1983, p. 173). The root of the problem, the large and growing US balance of payments deficit, averaged $742m. per year in the first half of the 1960s, and from then to 1969 it shot up to $3bn annually, not least because of Vietnam War expenditure (Moffitt, 1983, p. 30). The US ran down its creditor position with the IMF in order to finance these deficits to the point where the continental Europeans had to be called upon to supplement IMF funds in a whole series of initiatives to underwrite the dollar. The surplus countries had begun to look upon the IMF as an instrument that aided and abetted the reserve currency countries, the USA and Britain, in running inexcusable balance of payments deficits and accordingly they began to apply conservative, restrictive, conditions to the underwriting funds they supplied. Given the US interest in keeping the dollar on the gold standard, their dependence on the Europeans for support meant that their own power to underwrite sterling with dollars or through diplomacy with the Europeans was severely diminished (Stones, 1992, pp. 217–22). When viewed from within this network of relations a deeper and more intriguing framework of understanding is provided for an anecdote that Barbara Castle recounts in her diaries, concerning a putative exchange between Harold Wilson and Lyndon B. Johnson (LBJ). Wilson claimed that whilst in Bonn in mid-1967, at the funeral of the former German Chancellor Konrad Adenauer, the US President 'told me that if only I would put troops into Vietnam my worries over sterling would be over' (Castle, 1984, p. 282). Seen from afar, a funeral scene would seem, *prima facie*, to be somewhat marginal to an analysis of the broad situational tendencies and causal influences bearing down on the non-devaluation of sterling. Seen from close up, such a face-to-face interaction transpires, seemingly, to be at the heart of an analysis of what was and wasn't possible, of the relative impregnability and likely durability of the sterling structure.

Seen from within the intermediate zone of structuration, from within the relevant network of position-practice relations, one begins to have doubts about the simplicity of the 'great man', voluntarist conspiracy, version of history implied by this anecdote. The proverbial issue of the relevant weight and impact of great or small actors, on the one hand, and seemingly immutable historical trends, on the other, is a terrain that strong structuration is able to open up. It is able to formulate its objects of study in a way that combines analytical manageability with a refusal to over-simplify the field and processes at hand. It does this whilst paying careful and systematic attention to the often indeterminate inter-relations between claims, evidence and concept. The event in this case, a conversation at a graveside, is certainly of a suitable size for analysis on the basis of structuration. But as with so many other interactions that are thus amenable, especially between actors within highly differentiated modern societies, the structural content of the manageable moments soon begin to stretch outwards, to the inner workings and networks of the US Government, a range of its interested Departments, Committees, and the Federal Reserve to name a few.

Inside the heads of these variously positioned Americans, the more or less spectral awareness of the networked ghosts of IMF, G10 and European Bank officials and their concerns can be traced through, in turn and more or less adequately, to the palpable corporeality of the real inhabitants of those positions who, themselves, have their own situated legions of networked ghosts to contend with. We soon find that we have chased and transformed one part of the *frame* for structuration studies into an object of attention in its own right, itself suggesting rewards from an analysis on the basis of structuration. But once here the exact choice of focus is not immediately obvious. Due to the practical problems of scale only limited parts of an initial frame could be subjected to analysis on the basis of structuration. There are always choices to make as to which path to follow. The one we choose to take, if we choose to take any, will be linked to the questions we are most interested in pursuing. In trying to decide whether the USA would have continued to support sterling if Wilson had put troops into Vietnam, strong structuration draws my attention to the characteristics and complexity of the relational field and also to the relative paucity of the empirical evidence in my possession. My conclusion is that the question remains open. When LBJ's coaxing has been placed within the relevant networks of relationships it is not at all clear to me whether we will feel that he did indeed have the power to deliver what he promised.

On this note let us turn to look in detail at two further applied examples to highlight and explore the variety of relations between the strong structuration ontology and concrete substantive cases.

5

Case Studies in Structuration: Morawska's *Insecure Prosperity* and Ibsen's *A Doll's House*

The two extended substantive case studies presented in this chapter are both instances of the composite research strategies described in the previous chapter. The first case study, Ewa Morawska's *Insecure Prosperity: Small Town Jews in Industrial America 1890–1940*, is a detailed historical and sociological study, theoretically informed by structuration theory, of the emigration of East European Jews and their resettlement in Johnstown, Pennsylvania. The second case study involves an analysis of Norwegian dramatist Henrik Ibsen's late nineteenth-century play *A Doll's House* in terms of strong structuration. As both case studies are composite they afford examples of structuration theory 'in action' in ways that embrace many of the different methodological steps outlined in chapter 4. They involve aspects of the four parts of the quadripartite character of the duality of structure. In both cases one can see how ontology shapes empirical insights, and how ontology can show the researcher what is missing from an account, can point to the limits of what she knows. It is important to be clear with respect to Morawska's study in particular that we are not dealing only with an empirical case study, as in Giddens's discussion of empirical research, in order to illustrate the concepts of structuration theory (although it is determinedly intended to be this as well in the present context). The case study also shows how structuration theory directed at the ontic allows one to address particular questions concerning particular substantive processes of *in-situ* structuration in novel and critically challenging ways. In the process one can see how the quadripartite framework would:

- allow one to address such questions in a more precise manner;
- aid a more precise explication of what is happening within an existing explanation;
- help, by means of the ontological shaping, regulation and assessment of empirical evidence, to show what is present and what is absent across the various aspects of a proffered explanation.

Further, the two case studies provide a striking and illuminating point of comparison and contrast. Morawska's study does involve conjuncturally-specific internal structures, but it is much more focused on both networks of position-practices and general-dispositional internal structures. It deals very much with routines and their relative durability. It is also about change, but this is slow change over years, changes in position-practices and changes in habitus as the migrants slowly blend the socio-cultural patterns of life inherited from the old (Eastern European) country with the traditions and lifestyles of the dominant host society of the USA. Ibsen's play is much more about contingency, instability and the unsettling of routines, and as an almost necessary consequence of this (and of its dramatic form) it brings the question of conjuncturally-specific internal structures to the fore. Finally, there is another comparison to be made. *A Doll's House*, approached without accompanying historical notes and companion studies, lacks much of a grounding in those wider currents and networks that could provide a framework for locating it within a historical and social perspective. The focus is on a very localised slice of life, even though the spirits of some influential networked ghosts from times past play a significant role in the unfolding present. *Insecure Prosperity* roots the lives of its characters much more firmly at the intersection of history, geography and social structure. And its account of the latter is a relatively holistic one in the sense that it embraces many of the different projects and spheres of life pursued and inhabited by the Johnstown Jews, from the economic to the religious, and from the political and civic to family, gender and education. A further use of comparison is evident within *Insecure Prosperity* itself. Morawska uses the comparative method to striking effect throughout the book in order to reveal what was distinctive about both the particular configuration of relations between Jews and non-Jews in Johnstown, and the circumstances of different groups of Jews in varying US towns and cities. She not only reveals much of what is distinctive about the structural configurations of position-practices in these different cases but also provides a good deal of insight into the respective causal roles played by particular internal and/or external structures and by the conduct of particular agents or groups of agents.

Ewa Morawska's *Insecure Prosperity: Small-Town Jews in Industrial America 1890–1940* – An Ethnicisation *qua* Structuration Approach

Morawska writes that the duality of structure, or what she calls the 'double structure', informs her study such that human action and its social environment are 'substantively and causally equivalent' (p. xviii). On the other hand, in points that echo John B. Thompson, she notes that in dealing with particular groups in particular places one would expect to find unequal distributions of power. Faithful to Giddens's general points about power she writes that a clear conception of 'power to' – the understanding of power as the generic capacity of human agency to act upon the world – 'informs the structuration analyses throughout this study'. But she is clear about the differential impact of such general points when applied to situated practices:

> The capacity to produce the effects on the sociocultural environment, however, is usually unequally distributed among different collective and individual members of society, and these power disequilibria among social actors affect the processes and outcomes of structuration (Morawska, 1996, p. xvii).

One of the main emphases of the study is on the way that there are clear limits to the Johnstown Jews' 'power to' set by the existing economic and sociopolitical order in the town. Morawska is also interested in how these 'limits of the possible' are compounded by routinely accepted authority relations and cultural dispositions within the Jewish community itself (pp. xvii–xviii). In her introduction Morawska stresses the gender and intergenerational forms of 'taken for granted' or pre-reflective power within the Jewish community, but her study also brings out many other dimensions of the role played by the general-dispositional, both within the Jewish community and with respect to their relations with the wider community. In addition, Morawska emphasises what she calls the hidden and open transcripts used by the ethnic Jewish actors in their relations with others both within and outside their ethnic community 'to maneuver in their situation in the pursuit of their desired goals' (p. xviii).

The work draws on structuration to address substantive debates about ethnicity in the light of the Johnstown case study. Morawska argues against the *assimilation* model of immigration and ethnicity, and also against an overly voluntaristic approach in which ethnic groups are seen as having *invented* their own ethnicity (p. xviii). Rather her 'ethnicisation *qua* structuration approach' argues that the eventual lifestyles and sociocultural patterns of the Jewish settlers in Johnstown gradually emerged over time in an interplay between the cultural and practical schemas they brought with them and the socio-economic, cultural and civic-political circumstances of their new American environment (pp. xviii–xix). There was:

> a process of blending from inside the ethnic group of the old (country of origin) sociocultural patterns with the new – traditions and lifestyles of the dominant (host) society (Morawska, 1996: xviii).

Insecure Prosperity is based on 'twelve years of labor' (p. xx). It draws on very extensive primary ethnographic, interview and archival sources and on largely secondary comparative sources. A 30-page appendix at the end of the book is devoted to reflections on methodology and Morawska's general interpretative approach. The names of about two hundred participants in the study are listed in a second appendix. In the course of the study itself Morawska painstakingly and vividly traces continuities, gradual changes and hybrid articulations within the general-dispositions of Johnstown's Jews as they swapped their old conditions of life in the shtetls of East Central Europe at the end of the nineteenth century for resettlement in small town Pennsylvania. Morawska follows the migrants and their children through the process of ethnicisation from the initial periods of immigration through to the more established periods of still insecure, but less insecure, prosperity of the 1920s and 1930s. To paraphrase the title of one of her chapters, the slow pace of small town life led to slow but discernible transformations in ethnic lifestyles and sociocultural patterns of life, attenuations that 'emerge[d] in the interplay between newcomer-actors and the host environment (the ethnicization approach)' (p. xviii).

Morawska follows William Sewell Jr in speaking of schemas, seeing them as the 'practice-organizing symbolic resources of Johnstown's Jews'. She sees these as consisting of a variety of representations and prescriptions shaped both by group past history and by present experience. In terms reminiscent of Giddens's distinction between discursive and practical consciousness, Morawska notes that some of these ways of seeing the world are near to the surface and readily amenable to discursive articulation whilst others are 'so deeply sunk in everyday life that conceptualizing and verbalizing them requires a considerable effort' (p. xix). Her conceptualisation of the latter, however, is deeper and more developed than that of Giddens, and she explicitly conceives it as akin to Bourdieu's notion of habitus. Morawska considers the schemas to be generalisable, transposable and flexible – 'that is, transportable and adjustable to new situations by reconfiguring, absorbing new elements, and forming different patterns' (p. xix). Like Sewell, Morawska does not distinguish between the two forms of virtual, internal, structures within the agent. In describing her study I will, nevertheless, make this distinction and will try to indicate the critical advantages of doing so. Like most structuration theorists who have applied the approach at the empirical level Morawska, quite rightly, takes the existence of external structures and outcomes for granted. Empirical investigation into the detailed nature of those structures plays a major role in her analysis.

The Emergence of General-Dispositions in Eastern Europe

It is important to reiterate the point that whilst the general-dispositional is, in a certain sense, more transcendental than the specific-conjunctural dimension of agents' frames, the general-dispositional frame should not be seen as somehow separated from the external conditions of action. Rather, there is a discernible relationship between the agents' experience of interacting with these conditions of action and the emergence of their general frame. Many of the longest standing and most durable aspects of this frame had been formed in turn-of-the-century rural shtetls where Johnstown's Jews – or their parents when we are talking of the town's second generation Jews – lived Orthodox lives based on 'ethnoreligious ascription' in small shtetls of 2000 to 2500 Jews that were dotted around a countryside populated by dominant majority populations of Russian, Polish, Ukrainian, Slovak, or other, Christians. It was practically impossible to be a Jew other than 'among, with, and like other Jewish people' (p. 18). Between 1880 and 1914 seven million immigrants arrived in the USA from Russia and Austria-Hungary. Jews were disproportionately represented in this exodus. Thirty per cent of the emigrants to America from the Russian Pale, Galicia and Hungary were Jewish even though they only made up one tenth of the population. About 27 per cent of all East European Jewry left for America between the 1880s and the First World War (p. 26). Whilst the future Johnstowners shared many characteristics with the other Jewish emigrants they also had certain distinct features, and one of the most significant amongst these was that 80 per cent of them had been occupied in petty trade and rural artisanry. This contrasted clearly with the large majority, two thirds, of the Jewish emigrants to the USA as a whole (between 1880 and 1914) who had been employed as skilled workers prior to emigration (referred to by Morawska as 'protoindustrial wage workers'). Most of this majority had also lived in urban centres (pp. 26–30).

Morawska notes that the future Johnstowners were more or less exclusively bound by tradition. This was a version of the Orthodox tradition that was 'religiously unlearned by the standards of Judaic scholarship'. Amongst the characteristics of the traditionalism of the shtetls were:

> virtually complete nonvoluntarism of group membership; undifferentiation of folk (ethnic) and religious identity and practices; a high degree of influence on social and cultural life exerted by group religious symbols and institutions ... and inclusive communalism (p. 18).

In turn, Jewishness was expressed through religion-related cultural symbols and social institutions, with the organisation of public life in the shtetls being communal, typically centred, spatially, around a large synagogue, two or three *boti medroshim* (smaller buildings for the men's daily prayers and religious study), a ritual slaughterhouse, a *mikve* (ritual bath) and a few *khedorim* (religious schools for children) (pp. 18–19). The prayer houses also served as centers of social and cultural activities. Women, for their part, had no place in the public sphere of Orthodox Jewish religion.

Morawska also mentions the *khevres*, charitable societies restricted to males, that 'were virtually universal in Jewish communities across the region', and various forms of alternative charitable activities engaged in by women, including the *pushkes*, charitable boxes at home whose contents were passed on to travelling collectors for Jewish causes (p. 20). Morawska notes that these forms of assisting others were not 'voluntary'. The Jewish term for charity, *tdsoke*, implies a 'social obligation intrinsic to membership in the group' whereas the Christian word *caritas* carries the differing connotation of a voluntary act of benevolence. Alongside their particular practices of *tsdoke*, the women were also responsible for the daily maintenance of *kashrut*, Jewish dietary laws – one of the prime precepts of traditional Judaism (p. 21) – and for the preparation of the weekly Sabbath: cleaning the house, preparing the customary meal and, something that stood out in the memories of Johnstowners, lighting the Sabbath candles and reciting the customary blessing. Religious observance for men included prayers at the beginning and the end of each day (*davenen*), a blessing over wine recited at the opening of the sabbath (*kidesh*), and the ritual of *havdole* at its closing. Morawska notes the high degree of social control over the observance of the Sabbath and other religious practices ('In Zager they would kill you for violating Shabes', writes Morawska quoting Hyman M an immigrant to Portage, Pennsylvania). She also notes that their Gentile economic partners in the surrounding country-side – their general animosity notwithstanding – helped to sustain the conditions for these practices by adjusting to their rhythm and to the Jewish liturgical cycle (p. 22).

As rural traders and artisans the future Johnstowners had 'everyday dealings and familiarity with peasants who were later to migrate simultaneously to America in great numbers' (p. 30). The main area of relations between these Jews and non-Jews in Eastern Europe was in the sphere of economic exchange. Jews were generally traders who bought peasant produce and distributed it across the region and beyond, and they also sold both services and manufactured goods – from the city or from local artisans – to rural households. The shtetls thus served as:

> centers of this two-way market exchange, tying the countryside to the larger network of production and distribution. Propinquity and familiarity with peasants, and knowledge of the local languages learned through contact with the non-Jewish residents of the countryside – these were recurrent themes in the recollections of the immigrants themselves and of their American-born offspring reporting on their parent's memories (p. 13).

There were other forms of contact between the two groups around a variety of forms of economic exchange – peasant women working as maids in Jewish households, for example – but there was also mutual suspicion and a 'profound cultural divergence' (pp. 13–14). In the peasants' attitudes to their Jewish neighbours there 'predominated elements of disdain and resentment with an admixture of wondrous awe', and the routine daily relations based around economic and service exchange easily broke down into 'acts of verbal abuse and behavioural aggression' (p. 15). Jewish views of the peasants saw them as uncivilised and uncultured. They felt a certain disdain towards them, partly based on a sense of religious superiority, and this was inculcated in the children from infancy (p. 16). This was mixed, however, with feelings of fear and mistrust, inspired by a range of experiences from hurtful 'jokes' played out by children, through individual acts of verbal or physical violence, and finally to pogroms. Morawska writes that this 'kept the Jews in a state of ever-present anxiety' (p. 17).

These were all aspects of the everyday routine lives of the shtetl Jews through which their overall frames of meaning were conditioned and developed. The interactional frames necessarily drew on both general-dispositional and more conjuncturally-specific dimensions, with each supporting and informing the other. On the other hand, both also cohered to help constitute the more enduring, transposable and general-dispositional structures of the Jews. In this latter sense, the generalised stocks of knowledge and embodied skills derived from both dimensions can be thought of as the 'sedimentation of past practices' in their minds and bodies (cf. Jessop, 1985; and Bourdieu, 1980/1990). Or, to co-opt the conceptual language that Habermas uses, one can say that whilst both dimensions were clearly involved in the *a fronte* moments of everyday interaction in contextualised situations, they both also fed, *a tergo*, into the general and enduring constitution of the individual's habitus (Habermas, 1987, p. 135).

The routine economic, religious and communal practices thus gave rise to enduring general-dispositional schemas. One aspect of such schemes was a particular stock of folk wisdom[1] (p. 23). This was expressed in customs, sayings, proverbs and such like, all of which were deeply penetrated by religious symbolism and references: 'an unusually large portion of the Great Tradition was absorbed into the popular religion in the shtetls, although most residents would not have been able to articulate it in a coherent way' (p. 23). Aspects of these schemas included the taken-for-granted assumption of God's creative presence in the universe, of confidence in his beneficence and fundamental goodness, combined with a range of different degrees of hopefulness as to whether he would provide (Morawska quotes the popular Yiddish saying *'vi helft nor Got biz Got vet helfn'* – 'if only God would provide until He provides'). All this was combined, nevertheless, with the placing of a significant onus on the individual to be responsible, an emphasis caught in phrases such as 'God [may] grant one a successful life, but one has to work hard' (p. 23). Other popular directives for human conduct in Jewish life included the 'call to sustained and purposeful action' (p. 24).

Conduct required *takhlis* – concrete purposes within a range of social parameters within the Jewish community. Such purposes should be pursued, however, with a sense of the intrinsic ambiguities, uncertainties and potential reversals of human experience, with a sense that the world revolved in a wheel of fortune (B. Talmud; *Shabbat*, 151b; cited in Morawska, p. 25):

The Jews' precarious situation in turn-of-the-century Eastern Europe furnished experiential credence to the recognition of limits to rational mastery of life and the vicissitudes of fortune encoded in the Great Tradition, and generated similar acknowledgements in Yiddish popular culture. There were sayings familiar in all shtetls, such as *Yidishe ashires iz vi shney in merts* (Jewish wealth is like snow in March, here today, gone tomorrow) ... express[ing] a sense of chronic uncertainty and limited control over the course of their lives as middlemen in a sluggishly changing and impoverished economy, and as a politically dependent, and usually unwelcome ethnoreligious minority (p. 25)

All of these aspects were embedded in a general-dispositional frame on life in which goals and objectives were not thought of rigidly, as though they were set-in-stone, but as more provisional, fluid, goals to be re-assessed through 'intelligent evaluation of changing situations', and to be approached by 'twisting paths' (p. 35). The style of ethno-methods embedded within this general-dispositional frame was thus an adaptive, flexible, one, culturally alert to changing situations, constraints and possibilities. From within the perspective of the wheel of fortune, in which economic and social security today could be gone tomorrow, the religious injunctions to collective responsibility and mutual assistance took on the dual role of altruistic generosity and individual insurance (pp. 25–6).

Ethnicisation: The Interplay between Newcomer-Actors and the Host Environment

As noted above, the *ethnicisation qua* structuration approach that Morawska argues for works on the view that the eventual lifestyles and socio-cultural patterns of the Jewish settlers in Johnstown gradually emerged over time in an interplay between the general-dispositions they brought with them and the new circumstances of their American environment. Within this dialectical interplay the schemas of the Johnstown Jews are seen to have a relative autonomy of their own, just as the various social conditions and exigencies of Johnstown and the USA more widely – the external structures confronting the Johnstown Jews – are seen to have their own relative autonomy. In the early years the Johnstown Jewish settlers were able to draw on a number of the agential resources (their general-dispositional frames and embodied skills) brought with them from Eastern Europe as they established themselves as self-employed traders and shopkeepers in Johnstown. Indeed, it was a general sense of what they had to offer and of what they would feel comfortable with that led them to Johnstown in the first place. Those that had spent time, for example, in New York's Lower East Side before moving on were alienated and overwhelmed by the big city environment and were attracted to a smaller town, more rural, environment. There was also no appeal in the manual work available in the huge garment and other kinds of manufacturing enclaves in the big cities. By way of contrast, the future Johnstowners were advised by relatives and others that the steel and coal towns of Cambria and the surrounding counties in western Pennsylvania were good places to set up in business themselves (p. 37).

In establishing themselves in Johnstown, in what Morawska calls their 'ethnic entrepreneurial niche' the migrants drew on their 'natural' inclinations (p. 37) and know-how derived from the old country. The know-how related, of course, to the field of trading and commerce, but it also connected to their familiarity with the ways, needs, customs and languages of the East-European peasant-immigrants who were now industrial labourers in local mills and coal mines and who needed to be clothed and fed. Good prospects for employment, familiarity with the prospective customers and knowing their languages was the attraction for many of Johnstown's Jews. Jack S's father, who was working as a salesman in a Jewish store in Richmond, Virginia, was advised to check on Johnstown by a wholesaler from Baltimore who knew of his wish to be in 'business for himself':

> [H]e went there in 1910, and seeing 'how many people [there were] on the streets, immigrant workers coming and going with their lunch buckets, going to the mills, to the coal mines ... I made up my mind to stay' (p. 39).

The sense of the socio-cultural resources that they themselves embodied was thus combined with a flexible, 'intelligent' use of initiative in looking for the most suitable specific conditions in which to employ them:

> Such initiative served many immigrants well as a schema-resource in finding opportunities suitable to their skills and current circumstances ... Samuel I., immediately after his arrival in western Pennsylvania, 'looked around for the places that were similar to [his native] Lithuania, found a small niche [in a coal mining town], bought a little store and the right merchandise [i.e., wares suitable for the needs of his prospective customers as he knew them], and started to do business. From that he ventured out, went into hides and sheepskins [his occupation in the old country] ... This was intelligent: look around and find an opportunity'. (p. 45)

Whilst the migrant Jews drew on their general-dispositional resources in establishing themselves in an entrepreneurial niche, the external structural conditions in which they did this were very different from those of the shtetls where those dispositions had been developed. On the one hand, there was the sense that the marketplace in America was orderly and legally protected, more amenable to purposeful action, less vulnerable to non-economic vagaries, than the old country equivalent. On the other hand, the local market was itself structured in clearly discernible ways by particular sets of power relations. Johnstown itself was dominated by the Cambria/Bethlehem mills and coal mines where two-thirds of the town's male labour force worked as manual labourers. Another ten per cent of male manual labourers were involved in establishments servicing the mills and coal mines. There were few economic opportunities for women, and a much lower number of white collar workers than in the big cities.

Morawska notes that the influence of the 'local potentate', the Cambria/ Bethlehem company, whose managers were mostly members of the established Anglo-Protestant elite, stretched far beyond the economic sphere into the social, political and cultural realms (pp. 34–5). The native-born made up over three quarters of the local population despite the influx of new immigrants in the three decades preceding the First World War. The former were 'openly nativist and strongly conscious of their separateness and superiority' (p. 35). The social organisation of the town was based on 'pronounced ascriptive divisions between the old and the new ethnic groups'. Of those within the new, and at the lower end of the power spectrum, southern and eastern European labourers constituted about 50 to 60 per cent of the local miners and 30 to 40 per cent of the steel workers by 1914 (p. 35). By 1910 between 700 and 750 Jews, including immigrants and their children, resided in Johnstown from a population of over 50,000 (pp. 34 and 39). Most new immigrants lived in a few sections of the town known as the foreign colonies, and social and cultural interaction was similarly compartmentalised. There were virtually no institutional channels for socialising between ethnic groups and

> [e]ven if they shared the same class position, new immigrants from southern and eastern Europe remained quite separate from Americans and West Europeans, routinely frequenting different houses of prayer, social halls, and picnic grounds ... In sum, fragmented, ethnic-based ties and identities prevailed in the social and cultural organization of Johnstown and vicinity (p. 35).

The Creation of an Ethnic Economic Niche

Most new arrivals in Johnstown started as peddlers, drawing on the social capital of mutual dispositional schemas to obtain their supplies on credit from Jewish wholesalers, first in Altoona, thirty miles away with a more established Jewish community, and then later from within Johnstown itself (p. 53). This lasted from two to five years before most immigrants moved to a stationary business, opening small stores or artisan shops. Morawska relates how this course of action was aided by what she calls 'an intragroup network of information, reference and financial help that plugged the immigrants into the emerging ethnic grid of trading in the specialties of the local wholesalers' (p. 54). This network built up on the basis of shared general-dispositions provided the newcomers with the necessary 'capability' to – the 'power to' – get on their feet. Such 'ethnic-resource' networks were drawn on both for starting up initially and as a means of remaining in business, or of starting up again after a failure. The first port of call for help with financial assistance usually involved relatives. Morawska estimates that by the First World War more than 40 per cent of East European immigrant families in the area were related to each other either by blood or by marriage, and 'so the pool of potential assistance was quite large' (p. 57). A secondary source of resource support was from mainstream local banks and commercial credit, but this was very limited in the early years in Johnstown, partly due to the perceived instability of the small enterprises and partly due to the credit companies' typified wariness of Jewish traders attendant on their belief in a 'deviousness inherent to that race's market-place conduct' (p. 56).

The kinship network of support was often combined with help from the immigrants' closer acquaintances. In the early years there were no formal network associations to draw on but such avenues developed over time. By 1915 there were five or six better-off merchant-synagogue officers and community leaders who provided economic assistance and also assisted in arranging for citizenship papers, collateral to purchase a house, and such like (p. 57). Not only was the ethnic habitus very closely associated with the economic, the close intermeshing of ethnic and religious spheres apparent in the shtetls of Eastern Europe was still very much in evidence in Johnstown. The small number of Jews in the town, together with their sociocultural homogeneity fostered a 'continuation of the old-country tradition of the inclusive *khevre*, the religious congregation, as the main institutional center of communal activities' (pp. 50–1). This role was played by the Rodef Sholom Orthodox Synagogue located in the town's most Jewish neighbourhood. Three other organisations were closely associated with the synagogue: a society for the religious organisation of children; a fraternal organisation that provided insurance and *ad hoc* business assistance to its male members; and a society for the assistance of transients, which performed a traditional function but with a novel departure from 'the shtetl tradition of excluding women from even the most loosely organized activities' (p. 51) in that it was staffed and managed by women of the *khevre* Rodef Sholom. In 1922 a splinter group of residents from one part of the town, Hornerstown, founded their own small Orthodox *shul*, Ahavath Achim, but Rodef Sholom continued to be by far the larger through into the 1930s and 1940s, 'remaining the center of organized Jewish life in Johnstown and vicinity' (p. 94).

The more Reform minded Beth Zion Temple only became institutionally organised in 1924, but before then met for services in the private quarters of one of its members (p. 50). In the early years its members were the small and tightly-knit group of German Jews in Johnstown, but in the 1920s and 1930s Eastern European migrants also began to join. Some were post-war migrants, and others were American-born couples from larger cities, or, a little later, from Johnstown itself, who chose the Reform Temple in preference to the 'old fashioned' practices of Rodef Sholom (p. 152). Whilst the Johnstown

Jews could draw on economic resources derived from their ethnic and religious affiliation, and there was a limited degree of religious variation, it is clear that the plural differentiation of social spheres characteristic of modernity identified by Whittington as providing agency with much greater latitude for choice and selectivity was here conspicuous by its absence.

It was predominantly from within the Jewish business network, from large wholesalers, that merchandise was purchased for the stores and credit obtained. Morawska recounts the details of particular examples of stores whose supplier-creditors were mainly Jewish, either local or from large cities further afield such as New York, Philadelphia or Pittsburgh (p. 58). In the later period covered by Morawska's study a considerably greater proportion of debt was owed to local banks, 29 per cent between 1920 and 1940 compared with 12 per cent in the earlier period (p. 99). Morawska sees this as an indicator of ethnicisation, of the East European Jews supplementing their ethnic-class resources by being increasingly – if gradually and slowly – incorporated into the mainstream financial system. On the other hand, the majority of business operations of Johnstown's Jews continued to be financed within the group, by fellow ethnics. Bankruptcy records indicate that the creditors of Jewish stores in Johnstown and vicinity were intra-group wholesalers from the town or nearby Altoona or, revealing a marked sense of continuity, Jews from Pittsburgh, Philadelphia or New York (p. 99). The immediate face-to-face settings in which these networks of resource-relations were built brought the personal and the social into close proximity with the economic. Contacts between out-of-town jobbers and retailers involved visits to homes, stays overnight, and the sharing of food and conversational confidences about subjects ranging from family, through 'Jewish matters', to information about people and trade. Participants became entangled in a fine interpersonal 'web of reciprocal obligations' (p. 100)

Morawska presents the growth and consolidation of the ethnic entrepreneurial support networks in Johnstown as being founded upon a mixture of group institutional and normative tradition, on the one hand, and conjuncturally-specific pragmatism on the other. The pragmatism was the newcomers' response to their vulnerability to a specific range of external economic forces. The immigrant stores relied heavily upon the custom of the East European peasant-immigrants who worked in the steel mills and coal mines and so their custom was particularly vulnerable to the fluctuations in the local steel and coal industries, reflecting national trends, that caused massive layoffs alternating with a rapid expansion of the labour force (p. 59). The support networks were mobilised to allow store holders to spread their commitments over time in such a way that they could cope better than otherwise with these fluctuations.

External structuration sequences affected Johnstown's Jewish traders in many different ways over the years. These were sequences powered by structural complexes of either local or of wider origin, usually outside the control of the Jewish retailers. Samuel I's clothing and dry goods store in Boswell did very well with annual sales of $40,000–$45,000 until 1922 when a prolonged coal strike started in the area and the shop fell into trouble. Moses L's business records, to take another example, show that when, between 1927 and 1928, the volume of steel production decreased by 10 per cent, his weekly receipts ranged widely from a high of $900 to about $300 (p. 124). The Depression, of course, represented a causal sequence whose main thrust was well outside the control of all the agents within the immediate locality. This overlaid the usual sources of periodic instability and the number of East European Jewish businesses rated as 'major merchants', those having a net worth of over $20,000, dropped to 10 per cent in 1935 compared to a figure almost three times as large in 1925. At the lower end of the spectrum, amongst businesses receiving 'no rating' the numbers increased from 19 to nearly 40 per cent between 1925 to 1935 (p. 124). The average annual trade in 'Jewish' lines of trade decreased by nearly 45 per cent between 1929 and 1933 and then increased by 29 per cent by 1935. A disastrous flood in 1936 caused over $28 million worth of damage to business and residential buildings in the section of town where many Jewish stores were located (p. 124). Out of a total of 248 Jewish shop owners between 1920 and 1940 more than 30 per cent filed for voluntary or involuntary bankruptcy, nearly 60 per cent of these filings taking place during the Depression (p. 125).

The various external factors combined to undercut the limited financial capital of all small businesses whose continued survival depended upon a finite number of sources of revenue coming into the business unit from a range of actors located within the external structural context. Thus, unpaid customers' bills and overdue credit could soon undermine the conditions of reproduction for a small business. With the help of a Xeroxed list of just some of the mainly Slavic and Hungarian credit recipients in David G's clothing store in the 1920s (recovered from the Philadelphia Federal Archives and Records Center), Morawska illustrates how often a hundred-odd non-paying debtors of often very small amounts would be enough to undermine a business (pp. 125–6). These actors, in turn, were unable to pay their debts because of influences outside *their* control: irregular work in the mills and the coal mines, together with seasonal layoffs, or prolonged strikes (p. 125).

Morawska points out that despite the independent causal impact of these various external forces, information supplied by business censuses conducted in 1933, 1935 and 1939 indicate that annual sales of 'Jewish' businesses remained on average 17–18 per cent higher than 'Gentile' trade lines (p. 125). It was also the case that Jewish small businesses were more persistent through the inter-war period and the Depression years than non-Jewish stores. About half the Jewish merchants had stayed in the same line of business, compared to much lower figures of between one-third and one-quarter amongst non-Jewish merchants. Moreover, three-quarters of those who were unable to stay in the same line of trade managed to remain in the ethnic economic niche.

Nearly two-thirds of Jewish bankrupts either resumed the same line of trade or took up a different one in Johnstown or the vicinity, whilst about one-fifth went to work for other Jews in the area (p. 127). Comparative figures cited by Morawska show that the number of small retail persisters in the general population of Chicago and Poughkeepsie, New York, in the same period was less than 30 per cent. In avoiding bankruptcy or in setting themselves up again after bankruptcy, the Jews of Johnstown were undoubtedly aided by the 'social capital' of their networked business resources in which, to quote a comment that Morawska repeatedly heard from her informants as they talked about keeping their businesses afloat during the Depression, everybody owed everybody (p. 128).

The Cultural and Normative Consolidation of the Jewish Niche

These immediate pragmatic considerations of economic position, however, 'blended with a group-specific or ethnic component, a multilayered one' (p. 60). The many layers included the general-dispositional sense of the precariousness of fortune embodied in the idea of the world 'revolving in the wheel of fortune', a world-view that paralleled the precariousness of their class position both in the shtetl and in the new environment. The patterns of thought developed through living in hostile or, at best, indifferent environments meant that the immigrants turned to each other 'just in case' – 'an "automatic reflex" and a "natural impulse" as my informants called it' (p. 60). A less defensive aspect of this, again derived from the general-dispositional habitus of agents, was a desire to re-establish, to reconstruct, as one of Morawska's informants put it, 'the Jewish environment to live in and make friends, and [for] the Jewish community here to grow, and so the more people [were] helped in starting and staying in business, the better [for these purposes]' (p. 60).

A further layer that consolidated the development of the Jewish niche involved the ascriptive divisions of Johnstown's economic and socio-cultural life (p. 60). Morawska notes how her informants referred to a deep-rooted impulse to 'close ranks' based on a shared sense of group insecurity stemming from these ascriptive divisions and the compartmentalising of social activities and interaction along ethnic lines. Morawska relates how by the 1920s and 1930s a remarkable 80 per cent of young men and women were employed in the Jewish entrepreneurial niche. She links this explicitly to the group's phenomenological horizon in which there was a close, taken-for-granted, relationship between taking refuge within the ethnic community and their marginal position within the dominant local society: 'As Betty and Helen N explained it, the reasons for this proactive withdrawal were twofold: 'We didn't want to test anti-Semitism, although perhaps there was a little less of

this than we thought, and besides, it was natural, Jews were in business'
(pp. 94–5). Finally, 'the most explicitly "ethnic" ... reinforcement of internal
mutual assistance derived from the religiously grounded normative schemas-
prescriptions regarding social conduct within the Jewish community' (p. 60).
By this Morawska is referring to the general-dispositional precepts of mutual
help, set out in scriptures, religious manuals and pedagogical readers, such as
Tz'enah Ur'enah, of assisting fellow Jews to help themselves, with assistance
in becoming and staying economically self-sufficient considered to be the
most meritorious *mitsve* (p. 61).

The blending of conjuncturally-specific pragmatism and general-
dispositional inclinations provided the driving force behind actions that
combined to steadily crystallise the ethnic economic niche as the outcome of
this structuration cycle. This was an outcome – an emergent one – with a
discernible structural reality that was characterised by a cross-cutting and
overlapping network of position practices:

> As more immigrants settled in the area and joined the group's business support
> network, it expanded and solidified into an ethnic entrepreneurial niche wherein
> small stationary merchants and owners of artisan shops, employees of these
> enterprises, and travelling vendors were *tied to each other horizontally by kin-cum-
> business connections and vertically to the suppliers of credit and merchandise*.
> These bonds were reinforced by *shared participation* in the religious and social life
> of the community. This combination of horizontal and vertical interconnections
> channelled most Jewish entrepreneurs into a few lines of trade and services, in
> which they came to occupy a share much greater than their proportion among the
> local workforce in this sector ... By the outbreak of World War I, Jews,
> constituting about 1.5 per cent of the local population, made up somewhat one-
> tenth of the total numbers of self-employed in the trade and service sector in
> Johnstown (Morawska, p. 61, my emphasis).

These networks also served as an important employment resource over the
years, not only for Jews, as noted above, but also for, mainly female, Slavs
and Hungarians, many of whom worked not only as maids in more affluent
Jewish homes but also as hired employees in larger Jewish-owned establishments of which Morawska singles out the Glosser Brothers' department store,
a cigar factory, and a ladies' garment factory where Slavic, Hungarian and
other East European Gentile workers made up from between one third to a
majority of the workforce (pp. 92–3). The Glosser Bros.' store was, by the
1930s, the second largest department store in the town, after the one owned
by the Bethlehem Steel Company, the local 'Saks Fifth Avenue' (p. 95). Not
counting part-time and seasonal help it employed about five hundred
workers, of whom nearly one third were Jewish. Referred to colloquially as
Gee Bee Tech, it 'apprenticed to business the majority of American-born
Jewish young men and women in the town' (p. 95). The role of the networks
as sources of apprenticeships meant, of course, that they played a key role in

the formation of the skills and dispositions of the next generation. This function can thus be added to the others in which there was a gradual consolidation of the channels and possibilities of support in trade credit, financial loans, and business information.

'A Much, Much More Secure Insecurity': Emergent General-Dispositions in the New Country

Morawska argues that the experience of the Jewish community of Johnstown was one of relative prosperity compared with the days of the shtetls. But this prosperity, as the title of her book reminds us, was always an 'insecure prosperity'. Whilst for the majority of Jewish households the annual budget of between $2000 and $2600 (from businesses that brought in between $20,000 and $50,000 in net sales) gave family members a materially comfortable existence at a 'fair American standard' (pp. 112 and 122), it was still the case that enterprises did often go bankrupt, revenues were often affected badly by external vagaries, mortgages did go unpaid, debts were often heavy, retrenchment was a recurrent experience, and finances had to be skilfully and constantly juggled. It was, in Morawska's simple phrase, 'comfort without slack' (p. 122). Standard everyday expenditures from a budget of $2300 would:

> [leave] nothing for savings, a down payment on a house, or (in the case of immigrant parents) for college for the children. (In the 1920s and 1930s, the annual cost of maintaining one child at the University of Pittsburgh was $400–$500, including tuition, room and board) (Morawska, p. 116).

Mortgage payments, for their part, would also typically have added about $500 to the budget (p. 117).

Morawska believes that the Jewish community had a keen sense of the limits of the possible and of the uncertainties within their context. She argues that it was precisely the shared insecurity of their households' prosperity, embedded in their position within the external economic structures, that 'fixated the model of accomplishment placing the main emphasis on the goal of a comfortably material existence', a 'decent' lifestyle (p. 131). The significance of this goal in terms of the overall frame of meaning can be seen by placing it alongside the parallel desire of the group to remain inconspicuous and low profile in order not to draw attention to themselves (p. 195). Drawing imaginatively on a comparative analysis of Jewish involvement and experience in small towns and large cities in the USA, Morawska writes of a type of collective insecurity amongst Jews that was typical of small towns. This insecurity combined a sense of anxiety accompanying the perception of potential or actual threats to Jews with a sense of responsibility to provide a positive image to non-Jews in public and private life, to fulfil a positive role as 'ambassadors to the *goyim*' (p. 216). The Johnstown 'mix' of this combination was, unusually, weighted towards the former, anxiety, side of the combination. Local circumstances sustained a greater sense of civic insecurity than that of fellow ethnics in other small towns (p. 219). There were a number of reasons for this, many of which we will broach in a subsequent section. Above all, however, the configuration in which, in a company-run steel town, they had an occupational position as small business traders within an ethnic niche serving workers at the lowest end of the town's economic structure was 'the primary source of Jews' economic marginality and thus relative powerlessness' (p. 192).

Overlaying and infusing this continuing anxiety and fear, however, was a more positive disposition with its roots in the past. More precisely, the hermeneutic frame of the Johnstown Jews was deeply informed by an enduring and slowly evolving phenomenological comparison between the fears and insecurities of the old country and those of the new. In speaking with former East-European-Jews about their perception and appreciation of the civic situation of Jews in pre-Second World War Johnstown, Morawska found that overwhelmingly and spontaneously their recollections went first towards 'a comparison with their experience in Eastern Europe, either personally remembered or transmitted by family and group members' (p. 220). The sense of insecurity in Johnstown was implicitly and positively compared with conditions in the shtetl where, in the words of American-born Ben I repeating the engraved reminiscences of his father, '[Jews] did nothing antagonistic, and there comes an *ukaz* [edict] and all Jews must pay so much extra in taxes, or say *muzhiks* [peasants] got drunk after a market day and went around breaking windows [in Jewish homes]' (pp. 220–1). Likewise, Ukranian born Louis G told Morawska that he understood why she might suggest a parallel between the felt insecurity and anxiety in inter-war Johnstown and that experienced in the old country, but he insisted that 'it was quite different, [here] it was a *much*, much more secure insecurity!' (p. 220, original italics).

Over time the Johnstown migrants had been taught by experience to have a significantly comforting and bolstering faith in the guarantees of the American legal system, and in the official American ideology on the positive treatment of minorities. Their position as petty capitalists within a dominantly capitalist economy also meant that the significance of their ethnicity was reduced compared with their rural 'middleman' position in the midst of the peasant-based social structure of their milieu in Eastern Europe (p. 221). These factors, in turn, were linked to a gradual diminishing of the old country diffidence and accommodating deference to their Slavic customers (once peasants, now working-class) that had been their way of coping with an 'ever-present fearful and mistrustful anxiety'. Amongst the American-born generation this 'undercurrent of fear' had practically disappeared. On the other hand, the emergent and consolidated phenomenology of a much less insecure insecurity informed the dispositional inclination of Johnstown Jews not to risk endangering their *modus vivendi* with the dominant groups. The goal of a 'decent' lifestyle and a comfortable material existence should not be considered in terms divorced from this wider phenomenological frame. It is from within such a frame that the ordering of concerns in relation to particular predicaments, to be discussed in a subsequent section, should be interpreted.

An important reason why the Johnstown Jews' 'mix' of collective insecurity leant towards the desire to remain inconspicuous rather than towards diplomacy and the lessening of anxiety through positive interaction was precisely because of the strong communal ties within the Jewish group and the attendant inwardness of the community (p. 219). This communal source of support helped to assuage their insecurity but it also 'contributed to the social enclosure of their ethnic group, ... added to the persistence of its marginality, slowing the integrative processes, and thus perpetuating the whole pattern' (p. 243). One consequence of this was the slow pace of socio-cultural adaptation to the American way of life, with the ethnic content of the Johnstown Jews' 'sociocultural life contain[ing] a more substantial, and more visible, component of old-country traditional patterns, or, differently put, a proportionately larger share of continuity than change' (p. 185).

Change was both slow and, for the most part, nuanced. Morawska devotes an entire chapter at the end of her study to an account of the continuities and changes in what are, in effect, the general-dispositions of the Johnstown Jews. Morawska treads very carefully along a path that sees the American experience of this group of migrants as having intensified and enhanced some already existing orientations, as having led to the falling away of other dispositions, and as entailing a simple continuity in other, religious, ethnic and cosmological, dimensions of their outlook. The resultant, emergent, set of general-dispositions combined all of these elements, each of them affecting the others, and each existing within a blend of the old and the new countries. A central theme here is the extent to which the kind of instrumental, purposeful rationality associated with the modern 'American spirit' (p. 243) was to be found also within the habitual dispositions of the Johnstown Jews at different times in the history of their migration and resettlement. Thus, the 'intelligent evaluation of changing situations', with goals to be pursued by 'twisting paths' that was mentioned earlier with respect to the habitus of the Jews in Eastern Europe, was still evident in the habitus of the inter-war Johnstown Jews. But Morawska marks a subtle change as, drawing on notions crystallised by Ernest Gellner (1985, pp. 77–8, 81–2), she characterises the old country mentality as traditional and 'fixed' with limited elements of the 'variable' in the capacity for adaptation and flexibility. The general-dispositions of the later years, by way of contrast, are seen as having moved further over towards the variable pole whilst still retaining significant, but fewer, elements of the fixed. This 'variable cognitive capital' is an 'evidence-sensitive, relativizing, and circumstantial way of conceiving of human affairs and the surrounding world' (p. 244).

One of the ways in which Morawska identifies this shift in emphasis towards the instrumental and the positively adaptive is in the relative, and only relative, secularisation of outlook as evidenced in the falling away of certain traditional expressions. She sees an increased sense of control over one's life and a sense of the environment as much more amenable to purposeful action in the disappearance from, or marked decrease in, everyday use of phrases such as '*Dem yidns simkhe iz mit a bisl shrek*' (A Jew's joy is not without fright), idioms mentioned above such as '*Yidishe ashires iz vi shney in merts*' (Jewish wealth is like snow in March: here today, tomorrow gone), '*Got vet helft nor Got biz Got vet helfn*' (God will provide but if only God would provide until He provides), and also of 'a generalized *yidishe mazl*, all-round Jewish (mis)fortune' (pp. 230–2). This declining sense of being at the mercy of fateful forces was combined with a modulated view of the role of God in everyday affairs, a 'limited secularization' that maintained the religious cosmology for the 'bigger picture' but felt that in the 'smaller picture' of everyday life God left 'people alone to their personal and group devices, grabbing chances presented to them by the much more opportune American circumstances' (p. 232). There seem to have been interesting variations amongst the Johnstown Jews in the extent of their adhesion to such dispositions, with Morawska briefly noting divisions along synagogue and residential lines (p. 232).

Overall, the greater sense of purposeful control was in spite of the various economic and other insecurities faced by the Jewish community in Johnstown, and reflected a perception of more stable and orderly legal, civic and market conditions, and of the more secure insecurity already discussed. The sense of purposeful control, however, was always relative, the traditional wariness of external conditions was modified rather than expunged. They were well aware of the 'limitations of planning and control in their lives' (p. 228), and whilst the greatly improved life opportunities in America provided them with what Peter Berger calls a 'plausibility structure' for their greater optimism (Berger and Luckmann, 1966; cited in Morawska, p. 242), the 'whole situation could not but sustain in the people affected a sense that the goal of unqualified, perfect rationality would be self-defeating' (p. 228).

The fact that the beginnings of the Jewish Johnstowners 'flexible and fluxible' approach to life were already there in the early years of settlement, transported from Eastern Europe, meant, argues Morawska, that they had a distinct advantage over other groups such as the Slav migrants to Johnstown in adapting to the surrounding environment. The 'alert attentiveness' (p. 244), unwavering sense of commitment to the *process* rather than the success of goal-achievement, their readiness to pick themselves up and 'keep trying' through fluctuations of fortune, and the often ironic and sometimes sarcastic ingrained humour, were all habitual ethno-mechanisms that helped them to cope with the exigencies of their new life. The migrant Slavs, whose adaptation in the same town Morawska had studied prior to the project of *Insecure Prosperity*, lacked the extra driving edge of the Jews:

> Their lives as peasants in Europe and later as unskilled industrial laborers in Johnstown were full of insecurity and hardships; in the Slavic cultures, however, these attributes of existence seem to have been experienced more as a datum, a condition to which one succumbs 'floating along' as it were, until circumstances changed. As *Chranitel*, the local Rusyn-language newspaper, philosophized, depicting human agency as an object rather than a challenger to external forces: 'Life is like *morskoje plavanije*, swimming at sea [...] now the waves take us upward, then throw us downward again' (p. 234; also see Morawska, 1985).

An example of the kinds of changes that Morawska notes in the general-dispositions of the Jews through the years in America is that the relative emphasis placed on the process rather than the success of pursuing goals began to shift slowly, although unevenly, towards the ethic of achievement, although this was probably greater in the large urban centres than in places such as Johnstown. In Johnstown, notwithstanding the relative shift in emphasis, the second generation Jews continued to place significant weight on 'the continuing efforts rather than on the accomplishment itself', even though they began to express their attitudes in the linguistic idiom of the American success ethos – 'Tie, knot and hold on'; 'Winners never quit, quitters never win' (p. 234).

The Conjuncturally-Specific Structures: Mediators of Continuity and Change

As noted, the nature of Morawska's study is such that, when measured against the quadripartite framework, she spends relatively less time on the detailed analysis of the conjuncturally-specific dimension of an agent's frame of meaning and more on both the general-dispositional schemas of Johnstown's Jews and the networked patterning of their surface conduct or practices. This means that Morawska's account of the conjuncturally-specific internal structures is relatively thin. It also means that her account of agent's conduct relies more on the general-dispositional than the more conjuncturally-specific aspects of its constitution. There is thus a relative lack of emphasis on the important mediating processes between the general-dispositional resources and schemas of the agents-in-focus and the way these agents confront the immediate context of action.

Having said this, the neglect of the conjuncturally-specific is, as stated, only a relative one. Morawska's study contains several illuminating discussions which highlight the various roles that the conjuncturally-specific internal structures played as influential mediating links between general-dispositional structures and the external structural context. It is worth looking closely at what these discussions reveal about the uneven and structured processes of ethnicisation; about the processes and mechanisms of change, continuity, resistance and adaptation. It is also instructive to direct attention to what they reveal about how much, and how little, we know about these processes. It is particularly appropriate to discuss these mediating instances at this stage in the account of *Insecure Prosperity*. This is because it is possible by now to locate the micro-level lived experiences of the human beings in-focus within the frame not only of their inter-continental migrant history but also within the socio-structural matrix of Johnstown's position-practice relations. It is also possible to think through their phenomenological perception of the detailed constraints and opportunities of conjunctural moments in terms of their evolving general-dispositions. In short, the combined hermeneutic-structural diagnostics at the heart of structuration theory can, by this stage, further the understanding of lived experience by providing the mediating hinges between the micro-moments of an individual's practices and the larger historical, institutional and dispositional forces that have played their powerful roles in bringing them to that moment. These mediating hinges provide the invaluable final pieces in the critical apparatus that, to paraphrase Bourdieu, can make events, experiences and outcomes, truly understandable by picturing them within the relevant networks of hermeneutically-infused structures that make them what they are.

Adaptive Ethnicisation and Sabbath Observance

An empty chair, an absence at the table as the traditional family meal of the Sabbath begins, is the kind of surface appearance – surface absence – for which a causal explanation can be sought. It is an agent who is missing, the father or husband of one of Johnstown's East European Jewish families. In fact, many fathers are missing, may be missing. The explanation lies in the irresistible causal power (see pp. 111–15) of the host community's processes of structuration. It lies in the power of the conjuncturally-specific social circumstances to alter, in this instance, the religious culture of a minority community so that Jewish ritual practices accommodate themselves to the structures of the dominant milieu. It is an instance, to now paraphrase Marx, of social being, dominant social circumstances, determining culture, rather than the other way around. The fathers and husbands were often 'occupied in the store after the start of the Sabbath, he was often absent or arrived home late' (Morawska, p. 156). The father, in his status^2 of shopkeeper, was working after the start of the Sabbath, something that would have been inconceivable in the old country. In turn, a noticed but unintended consequence of this adaptation of the cultural-religious to the immediate social conjuncture was a further departure from traditional practices and consciousness: the placing of the observance of the Sabbath ritual within the home more fully under women's guardianship (p. 57). This was thus part of the slow – much slower than in the large cities where the complex division of labour accelerated such developments – but perceptible aspect of 'ethnicisation' that saw an increase in women's involvement and autonomy in social spheres that had previously been male preserves.

The absent husbands and fathers signified a compromise, and a negotiation, between the old ways of the East European shtetls and the exigencies of the new external structures. For whilst in the agricultural, pre-industrial, context of the shtetls the rural Christian population accepted and adapted to the cessation of trade on Saturdays, such an arrangement was impossible in Johnstown. The power relations embedded in economic relations and their temporal routines meant that Saturday was the busiest trading day of the week, 'the day the mill workers and coal miners were paid their wages and went shopping with their whole families' (p. 155). The stark phenomenology of the shtetls contained within it the inexorable consequence of punitive sanctions for transgressors: 'they'd kill you for violating Sabbath' (Hyman M). But the Johnstown Jews worked on the Sabbath. Morawska records the change bluntly, 'by consensus they altered the norm prohibiting Sabbath work' (p. 155). The generalised-dispositions of the Johnstown Jews on this core issue began to change, to adapt – not without emotional tension – as the exigencies of the 'out-there' of the new situational milieu was interpreted 'in-here' within the duality of structure and agency: 'Here in Portage I did work on Shabes, although I did not feel too good about it at the beginning, but I had to, to make a living, and Saturday was a business day.' (Hyman M, in Morawska, p. 155).

The external structural milieu of Saturday trading, and the networks of key social practices that fed into the constitution and intractability of this milieu, were perceived as a particular complex of internal structures within the overall frames of Jewish shopkeepers and artisans. The power, the normative frames and the routine practices of the key situated actors (not least the owners and managers of the Cambria/Bethlehem Steel Company, themselves situated within wider legal, cultural, religious and economic structures with their own powerful trajectories) within that conjuncturally-specific milieu were perceived to allow only some possibilities for the Jewish actors. This perception of limited possibilities contained a temporal dimension in which the Johnstown Jews' perception of the current external conditions of action looked forward also to the future, to what would happen to their interactions with customers if they refused to work on the Sabbath. In other words, there was a set of expectations about what would happen if they worked and what would happen if they didn't work. The phenomenology of the Jewish agents-in-focus was thus such that they perceived the external structures as embodying a set of constraints, limits to the possible, of which one was a curb on continuing the old-country ways of Sabbath observance in this American context.

On the other hand, if one looks at this situation from the angle of Giddens's 'agents who could choose to do otherwise', and from that of Archer's notion of dualism at time 1, then one can see that the external structures by themselves didn't, strictly speaking, make it impossible, at time 1, for the Johnstown Jews to observe the Sabbath. If they had been determined that their religious-cultural values were not to be compromised then they could have stopped work on the Sabbath and waited to see what the consequences were. The likely outcome would have been much reduced takings or bankruptcy at time 3, after the various interactions (times 2 to 3) between mill workers, coal miners and Gentile shop owners on a number of Saturdays, and a consequent change in the income and profits profile of the Jewish community and in the structural composition of traders in the Johnstown area at time 4. They didn't take this course of action partly because their knowledge of the external structures was such that they could anticipate the consequences at times 3 and 4. But, also, because the overall hermeneutic frame on the basis of which they made the decision to compromise and work in their businesses on the Sabbath, contained a hierarchy of purposes. Within this hierarchy, the forfeiting of this one element of Jewish religious life (not by any means, of course, the whole of Jewish religious life) came lower down in the hierarchy than the goal of making a better living for their families, the goal they came to America determined to achieve (see p. 155). It was also framed by the desire to remain inconspicuous within the larger community.

The extent to which this was a pragmatic and reluctant move, rather than a wilful and enthusiastic movement towards the secular and towards a splitting of the religious from the ethnic character of Jewishness, as was seen in many of the large cities, can be seen from the extent to which private, home-based observances were maintained. There was both a common core and a degree of variability around observances in this domain, with the Sabbath being most strictly observed amongst the members of the Orthodox Ahavath Achim, least strictly amongst the East European members of the Beth Zion Temple, and with Rodef Sholom families falling somewhere in between:

> at home there was no work, or it was deliberately limited. Women's abstention from cooking was a prevalent observance, even in Westmont homes ... there was also a total or partial abstention from sewing, repairing, gardening, piano playing, and writing ... even in prestigious Anglo-Protestant Westmont, a considerable number of immigrant households with grown-up coresident children kept the truncated Sabbath in a stringent manner (p. 156).

The agent's conduct of the traders in deciding to do business on the Sabbath would have depended upon an interaction between the general-dispositional commitment to making a good life for the family and the conjuncturally-specific appreciation of the sanctions that would follow from refusing to do business on the Sabbath. Thus, whilst it was not physically impossible for the agents to observe the Sabbath, their value commitments and the hierarchy of priorities within their phenomenological frame meant that they did indeed experience the external structures in terms of, firstly, a constraining and intractable dualism immune to their wishes, and secondly, in terms of duality, as an irresistible causal influence they felt compelled to draw from as the medium of their conduct. Both dualism and duality were experienced as such from within a culturally rich, particular, complexly hierarchical, hermeneutic frame:

> Benjamin I. recalled the reasons articulated by his father, an otherwise highly observant man, for working on Saturdays in his store in Boswell: "[I knew] he regretted it, but he worked on Shabes, because otherwise he would have made for us only a meager living ... He told us, 'One has to act in the form of *derekh erets* [way of the land, or in keeping with locally accepted social standards of behavior],' and he came to America to make a good life for the family" (p. 155).

Morawska doesn't say much about the process through which the Jewish community arrived at the 'consensus' to alter the norm prohibiting Sabbath work. There is the implication that it would have seemed 'natural' given the combination of external structures and the traders' overall cultural schemas. She does present, as we have seen, recollections of her first and second generation informants, but these are about the individualised responses of Jewish traders to the external situation. They are not about how these individuals perceived the intra-group norms and how they ascertained that these were changing. This is an important point given that in the shtetl 'they'd kill you for violating Sabbath'.

One can soon come up with suggestions as to the relatively banal processes involved, no doubt involving many conversations at home, at work and in the shul, as well as self-reflection, knowledge of the different legal context of the new country, and an implicit mutual understanding of the hierarchy of purposes and pragmatic orientations embedded within the general-dispositional frames of fellow Jews. Whilst we know that it was virtually 'from the beginning' that conducting business on the Sabbath became 'the accepted norm among Johnstown's Jews' (p. 155) one can still wonder about the manner and the pace of the change; whether a single shopkeeper was the first to test the water alone, or whether a number did so on the same day, whether there was a collective agreement by a committee attached to a synagogue or a cultural movement that was less formally co-ordinated. One can also imagine what might have been the content of the conversations and the self-reflection, the texture of the emotions and the degree of self-doubt, and the extent to which there was a sense of risk and uncertainty involved in the minds of the first not to observe.

Resistant Ethnicisation: Restaurants, Dating and Christmas

Similar kinds of questions to those asked about the Sabbath, about the co-ordination of mutual responses to changing times, can be asked about the Johnstown Jews' intra-group responses to other forms of social behaviour such as nonkosher eating in public, dating or marrying Gentiles, or the display of Christmas trees (pp. 158–9, 168, 210–11). There is clearly some kind of pattern in which there is greater change and 'ethnicisation' in areas where the Jews felt their livelihood may have been threatened if they failed to adjust their norms, and less, or slower, change in other areas. Many interesting questions remain, however, with respect to these other areas. Most of them revolve around the ways in which individuals and groups embedded in the Jewish habitus and with varying degrees of reflective distance from the more traditional norms, apprehended their own context of action and the limits within which they felt they could act. The process of ethnicisation took on different forms and crept forwards at different speeds depending upon the area of life concerned and, sometimes, upon nuanced differences within groups. Appeals to the various components of the quadripartite cycle of structuration can provide causal accounts of this uneven ethnicisation process with greater analytical clarity, drawing attention to the reality and perception of conjunctural constraints.

Morawska notes that 'eating out' was a form of social behaviour that only emerged slowly amongst the Johnstown Jews, especially when compared to the Jews of large cities like New York. When it did appear in Johnstown it was 'closely monitored by local opinion' (the commercial and recreational life of the Johnstown Jews centred on just a few blocks), with the news of any 'unusual actions' being circulated by word of mouth. By the 1930s 'more modern liberal' Jews, mainly from Rodef Sholom, were seen eating in nonkosher restaurants, 'but not the forbidden foods'. Traditionalists explicitly expressed their disapproval of this but still such behaviour did not elicit the social anathema that it would have done in the shtetls. Morawska notes two instances of 'outright condemnation of nonkosher eating in public view' by people in positions of leadership at Rodef Sholom who, it was said, 'should have known better', should have understood the significance of their action within the Jewish community (p. 159). It seems, from Morawska's account that there was some kind of relationship between structural positioning as members of particular synagogues and the hermeneutic frames of meaning that informed actions in this sphere, with members of Ahavath Achim not practising *oysen* (eating out) at all. Interaction and adaptation within different synagogue communities, and within different residential groupings, could certainly account for some of these differences, and could indicate some of the likely processes of mutual adjustment involving the sounding out of fellow Jews and the gradual modification of behaviour and core scheme-value concepts.

It seems that similar religious variations within families accounted for some of the differences in parental attitudes to their sons and daughters dating Gentiles, with, for example, more traditionally Orthodox homes having a more strictly prohibitive attitude, with generally more acquiescent children. There were, however, instances of defiance and transgression of parental wishes in some families with respect to dating, although the Jews' shared general-dispositional frames seem to have contained a routine taken-for-granted acceptance that such transgressions would stop this side of marriage, with a striking 98.4 per cent of all marriages before the Second World War being within the community:

> Unlike adolescent dating ... intermarrying was unanimously regarded in the Jewish community as a 'social disgrace' and 'looked at with contempt,' so that 'such couples tended to stay away,' and in fact the majority of them left town (p. 211).

The case of the missing Christmas tree in the homes of Johnstown's Jews, something that was taken-for-granted, follows the same general-dispositional logic (the logic of doxa) as the taken-for-granted disapproval of intermarrying. In this sense, both phenomena have a directly opposed character to that of the missing father at the family's Sabbath meal, which was, especially in those early years, the result of a painfully aware, explicit, pragmatic response to recalcitrant circumstances, what Heideggerians refer to as the experience of 'unready to hand' circumstances – circumstances in which a practice that has previously been routinely performed without conscious awareness is suddenly jolted into conscious awareness through being rendered problematic[3] – whose perceived imposition was experienced as an acute source of discomfort. Value-schemas with respect to intermarrying had remained, by way of contrast, 'ready to hand', taken for granted. The same was true for Johnstown Jews' eschewal of Christmas trees. Whilst in the late 1930s and early 1940s a Christmas tree 'for the children' had become increasingly common in Jewish homes in the Upper West Side of Manhattan, where it was stripped of its religious, Christian symbolism and secularised to 'signify participation in a national American festivity', for the Johnstowners

> the tree retained its inherent Gentile religious symbolism and could not be adopted as an ethnic custom. My American-born informants emphatically denied even contemplating such an idea (Not even an Easter egg!) (p. 168).

One can look at this in terms of the long-standing significatory structures within the shared frames of meaning of the Johnstown Jews retaining their enduring quality and essential integrity in terms of signifier, signified and position in relation to other significant meanings within the paradigm. These structures seem to have remained unquestioned and taken-for-granted, embedded in habitus and practical consciousness. There was also an implicit action-informing normative sanction attached to these structures of signification expressed in Morawska's comment that it would at that time have been 'socially impossible' for a Jew to install a Christmas tree in Johnstown. The Manhattan Jews, on the other hand, in external structural conditions of employment outside the ethnic niche, greater secularisation, and greater diversification of practices within the Jewish community and a correspondingly reduced level of social control, had clearly established a greater reflective distance from the inherited structures of signification within their general-dispositional schemas.

Indeterminate Fear, Comparative Sociology and Civic-Political Quiescence

Having sketched some of the elements of the emergent position-practice relations of the Jews within the wider community, drawn attention to the slow process of ethnicisation, of the blending between the old and the new in terms of general-dispositions, and of the role of conjuncturally-specific structures in the mediation of continuity and change, I now want to add some additional factors into the equation, factors that focus on the civic-political quiescence of the Johnstown Jews. In doing so I hope to bring out further the advantages of the broad, relatively holistic, and comparative approach pursued by Morawska. In particular, the consideration of further factors can help to 'round out' our appreciation of the range of structural clusters that may have played a part in the Jews' perceptions of the external structural field that confronted them. These further structural clusters are important in thinking through issues of possible sanctions and constraints that we, as researchers, may not yet have considered but which may well have informed the hermeneutic frames of the Jewish actors. For the marginality and relative powerlessness stemming from the Jews' position within the town's economic structure was, in fact, compounded by a political climate and civic life in Johnstown that were 'anything but liberal' (p. 192). It was a Republican stronghold with a subservient press and an accepted exclusionary culture with associated practices in the civic sphere that reproduced and consolidated the stratification along ethnic lines of both institutional and informal social life. Albeit of 'a subdued nonvitriolic kind' there was a 'detectable undercurrent of anti-Semitism among both the upper socioeconomic strata and those at the bottom of the local stratification system, who themselves faced severe ethnic prejudice' (p. 193; see pp. 193–5). The anti-Semitism took a primarily religious form amongst the Anglo-Protestant elites (the 'Invidious Jews have accused Jesus ...' being a representative extract from one Catholic-Slovak-Rusyn parish bulletin echoing the protestant voices from the *Johnstown Tribune*) whereas the Shylock motif surfaced amongst the working-class Slavic communities (p. 194). The ethnic-divisive social organisation of the town was in the main accepted as a given, with the civic participation of the Jews constrained within very restrictive limits.

Indeed, Morawska discusses two areas in which the Jews' analysis of their external context led them to act in ways that were contrary to, or in tension with, significant general-dispositional values. The first case involved their registration with the Republican Party. Over four-fifths of Jewish Johnstowners were registered Republican in the latter half of the 1930s at a time when the majority of American Jews had sided with Roosevelt (FDR) and the Democrats, especially for the New Deal social policies and for FDR's stand against Nazism in Germany (pp. 198–9). Morawska uses the results of her research in this area to emphasise that the feasible political options perceived by Jews in the USA were moulded – arguing against conventional interpretations that simply linked Jews' marginal status with their political liberalism or even radical revolutionary-ideologies – by a combination of the local situation itself and their interpretation of this on the basis of current experience and collective memory (p. 199). Thus, the four fifths registration with the Republican party in Johnstown was far higher even than the percentage – about two-thirds – of all registered Republicans in the town as a whole, and is linked by Morawska to the Jews' probably justifiable interpretation of their local circumstances, to their much less insecure but still insecure prosperity, and to their resultant pragmatism and desire to remain inconspicuous (see p. 219).

This emergent and enduring general disposition was closely tied – as we have noted – to a sense of dependence and vulnerability based on their position within the various horizontal and vertical economic and social power networks in the town. This can be seen in the reflections of Elmer M on political affiliation in Johnstown: 'to be a registered Democrat in Johnstown – and in a small town people knew such things – where the mighty, the WASPS [White Anglo-Saxon Protestants], were all Republican, it lowered your class position, and not to be part of it [the Republican majority] could also hurt your situation' (p. 200). The sentiments here are expressed in terms of an agent who perceives the external position-practice relations facing him – the ghosts of networked others – as one of, to use Mouzelis's conceptualisation, intractable dualism. This external context is taken as given, and Morawska, drawing on her interviews, summarises some more of its networked contours and the perceived advantages of simply adapting to them, in the following way:

> Siding with the powerful, especially since not doing so was readily perceptible, facilitated business-related matters such as a bank loan, mercantile license, or adjustment of tax levied on a store building – or, in the case of the more affluent merchants, when the county had some orders to place for clothing, shoes, dry goods, or the like. The insecurity of Jewish businesses closely tied to the production of the mills and coal mines, whose owners pretty much controlled the course of local politics, naturally increased this sense of dependence (p. 200).

A similar pragmatism was evident in the Jews response to the failed strikes of 1919 and 1937 at the Bethlehem Steel works, whose goal was the establishment and recognition of an independent union. This time the pragmatism in the face of a threatening external context was also marked by an uneasy and awkward ambivalence about their agential response to it. For on the one hand they didn't want to alienate their customers, who were on strike, whilst on the other hand their livelihood depended upon the workers getting paid, and also they 'dreaded antagonizing Bethlehem Steel management and the city government that supported it' (p. 200). The result was mixed. Whilst many of the congregational rank and file sat on the fence as well as they could, the rabbi of Rodef Sholom, the largest Jewish congregation, joined the Citizens Committee organised during the 1937 strike by the Westmont Presbyterian Church's council with the ostensible purpose of acting as arbiter, although in the event it 'actually promoted the company's interests' (p. 200). Most shopkeepers, like Irving L, realised that by 'keeping quiet, it meant supporting the company ... and they said amongst themselves how ridiculous this was, but they kept quiet' (p. 201). This is another example of the external social structures silencing and neutralising the ideal cultural values of the agents-in-focus. Beth Zion's rabbi, on the other hand, refused to join the anti-strike Citizens' Committee, angering his congregation in the process.

Morawska notes that Beth Zion's rabbi was apparently influenced by the radical pro-social justice orientation of the contemporary American Reform rabbinate, and so we are able to locate the rabbi – on the basis of the conceptualisation, introduced in chapter 3, of plural codes of conduct arising from involvement in a plurality of external structural clusters – at the intersection of three structural clusters (Whittington, 1997/92, pp. 377–82). For in the duality within himself as agent he combined knowledge and perceptions of the viewpoints and external position-practice relations of management and also of workers in the current conjuncturally-specific context of action, whilst also being informed at the general-dispositional level, by the pro-social justice discourse of the American Reform rabbinate. This additional ingredient of the social justice discourse within his agential resources would, all things being equal, have provided him with more autonomy than those without recourse to this. It would be an additional resource on which he could draw in gaining a critical distance from his immediate situational context. It would be interesting to know more about how he came to his decision to pursue a course of action that was to have the consequence of angering his congregation. That is, to know the extent to which the decision was a 'purist' ideological one and the extent to which, and the ways in which, the more trans-situational social justice values were combined with a context analysis of the likely consequences of his stance both for himself and for his congregation.

Morawska reports that most Jewish shopkeepers commiserated with the

Slavs and Hungarians 'slaving in the mills and coal mines', 'so exploited by these companies', and continued to extend credit to them until work resumed. Her informants remembered their lack of open support for the workers as 'the only rational option for people in their position' (p. 201), but at the same time a number of them 'sounded somewhat defensive, as if they also remembered having felt somehôw guilty of betraying a group ethical norm, namely, the traditional Jewish religious precept of acting for social justice' (p. 201). This tension between pragmatic action *in situ* and general-dispositional ideals ('a competition between business interests and the built-in Jewish idealism' – Samuel K) was probably reinforced and exacerbated by the exposure to other related external sources of influence on general-dispositional ideals, two of which merit special mention. The first was in the form of the Yiddish newspaper, *Forverts*, which was taken by 20–25 per cent of households. *Forverts* was 'socialist-secular' in ideological orientation although most Johnstowners denied that their reading it had anything to do with socialism, 'there were no socialists here'. They read it, they said, because '[I]t was a Yiddish paper, and had good stories, and Jewish news, [also commercial advertisements] that's why' (p. 144). Nevertheless, the paper consistently maintained a pro-labour orientation and this, combined with family and social contacts in New York, where both Democratic politics and unionism had a large Jewish following, probably added to the dissonance experienced by Johnstown Jews, expressed by Morawska as a 'sense of collective normative impropriety' (p. 201).

The second source reinforcing tension mentioned by Morawska came in the form of union officialdom. Labour organisers and lawyers from New York visited the town during and after the strike of 1937 and helped to set up the basis of what was to become the recognised steelworkers' union in 1941. Morawska's informants remembered 'the awkwardness of occasional encounters between quiescent Johnstown Jews' and these big city officials who tried to persuade them to take a more active stand (pp. 201–2). Extending Giddens's discussion of the relevance of Goffman's work to structuration theory it can be seen here that this face-to-face experience of awkwardness is closely tied to broader institutional forces (Giddens, 1987, p. 139). In this case the sense of emotional unease and impropriety was caused by the Jews' attempts to negotiate between the conflicting external pressures of local power structures and the New York officials. Morawska relates how the union visitors' appeal to the general-dispositional values of a collective 'ethnic' commitment to social justice caused the most embarrassment to the quiescent Johnstowners (p. 202). But, as she poignantly notes, this was still 'apparently not sufficient to prompt a change in behavior' (p. 202; cf. Archer, 2000, p. 232). Another small part of the inherited ethnic and religious tradition was thus pragmatically conceded to conjunctural exigencies.

The conjuncturally-specific dimension of the Johnstowners' overall hermeneutic frame, together with their commitment to creating a good material life for their families, over-rode the ethnic commitment to social justice when it came to overt political action (inaction). This combination of their context analysis and their inner negotiation of conduct over-rode their more generalised cultural ideals. And it did this at the same time as it created psychological discomfort and embarrassment in their social interaction with the New York visitors. The Johnstown shopkeepers experienced little room for manoeuvre in their day-to-day interaction as agents in the political sphere. Their perception of the immediate structural context of interaction was one in which the structural complexes most important as conditions necessary for the success of their most cherished goals were intractable. The external structures were experienced as impervious to change, and the action-informing schemas of the agents-within-these-structures were perceived as being sufficiently retributional to impose retaliatory sanctions – of one kind or another; it is hard to tell precisely what was feared, whether the fear was specific or diffuse, or the extent to which the fear was justified – on the Jews if they were to be seen not to stay within certain parameters of acceptable conduct.

Morawska brings these civic-political factors, and others, into relief through a comparative exercise that highlights the importance of multi-causality, of plural structures in 'open' interaction with each other such that they produce potentially unique configurations of position-practices in particular places. In discussing the involvement of Johnstown's Jews in the wider local society, Morawska compares their circumstances with the social integration of American Jewish communities in four other towns and cities – the two small towns of Charleston, South Carolina and Terre Haute, Indiana, and the two large cities of New York and Cleveland, Ohio. In all four places, and in stark contrast to Johnstown, Jews were actively involved in the mainstream civic-political process and in organised community life that was unrestricted by ethnic boundaries (p. 187). Given that Morawska was keen to study the causal influences on the quiescent attitude of the Johnstowners, the depth of their commitment to remaining inconspicuous, to not rocking the boat, this comparative framework is exceptionally helpful. It provides a good deal of critical purchase on the question-at-hand through reflection on the varying social conditions and processes within these other places that facilitated and supported greater Jewish participation, and which alleviated that fear of being conspicuous that was apparent in Johnstown.

The comparative exercise makes it clear, for example, that sheer impact of city size or the proportion of Jews compared to the overall population are not, on their own, necessarily determining factors (pp. 186–7). It also directs attention to significant variations in the economic character of the different places, with a much more developed and 'modern' division of labour in New York and Cleveland, and in similarly-sized Terre Haute a more diversified economy than Johnstown's including, besides coal mining, prosperous light industry and commerce (pp. 187, 192). Morawska suggests that a more diversified economic structure would dissipate the dependence and the economic insecurity felt by the Johnstown Jews in their ethnic entrepreneurial niche, and would in the process have withdrawn some of the conditions for the *gemeinschaftslich* intra-group traditionalism that itself perpetuated the absence of Jewish involvement in the wider community. In Terre Haute, for example:

> Jews had been well-established merchants or light manufacturers, and occupied such high-powered positions as the presidency of the local Chamber of Commerce or the directorship of a local bank (p. 192).

The existence or otherwise of pluralistic civic-political opinion is also picked out as a seemingly significant contributor to a 'diminution of status anxiety' (pp. 187–8). In terms of the general-dispositional frames of the non-Jewish community (the agents within the structural context), the position of Jews within the collective civic memory of townspeople – having a presence amongst the early settlers and amongst the 'revered patriot-heroes of the American Revolution' – is also singled out as significant, playing a palpable role in Charleston, as also, ironically, did the racist ideology prominent in this same Southern town, a cultural schema which made skin colour and race 'the major social partitioner, overriding ethnic divisions' (pp. 187, 188). In Terre Haute, the silent acquiescence of the dominant, Anglo-Protestant, elite in the symbolic manifestations of the activities of the Ku Klux Klan, served as a tacit reminder to Jews of ethnic and racial tensions, although the fact that the overt hostility in Indiana was directed against local blacks and Catholics, mitigated the effects of this on the civic-political participation of Jews (p. 190). A further factor conducive to Jewish integration identified by Morawska from this exercise was 'the presence of outstanding Jewish group leaders and activists' (p. 187).

Three other factors, specific to the Johnstown configuration, that could well have contributed to the Jews' sense of insecurity were:

- the illiberal political climate and quality of civic life in Johnstown, a republican stronghold of a type contrasting greatly with Cleveland's progressive and reform-minded tradition of Republicanism;
- the stratification of institutional and informal social life along exclusionary ethnic lines, with an absence of pluralism and, as we have seen, an undercurrent of anti-Semitism; and
- the density (with about nine-tenths of the total population of the town being church members through the inter-war years) and the depth of the taken-for-granted attachment to Christian values within the Anglo-Protestant elite. Christian references permeated most public affairs, from meetings, to newspapers to political campaigns, and explicit Christian values and morals also dominated the ethos of the public schools. Even in

the relatively rare, well-meaning and integrative, interfaith meetings 'the terms "Hebrews" or "the Hebrew race" used ... to refer to ... Jewish fellow citizens reconfirmed ... the deep-rooted Christian sense of Jews' inherent otherness' (p. 195).

All these factors indicate aspects of the general-dispositional world views of the agents within context, primarily of the Anglo-Protestant elite that must have constituted the most powerful background threat to the Jews' sense of security.

Broad comparative exercises cannot substitute for analysis of the specific configuration of causal factors in Johnstown, nor can they substitute for associated analyses of structuration *in situ*. On the other hand, the very process of setting up a comparative framework, of singling out a variety of factors and thinking of them in terms of different configurations in different places, helps one to think more clearly about one's own case. It provides a geographical comparative frame to complement the kind of historical framing of structuration cases discussed in chapter 4. It helps one to begin to think of the case in that broad, more holistic, manner just mentioned, precisely as a configuration of different causal factors, intermeshing and interacting with each other in what realists have called 'open systems' (Bhaskar, 1979; Sayer, 1984/1992, 2000a). And it also helps one to bring to the foreground the specificities of the case, alerting one to the *absence* of factors that made a difference elsewhere, and could have made a difference here, and doing the same for potentially influential factors that are *present* in the case at hand that one could look at in greater detail in order to ascertain more about their precise role in the structuration process. In addressing the specific question of the involvement of Johnstown Jews in their local society in *Insecure Prosperity*, Morawska uses the comparative framework as a guide and a backdrop to the construction of the position-practice configuration, or what she calls the 'constellation of factors' specific to the Johnstown case. This constellation 'slackened the processes of sociocultural transformation within the Jewish group' and 'kept Johnstown's Jews both in the midst and actually on the periphery of local society' (p. 191).

The Structuration of Instability and Contingency: Ibsen's *A Doll's House*

I devote the final section of the chapter to an analysis of some of the key structuration processes involved in the narrative of Ibsen's *A Doll's House* written in 1879. The content of this drama contrasts with *Insecure Prosperity* in that the micro interactions of its characters lack much of a grounding in those wider currents and networks which could provide a framework for locating them within a socio-historical perspective. Also, the connections between the actions of protagonists and the more immanent clusters of external position-practices that make up the socio-structural context are fragmentary and sketchy compared with the relatively holistic and detailed account provided for the Johnstown Jews. On the other hand, the case usefully contrasts with Morawska's study in that whereas *Insecure prosperity* charts adaptive and reconciled changes that take place at a slow pace over some sixty years, Ibsen's drama is focused upon intense and fraught transformations whose effects, whilst having some of their latent origins in a more distant past, are finally wrought in days rather than decades. On a more general point, one can see in the story of Nora Helmer one of those processes of structuration in which the characters are involved less in reproducing routine practices and more in responding to the heightened exigencies of the unique conjuncture.

Having made the point about the relative absence of the relations and networks of the socio-historical context, it is still important to recognise those points at which a broader non-reductionist type approach could establish points of contact with the kind of structuration process represented here. Thus, *A Doll's House* clearly involves the practices of the institutional complex of a family, with other (non-reductionist, plural) external structural clusters combining with the practices of the family to constitute the events and processes that take place within that family. These external structural clusters which enter into the practices of the family include: those associated with the bank for which both Helmer and Krogstad work, itself embedded (primarily but not only) within economic relations; the institutions and practices of medicine; those of law; networks of friendship outside the family; and the ideologies or discourses and practices of love, trust, honour, marriage and patriarchy. The ways in which each of these spheres impinge upon the structuration process of family events – both individually and in combination with each other, and as independent, irresistible or malleable causal forces can in principle be traced on the basis of a hermeneutically informed analysis, involving the elements of the quadripartite process.

The composite character of the plot of *A Doll's House* means that the case study itself is *relatively* broad, covering the dynamics of events across time and propelled by the networked interdependencies of a number of different situated agents who all contribute to the final denouement of the drama, Nora Helmer's decision to leave the 'Doll's House'. The structuration processes that are external to the agent-in-focus at any one time are seen to have powerful constraining, pressuring and empowering qualities in a variety of combinations. In tune with the central tenets of structuration theory, one can see that it is the agents who take things forward, but they do so in circumstances (of internal structures and external structuration processes) not (all) of their own choosing, being more or less in control, more or less aware of the dynamics at work around them. There are, within this broad focus, sub-questions or problematics addressed *en route* – the social constraints perceived by various agents, for example – all falling within one or other of the remaining categories of question-steps and question-types outlined in chapter 4, and all closely related to the wider dynamic. The attention given to any of these sub-questions is always dictated, however, by their relevance to the main question of attention: the various conditions and causal influences necessary to produce Nora's fateful decision.

I will analyse the particular sequence of events that forms the spine of the play on the basis of the strong project of structuration, including an emphasis on the duality of structure (and agents) within a relational nexus. The main explanandum, as noted, will be Nora's decision to leave her husband Torvald Helmer and her children, and the explanation will be a 'composite' one involving structuration processes that stretch backwards in time and involve a plurality of spheres and networked actors which together provide the conditions of existence for Nora's decision. An investigation of the causal influences on this outcome will reveal how important it is to separate out different stages of the structuration cycle. Doing this allows one to attend to the dynamism within the cycle by looking at the way the separate components interact. The focus can be placed on the relations between:

- particular external structuration processes and the conjuncturally-specific structures of the agents-in-focus;
- these conjunctural structures and the general-dispositional frames of characters-in-focus;
- the emergent properties of the rapprochement between these two inner dimensions of the agent and the ensuing agent's conduct;
- agent's conduct and the various consequences of this.

Both agent's conduct and context analysis are required in order to capture the various moments of this composite process. The latter is essential in that an understanding of the plot is impossible without taking a position on what the external conditions of action are in and of themselves. Without this it would be impossible to gain a sense of the overall nexus of perceived and actual obstacles, constraints and opportunities confronting the protagonists at various times within the sequence of events – or to develop a parallel sense of the likely durability, intractability or malleability of these.

Analysis of the plot of *A Doll's House* also reveals the necessarily shifting nature of the focus of structuration when dealing with a composite process, from this or that agent to another agent, then to another and so on; this is the necessary shifting back and forth between first and third persons that Kilminster highlights (see chapter 3). Each of these agents, situated as they are in differing positions within sets of position-practice relations, confronts a different set of external and internal structural conditions, constraints and opportunities. These external structural conditions feed into the conduct of agents by means of the mediations we have outlined. Noting this guards against any temptation to think of interaction and action as taking place in a period of 'time-out' from structures, and provides an immanent structural moment within interaction and action that is insufficiently conceptualised in many theoretical accounts.[4] In the final part of the play we observe a seismic change in Nora's outlook on the world, alterations in her general-dispositional perspective, values, sentiments, and morals. Enough to radically change her conduct. Her profound re-assessment of her situation is an emergent product, a cumulative product of her experience of events and interactions produced by a combination of the identifiable actions of the play's protagonists and more anonymous, structurally 'conventional', causal influences.

The character of Nora in *A Doll's House* is the central figure, the primary agent-in-focus, in a series of circumstances and events that she only partly brings about herself. Some years ago she secretly forged her dying father's signature in order to borrow money to pay for a holiday in the warmer climate of Italy, a trip that she believed saved the life of her husband, Torvald Helmer, who had grown sick from overworking. Confiding in her friend, Mrs Kristine Linde, Nora now describes the intensity of her knowledge that Helmer must never be told of this: 'That's the whole point. He wasn't to know. Don't you understand? He was never to know how ill he was. The doctors came to me, to me, and told me his life depended on it' (p. 17). Nora knew that her husband's proud sense of what it was to be a man and a husband would be irretrievably compromised by the idea that he owed something to his 'poor, helpless little darling' (p. 92): 'It would break us apart. Our lovely home, our happiness – all gone' (p. 17). So she pretended that the trip was for her, that it would be good for her condition, expecting as she was to give birth any day to her first child, Ivar. She had told Helmer that 'he had to be kind to me, humour me. I hinted that he took out a loan. Kristine, he almost lost his temper. He said I was featherbrained, and his duty as a husband was not to indulge my ... my little whims, he called them' (p. 17). In an earlier scene, more recent in chronological time, we have already heard Helmer assail his wife with the unequivocal incantation: 'No borrowing. No debt. When a household relies on debt, it's slavery, it's vile' (p. 3). Nora had decided, those years ago, to find a way herself to raise the money. But women were, by law, not allowed to borrow without their husband's permission, and so she needed her father's signature to guarantee the repayments for the debt she was to take out. She felt that her father was too ill, however, to burden with the knowledge that she needed the money because her own husband was at death's door. So she forged his signature. Her perception was that the situation allowed her no alternatives. Unable to confide in Helmer, Nora had been in debt ever since, struggling to meet the payments on time, each time – quarterly accounts, instalments – paying everything from her own small allowance and secretly taking on copying work, locking herself away into the small hours.

We begin to get a glimpse here of the distinctiveness and force of Nora's frame of meaning on these events. Her concern for Torvald's health and her father's peace of mind motivate her actions. These motivational grounds combine with her knowledgeability of the social context and with her own hierarchy of values in framing her decision to do what she did. It is this distinctive internal dynamic, this internal negotiation of personal values and predispositions with conjuncturally-specific internal structures (perceptions of external social norms, meanings and resources – themselves experienced in large part as forceful impositions) that agent's conduct analysis is designed, *inter alia*, to investigate. At the same time, however, the attention devoted to the analysis of the internal dynamics by which Nora aligns her personal dispositions and conduct with her conjunctural perceptions of norms, meanings and resources, needs to be complemented by a more exclusive focus on the *structural content of those perceptions*. This leads us into the domain of agent's context analysis. As we have seen, this form of analysis allows us to focus both on the more or less explicitly acknowledged content of Nora's perceptions of norms, meanings and resources – the conjuncturally-specific internal structures - *and* on the relationship of these perceptions to external structures. It allows one to ask, for example, whether her perception of Helmer's sense of normative propriety, or of her belief that she had the power to manage with impunity the forgery of a document guaranteeing a loan, was accurate or mistaken. Both these questions involve addressing issues of structural pressures, constraints and possibilities, both perceived and actual. Both involve dealing with the duality within the external structural context. Context analysis draws one back from Nora's conduct towards the structures within her, and from there to the structuration processes external to her. It allows one to look at the enabling and constraining conditions of action, as internally experienced and as externally existing.

As the narrative unfolds it will become clear to Nora and to the audience that she did not, after all, have the power to manage the repercussions of her forgery, whilst her reading of Helmer's character – at least in the respect mentioned – emerges as well-founded. What is striking about the plot's development from a structuration point of view is, firstly, the force of agents' characters, general-dispositional frames and choices upon the course of events. But, secondly, in complex tension with the first, is the support it provides for a conception of the independent and/or irresistible causal influences of particular structures on particular actors or sets of actors. As noted in chapter 3, the abstract, philosophical, form of structuration associated with Giddens's focus on 'ontology-in-general' has been regularly criticised by commentators for its apparent inability to make up its mind as to which one of these two sets of forces is to have priority and precedence in the approach (see, for example, Anderson, 1990, and Craib, 1992, p. 149). The key to this apparent conundrum is that such assessments of priority and precedence, and the prior identification of their respective contributions, cannot be undertaken at the level of ontology-in-general; they can only be meaningfully addressed in relation to particular questions about particular conjunctures addressed on the basis of ontology-*in-situ*. The co-existence of these two types of seemingly contradictory causal influences ceases to be problematic once one utilises the critical framework of strong structuration in this manner. With respect to *A Doll's House* this includes drawing from the insights of those authors discussed above who have stressed the need for a more developed – relational, networked, stretching away in time and space – conception of the agent's context, in order to emphasise Nora's limited, variable, power in relation to it, and to investigating her own grasp of it – always finite, often hazy, and elementally corrigible.

The dynamics of the narrative's resolution happen, to a large extent, 'behind the back' and 'beyond the control' of Nora, the agent-in-focus. The outcome for Nora of her act of forgery remains suspended in time, its power to affect her own circumstances remaining latent for several years. The processes in which her action continues to produce subsequent effects – its consequences no longer hers to determine – are played out by other agents within the context of action. These are agents linked together in particular social networks of position-practices. These other agents, playing contributory and essential parts in producing the outcome, neither know what the outcome will be nor have the power to control many of the other parts of that process. Nora's fate is in large part decided by the frames of meaning and situated actions of these others engaged in overlapping and articulating legal, work, economic, family, patriarchal and love relations of interdependence with each other. The impact of these relations are variable for differently situated actors whilst also they shift and vary over time.

Helmer, who was for many years a lawyer struggling to make ends meet, has procured a position as a Bank Manager, suggesting an end to the family's long-standing worries about money. The man responsible for the loan to Nora, Krogstad, himself previously a lawyer, turning to money lending some years ago when he had fallen into disgrace after he had forged a document, has since been attempting to re-establish his respectability with employment at the Bank as the first step. It transpires that Helmer's good fortune is Krogstad's misfortune as he is sacked from his position. Helmer could not forgive Krogstad for two things. His reaction to both these two things serves to reinforce what we have been learning about Torvald's embedded character dispositions and personality traits, whilst also being a clear example of how an agent in a position of hierarchical power has the ability to impose an external structure of particular norms on a third person or, in this case, the sanctions associated with transgressing these norms. The first unforgivable thing about Krogstad – related to the fact that the two men had been childhood friends – was that he was a 'tactless oaf' who used Torvald's first name 'even now, even when we're in company. Thinks it's quite in order to stroll up any time he feels like it – "Hey, Torvald, Torvald ..." Highly embarrassing. It would make my position in the Bank impossible' (pp. 49–50). But, also, Helmer can't forgive Krogstad his past misdemeanour, his forgery, saying that such people make him feel physically ill:

> Imagine someone like that. Lies, hypocrisy, tricking everyone in sight, his family, his wife, his children. That's the worst thing of all, the children ... An atmosphere like that, a stench of lies and deceit, poisons the whole household (p. 39).

Krogstad subsequently visits Nora, and produces the contract ostensibly signed by Nora's father but reveals that he knows about the forgery as he has discovered that the signature is dated three days after the death of the man whose signature it was supposed to be. Krogstad makes it clear that he would be prepared to use this evidence if Nora does not help him, he would be prepared to use the courts, to invoke the latent causal force of the law. He insists that Nora use her influence with Helmer to help him reclaim his job. In fear Nora tries to do this but is brought up against the intractability of her husband's fastidious dispositions. She is trapped, constrained by a reconfiguration of position-practices and latent structures that are beyond her reach. The outcome of this process is that Krogstad sends a letter to Helmer revealing everything.

Whilst the storm clouds of the past, present and future actions of others are gathering, *we are aware* (from the point of view of spectators, analogous to the point of view of the social researcher in the model of agent's context analysis) that until the late point at which she has things spelt out to her directly and unequivocally, *Nora remained unaware* of the immanent dangers contained within these external processes of structuration. The painfully finite, socially influenced and personally inflected, quality of her knowledgeability of these external possibilities is expressed with ironic eloquence in Act One. She converses with a family friend after learning that Krogstad works for the Bank, and in the context of envisaging that all the worries and anxieties about the debt and the schedule of payments that she has had to keep secret all these years are now at an end. She imagines a reversal of fortunes, a reversal of power, whose simplicity of profile reveals more about the limitations of her own internal structures than it does about the tendencies implicit in the external processes of structuration:

> What do I care about silly old society? I'm laughing about something else. Dr Rank, it's true, isn't it? Everyone who works at the Bank has to answer to Torvald now? ... Torvald has power over so many people (p. 22).

In a twist to the plot, the actions of a further agent within the web of interdependencies, those of Kristine Linde, also produce an intermediate outcome that continues subsequently to affect the whole causal sequence (these are actions that are, again, beyond Nora's reach). This intermediate outcome is that the letter does in fact come to be read by Helmer. At a crucial stage in the unravelling of the causal process, the recently widowed Kristine, who has rekindled an ancient love affair with Krogstad, dissuades him from asking Helmer to return the letter unopened. She does this because witnessing what she has in that household over the course of the previous day, she is convinced that there should be no more lies, tricks, they must understand each other' (p. 77). Mrs Linde's actions in halting the intrigue that would have prevented the letter from reaching Helmer also help to bring about, in turn and at a distance, the subsequent effect of this letter – Helmer's cowardly and self-interested reaction – simply because he would not have had a letter to react to without her intervention with Krogstad.

In one more turn of the structuration cycle, that bit further away in time from the initial event, Kristine's intervention was clearly also a necessary prior condition for Nora's own agent's conduct response to Helmer's emotional reaction. Nora's perception of the external process that is Helmer's cowardice astounds her, leaving her numb and momentarily dazed. Her numbness, however, quickly combines with a deep sense of anger at the betrayal of the idea of himself that Helmer had enunciated to her throughout their marriage. The whole woven fabric of her world-view begins first to unravel and then to weave itself anew as her general-dispositions are transformed as a direct response to the actions she has just witnessed. She begins to understand that Torvald is not at all the man he professes to be, the man who would give his 'heart's blood', his life, for her if she was ever in any danger (pp. 56, 87), the man who was 'always right' (p. 81), who would 'spread his wings' to shelter the little dove she was, keeping her safe from the claws of the hawk (p. 92). For as long as she believed the myths and fables of Torvald's own self-depiction, the less dignified and appealing aspects of his character had been experienced without question as indivisible parts of a whole held in adoration. Nora's loyal commitment to Torvald was total. When the foundations of her belief were undermined, the whole set of significations, values and emotions that informed her predispositions towards him also had to be rebuilt. Instead of continuing to play her role as the passive woman-child who exists to perform for her husband, she resolves to find the space to think things out for herself, to educate herself, to find her own answers (p. 96).

Both Helmer's craven reaction to the letter and Mrs Linde's action towards Helmer through Krogstad, can be seen in terms of independent causal constituents of Nora's predicament. This is not, of course, to say that their effect on her has nothing to do with her own dispositions and reaction. As we have seen, their ultimate causal contribution has much to do with her active, critically reflective, and emotionally fuelled response. Rather, it is to say that, as an agent *in situ*, she had no control over either of these external processes. These independent constituents are the prior causal grounds for the events that provide the external basis for Nora's immediate perceptions. Through this causal role they play an indispensable part in the consequent transformation of her general-dispositional frame, In turn, there is little in the routines and relationships of her present life that she now sees in the same way as she did at the start of the play. The change in dispositional frame means that she now sees the immediate conjuncture in an entirely different light. There is a complex process here in which all four aspects of the quadripartite nature of structuration are involved in successive cycles. Each aspect, in each cycle, involves both hermeneutic and structural moments in interplay with each other. One can see, focusing on Nora's own experience, that it is a process in which, firstly, changes in independent external structures have an impact such that familiar conjuncturally-specific structures are perceived anew within the agent. There is a revision in the understanding of already existing structures, some of these previously latent as in the case of Torvald's character dispositions. In turn, and again in conjunction with agency, the interpretation or re-interpretation of these conjuncturally-specific internal structures then have their own impact upon the whole general-dispositional frame. The change in this frame entails a phenomenological reconfiguration and re-evaluation of Nora's whole way of life, on a plurality of conjuncturally-specific clusters, way beyond those involved in the immediate events. The decisive outcome is the effect that this reconfiguration has on Nora's immediate conduct. That is, her decision to 'desert' Helmer and the children, to find the space to grow beyond the doll's house, as the only way to serve her own 'sacred obligations'. Subsequently, this is a decision that will clearly have its own impact upon the nature, relations and lived experience of the external structural cluster that is the rest of the Helmer family. This is, in Archer's terms, 'structural elaboration' with a very human face.

It is the reconfiguration and re-evaluation of her hierarchy of priorities that also allows leaving the 'Doll's House' to become a 'feasible option' for Nora. Previously, her intense and unquestioned commitment to everything the Doll's House stood for meant that she experienced all external provocations to protect it, and her life within it, as irresistible causal forces. With the subversive, wrenching, realignment of her world-view, many of the causal forces that once had this irresistible power to influence her actions now no longer have that causal efficacy. She now feels it possible not to live in fear of Torvald's displeasure, of transgressing his patriarchal, constricting and pompous norms of propriety. Her liberation, though, is not without acute pain, as in freeing herself from her marital and legal obligations towards Helmer she also relinquishes her right to be a mother to her children.

We see here, in detail and with a hermeneutic sensitivity, how nuanced aspects of the separate position-practice domains of law, banking, economics, medicine, and friendship are all involved, in varying ways, in the constitution of the general-dispositions, conjuncturally-specific structures and position-practices of the family. We see, also, how the discourses of patriarchy, love, gender, trust, honour, pride and situational propriety jostle and intermingle

with each other within the general-dispositional frames of Ibsen's protagonists, influencing in various ways their conduct and interactions. All of these
strands are interwoven in a narrative of structuration processes that, in
various measures, are constraining, empowering, and influencing, that are
partly controlled and partly beyond control, that are partly known and partly
unknown, partly expected and predictable, partly mercurial, unexpected and
deranging. They are structuration processes that provide Nora both with her
fate and her choice.[5]

Conclusion

Six Key Themes of Strong Structuration

In the Introduction I wrote about the distinctive contribution that structuration theory can make to social theory. From the subsequent chapters six key interconnecting themes have emerged. Their combination gives strong structuration its unique capacity to illuminate some of the most central issues of social life. These six themes are:

1. *The distinction between ontology-in-general and ontology*-in-situ.
2. *The quadripartite cycle of structuration* based on the structural-hermeneutic core of the duality of structure. This complex cycle includes the four elements of:

   - external structures;
   - internal structures;
   - active agency;
   - and outcomes of actions.

   There is a further key distinction within internal structures between the conjuncturally-specific and the general-dispositional.

3. *Systematic attention to epistemology and methodology.* This is in contrast to structuration theory's previous overly exclusive emphasis on ontology. Here epistemology and methodology are always attended to in tandem with issues of ontology. There is a foregrounding of:

   - the nature of the question or problem-at-hand;
   - appropriate forms of methodological bracketing;
   - distinctions between methodological steps in the research process; and
   - the specific combinations of all the above in composite forms of research (see chapter 4, pp. 120–7).

4. *The meso-level of ontological abstraction.* This is the meso-level of ontology between the abstract, philosophical level of ontology and the *in-situ*, ontic level. This is elaborated in terms of the possibility of conceptualising, at a meso-level of abstraction, a range of variations in abstract ontological concepts as they manifest themselves in specific empirical circumstances (see chapter 3, pp. 76–81).

5. *The meso-level of ontological scale.* This is the meso-level of ontology at the level of temporal and spatial scale. It rests between a focus on

individual agents at one end of the spectrum and on the large forces of history and 'conventional' social structures at the other. It is marked conceptually by the notion of position-practice relations (see chapter 3, pp. 81–4).

6. *The conceptualisation of 'independent causal forces' and 'irresistible causal forces'* (see chapter 3, pp. 109–15). The latter of these two notions, that of 'irresistible causal forces', builds upon the distinctions between external structures, internal structures, and active agency. It represents an avenue between the extreme dichotomies of voluntarism and determinism that Giddens's abstract rendering of agent's 'ability to do otherwise' failed to transcend. Central to the idea of irresistible forces are the interconnecting phenomenological notions of:

- a horizon of action with respect to the actions-in-hand; and
- a hierarchy of purposes or ordering of concerns with respect to the conjuncture.

These carry within them the weight of past and present social influences. On their basis the agent-in-focus often believes that she cannot resist perceived external pressures and injunctions without forfeiting core goals and ideals. Her experienced 'ability to do otherwise' is thus often much more highly circumscribed than an abstract treatment would suggest.

The major part of this book has been taken up with delineating, expanding, developing and illustrating the tenets of a stronger structuration theory. There is still much more left to do, however, and many valuable contributions to the tradition that I have not had the space to do justice to. Thus, although I have drawn attention – often by drawing on the interventions of other critics – to many aspects of Giddens's original formulation of structuration theory that were left under-developed, and hence in need of greater elaboration, there are still many areas that I have left untouched. Also, probably all the conceptual and methodological developments and innovations that have been touched upon in the book could themselves be further elaborated and refined, and would benefit from being so. Such refinements could emanate from research at the relatively abstract and philosophical level or at the *in-situ* level with respect to a particular case or object of study. I am particularly aware, to take just one example, that structuration theory's power and vitality would be much enhanced by a more extensive and systematic integration of the emotions into the model presented here. And it is also clear that there are many existing contributions to structuration that I have not been able to integrate into the present synthesis. Such studies include: Chris Shilling and Philip Mellor's work on structuration theory, embodiment and sensuality (2001; also see Shilling, 1999); Chris Bryant's extension of Giddens's notion of a dialogical model of the practical implications of sociology (Bryant, 1991); Sydow and Windeler's theorisation of inter-firm networks (1997); Kenneth H. Tucker's imaginative essay on structuration's relationship to play and aesthetics and cultural memory (1993/ 1997); the work of Orlikowski and her co-authors on structuration, technology and communication (for example, Orlikowski, 1992; Orlikowski and Yates, 1994) and both recent and more longstanding contributions to an exploration of the relationship between structuration theory and psycho-analysis (see Wilmott, 1986 and Groarke, 2002). There are also some significant studies inspired by Giddens's work as a whole that would be likely to repay close analysis of their status in terms of non-reductionism, abstract structuration, or strong structuration, or a combination of the three. One such study is McNally and Wheale's analysis of environmental and medical bioethics in late modernity (2001), judged by Chris Bryant and David Jary to be 'perhaps the most remarkable use of Giddens's 1990s writing' (2001b, p. 55). It would be instructive to determine the extent to which, and the ways in which, this study does and doesn't integrate the hermeneutic-structural core of structuration into its analysis.

The strong structuration synthesis that has been outlined thus far should therefore be seen as preliminary groundwork. I hope that those writers who have recently made gestures towards post-structuration, arguing that structuration theory has had its day, will be convinced that their concerns can be integrated into a strong structuration which continues to argue for the power of duality alongside a concern with dualism. My view is that structuration theory is still at the beginning of its career. I believe that it would be wasteful in the extreme if structuration theory's most productive days, as a theoretical approach and as a research programme, are not yet still to come.

The Normative Commitment of Structuration Theory

The commitment to the hermeneutic and phenomenological dimensions within the duality of structure is motivated by a strong normative commitment and it is worth making this explicit. This motivation involves a determination to make respect for the intrinsic value of human agents count for something in the way that social theory is done. This respect means cultivating an openness and sensitivity to the many ways in which situated human beings see their world, and to the social and cultural circumstances that have contributed to these ways of seeing. The respect at the heart of structuration's normative commitment encourages a desire to understand both the common humanity and the cultural differences within others. It encourages a reflex questioning of simple stereotypes and typifications, and an investigative commitment to reveal and to communicate the texture of cultural complexity. The hermeneutic revelation of this complexity is never, for structuration theory, the final word. Respect for the lived phenomenology and experience of an *in-situ* actor does not mean that her beliefs, opinions and judgments are epistemologically or morally incorrigible, beyond question. On the contrary, an agent's phenomenological perception of context will always be open to critique by structuration theorists on the basis of: their appreciation of the duality of structure within that agent; a sophisticated analysis of a context that may escape the agent-*in-situ*; and the relatively autonomous level of moral argument itself (see below, p. 196).

It is nevertheless essential that the *in-situ* agent's understanding of the world is never diminished or dismissed, *a priori*, as of no importance to a fully human understanding of what goes on. For this is both disrespectful and hubristic. Whilst causal and moral considerations will always go beyond the hermeneutics of a particular *in-situ* agent, or group of agents, one should never presume that one understands enough, from the start, about the ways in which agents apprehend the world, and about how they judge that world in normative terms. Such presumptuousness should be avoided just as much when we are dealing with those whom we believe have committed evil, perhaps continue to do so, as it should when victims are the subjects of study. One shouldn't be frightened off this road by the censor's warning that too much understanding will lead ineluctably to too much forgiveness. Rather, the deeper the understanding, the more opportunities there will be for clarifying the causal processes involved. The clearer these processes then the greater the possibility that moral judgments about them will be informed ones. And finally, the more we have of all of these then, *ceteris paribus*, the greater the possibility of desirable preventive or reparative practical intervention in the world.

In the course of the book I have linked respect for, and sensitivity to, others to C. Wright Mills' 'sociological imagination'. Like Mills, I have argued, that adherents of structuration are also keen to emphasise structures as well as the experiences of lives lived. The affinity is not only a matter of straightforward inheritance, however, for structuration is able to reinvigorate the sociological imagination by extending and deepening key aspects of Wright Mills' original conception. There is still the emphasis on lives lived at the intersection of large historical forces and social structures, but now these are joined by the fruits of more sophisticated and penetrating insights into what these intersections involve.

Armed with its panoply of concepts, ranges and potential alliances of approach, structuration has great potential. It can, to paraphrase Bourdieu, focus in on any set of surface appearances and make our understanding of them richer and more meaningful by elaborating upon the structures and agents involved and placing them in relevant networks of social and historical relations. This potential has been illustrated in the present volume by many examples pulled from studies directly informed by structuration theory and from those that can be fruitfully articulated with it. The examples show precisely that structuration can take us beyond surface appearances to provide social and historical depth, relational complexity, and a critical humanism to what would otherwise be superficially apprehended instances cut adrift from the antecedents, structural-hermeneutic complexes and consequences that can provide them with substantial meaning. The cases have included:

- Tony Spybey's account of the owners, managers and workforce of a leading Yorkshire based company in the British wool-textile industry in the late 1970s and early 1980s.
- Joan Scott's analysis of the discourses of the female Parisian garment workers of 1848.
- Travis Kong's analysis of young gay men in 1990s Hong Kong.
- the struggles of Paula Spencer to live in the shadow of an abusive husband in Roddy Doyle's demotic Irish novel, *The Woman who Walked into Doors*.
- Ewa Morawska's detailed study of the transformation of rural Eastern European Jews into the small-town American Jews of Johnstown, Pennsylvania, 1890–1940.
- Eamonn Carrabine's study of dominant alignments and experiences in a Manchester prison, 1965–1990.
- the framing perspectives on the lives of eighteenth century actors as diverse as Archbishop Lomenic de Brienne, Louis XVI, and Saint Just in Michael Mann's interweaving of the primary sources of continuity and change during the French Revolution.
- Ibsen's tragic *dramatis personae* from *A Doll's House*, written in 1879 for a predominantly middle-class Norwegian audience on the eve of a massively transformative era of rapid industrialisation.
- and my own account of personalities and interactions caught in the web of the international monetary system in the Bretton Woods era, including the shapshot of Harold Wilson and Lyndon Baines Johnson engaged in conversation at the 1960s Berlin funeral of one of the great post-war statesmen, Konrad Adenauer.

Structuration's constituents, including all the various strands of influence on the abstract-philosophical approach of Giddens and then the additional influences and strands brought to it by the various amendments, developments and empirical applications synthesised in strong structuration, are clearly inter-disciplinary. Its roots are in sociology but its final form is a rich hybrid of social and cultural theory reaching out this way and that to an extensive range of disciplines. It has been implicit in what I have argued throughout that this inter-disciplinarity can only be positive. It is the question at hand and/or the object of study that should determine the relevant conceptual, theoretical and methodological tools and relevant evidence, rather than a rigid and sterile commitment to the purity of a particular discipline (cf. Sayer, 2000b).[1]

This point has a close affinity with another argument made through the book, that structuration theory should understand not only its distinctiveness but also its limits and its consequent status as one theory amongst others. A correlative point, made explicitly in chapter 4, is that structuration should look for alliances with other theories that can help to frame, or to address more cogently, particular questions and objects of study, or particular aspects of such questions and objects. Other theories should not be dismissed too easily, as they often are, for reasons of fashion or expressiveness (cf. Rule, 1997). Nigel Thrift's combination of aspects of structuration with the work of Latour, Haraway, Law, de Certeau and others in engaging with substantive issues is a paradigmatic example of just how positive and suggestive creative syntheses along these lines can be. Thrift's work is very close in some of its emphases to the insightful formulations and insights with respect to the notions of networks, scapes, flows and fluids made by John Urry in *Sociology Beyond Societies* (2000; also see Urry, 2003). In critical comments aimed at Archer, however, Urry makes remarks suggesting an antithesis between his emphases and those of debates around structure and agency, implying that the latter are now outmoded and unable to respond to the dynamics at the heart of the new mobilities. On *prima facie* grounds it seems clear to me that notions such as fluids and flows help to capture much about mobilities *per se* that structure and agency would struggle to match. However, it also seems very clear that many objects of study and key questions related to mobilities – such as those dealing with constraints and possibilities, regulation and control, intractability and malleability, and to taken-for-grantedness and critical distance – would benefit greatly from also drawing upon the conceptual and methodological fruits of structuration. There is no exclusivity here and sociology will not be strengthened in the long run by too quick and easy a predilection to throw out the old as we bring in the new.

Just as inter-disciplinarity and theoretical alliances can enrich structuration and hence the sociological imagination, so too can the sociological imagination enrich what Martha Nussbaum in *Cultivating Humanity* (1997) has called the 'civic imagination'. This I interpret as an analytically distinguishable sphere encompassing the general understandings, sensibilities and normative ideals inhabiting the broader civil society and political spheres. The sociological imagination should feed into this sphere, informing it and raising the quality of social understanding within it, as much in terms of general sensibilities, orientations and intuitive methodologies for grasping the social as in terms of specific facts about particular scenarios. The information age has provided us with the latter in abundance; the quality of the former could certainly be much greater, much more sophisticated. The sociological imagination, however, will never provide all of the material for the civic imagination, even as the latter relates to issues at the heart of human lives at the junction with history and social structure. There are many areas that social theory and social science will always find hard to reach. This is true in a particular way at the *in-situ* level, where methodological, practical and ethical exigencies will often prevent the in-depth or experimental exploration of dimensions of social life that can be provided by the theory and practice of the theatre, film, the fine arts or literature, amongst others. It is important to be aware of this and to look to these other sources to complement, to inform and, at times, to inspire the role of the sociological imagination. I would place in this bracket the use I have made here of the work of Ibsen's *A Doll's House* and Doyle's *The Woman who Walked into Doors*.

The Politics of Structuration Theory

I would like to conclude with a few words about the politics of structuration theory. It has been famously argued by Richard Kilminster that Giddens's conception of the agent in structuration theory dovetails remarkably smoothly with the dominant post-nineteenth-century brand of liberalism. This was a liberalism that resonated powerfully with individuals freed from traditional *gemeinshaftlich* communities and thrown into complex urban milieux traversed by countless networks of interdependencies that were now more impersonal, anonymous. It was a liberalism with politics underpinned by an ontology of the individual 'seen as the unique, bounded and dynamic center of self-activity, set against arbitrary power in the political realm and against "society" in general' (Kilminster, 1991, p. 79; see also Loyal, 2003). Kilminster sees much of this reproduced in Giddens's conception of the actor and in the plea to recognise the dignity of these actors. This argument clearly has some force, but it needs also to be set against the diffuse societal-influences within the agent derived from the external structures of signification, domination and legitimation. This societally embedded dimension is consolidated when the latter emphases are explicitly linked not only to the *a fronte* consciousness of the conjuncturally-specific but also to the general-dispositions accruing slowly, *a tergo*, over the years. These are dispositions that harbour novel and hybrid, but nonetheless enduring, types of social solidarity, community, intimacy and commitment that survive and transmute in the context of the new urban divisions of labour and conditions of life.

This means that if strong structuration has a natural political correlate then it will be an appropriately messy one in which liberalism, community, and respect for the hermeneutic frames of different others will necessarily jostle with each other in complicated struggles. The sense of commitments to others and of the exigencies of co-existing with others in complex interdependencies mean that strong structuration's agents will almost inevitably be aware of the necessary limits to freedom that such commitments and connections demand of them. This is not to say that these lay agents will always move from the 'is' to the 'ought', that they will feel that these *de facto* demands are also legitimate at the level of principled normative commitment. One can experience all sorts of extra-individual pressures, constraints and demands on one's time, energy and concern as impositions. These pressures may be embedded in the normative expectations of others that would have the power and the inclination to impose sanctions on the agent-in-focus if she ignored their expectations. In terms of ideals, the agent-in-focus may well disapprove of these normative expectations of others, even as she pragmatically fulfills them. Ideally, she could well wish for a state of affairs in which she had more freedom and autonomy, and she could feel that this would be an ethically superior state of affairs. The *de facto* normative level is experienced here as *force majeure*. On the other hand, the agents conceptualised by strong structuration might well believe that many of the demands made upon them, and their freedom, by others are in fact normatively legitimate. The *de facto* relation between the normative expectations of others and the ethical principles of the agent-in-focus is an open, empirical, question that will vary across circumstances. Strong structuration provides a sophisticated basis from which to begin investigation into a plurality of different sets of such *in-situ* circumstances. The exact relevance of political-ethical principles drawn from either liberalism, communitarianism or multi-culturalism to the stances taken by agents in any one of these sets of circumstances cannot be decided in abstraction from the analysis of circumstances themselves, and from moral argument with respect to those circumstances.

It is important to keep a critical distance between two broad types of analysis. Firstly, there are the ontological, causal and social levels of analysis, levels that should embrace recognition of the *de facto* normative commitments, principles, deliberations and frustrations of situated actors. Secondly, there is the specific level of political and moral deliberations and argument, on the part of theorists, about how those situated actors 'ought' to behave.

Thus, for example, it is important to recognise that the argument that causal influences should still be thought of as irresistible even when they are partly produced by an agent's hierarchy of priorities within her general-dispositions (such that many of Johnstown's Jews felt it was impossible to resist altering some of the rituals of Sabbath observance or to openly register as Democrats – see chapter 5) is a rendering of the first level of analysis. Lay versions of such assessments often play their part within the pragmatic calculations of political leaders (perhaps of Democrat politicians in Johnstown) that it would be difficult to alter such a hierarchy. Such assessments need to be sharply distinguished, however, from ethical judgements on the part of the theorist that this or that hierarchy of priorities is acceptable, morally justified. Concrete moral judgements, where they are made, would ideally embrace a relatively autonomous form of reasoning based on moral and political philosophy, but one that is integrated with a rigorous analysis of how things actually exist at present, based on the best strictures of social theory. However, it is, as yet, a distant goal for social theory and moral and political philosophy to successfully join forces in this way. This is nevertheless a goal worth struggling towards (cf. Bernstein, 1989, pp. 32–3).

These comments on the relative political indeterminacy of structuration theory should be added to what I have already argued about the difference between strong structuration theory and non-reductionist pluralism. The primary influence at the theoretical level on Giddens's writings on politics from the 1990s onwards has been his commitment to non-reductionist pluralism. Given this it would be very careless to simply read what he says explicitly about politics in these writings and then to interpret this as the politics of structuration theory. Even less could one assume this to be the politics of strong structuration. Having said this, I find that my own structuration informed sensibilities do have at least an elective affinity with central aspects of Giddens's 1990s writings from *Modernity and its Consequences* and *Beyond Left and Right* onwards. The key notion informing this sense of affinity is that of 'utopian realism', an evocative phrase carrying the sensibility that utopian ideals should be balanced with realism. This includes a restatement for contemporary times of the Marxian principle that 'avenues for desired social change will have little practical impact if they are not connected to institutionally immanent possibilities' (Giddens, 1990, p. 155). 'Utopian realism' thus combines an anti-voluntarism with a commitment to imagination. In doing so it raises issues of great significance. However, when used at the level of pluralistic non-reductionism, and informed at best only by the abstract level of structuration, it is no more than a vague and highly indeterminate catch-phrase. It could become more than this, however, if the broad schemas of modernity and politics were to be subjected to the greater rigour, precision critical penetration and substantive bite of strong structuration. A utopian realism re-interpreted on the basis of strong structuration would truly mean something. It would be understood as an injunction to combine together: an informed and sympathetic critical humanism; a hard-headed, systematic, *in-situ* realism about what can and can't be done; and an idealistic, imaginative, creativity set to work on conceiving the other, better, things that it might just be possible to do.

Notes

Introduction: Structuration Theory

1. For reviews of this material and for specific references see Bryant, 1999; Bryant and Jary, 2001b, pp. 43–61, and the four volume collection edited by Bryant and Jary, 1997.
2. See Bryant and Jary, 2001a, and see Giddens and Pierson, 1998.
3. Comments made as one of a panel of speakers in the Old Theatre of the LSE in an event to mark the publication of Chris Bryant and David Jary's collection *The Contemporary Giddens* (29 May 2001).
4. See the further reading section at the end of the book.

1 Giddens's Structuration Theory and its Influences

1. If resources, as defined in the first case, were instantiated in action in the second case then they would also have to have an existence as prior potential in that case. This would make the definition of structure in the second case inadequate and misleading.
2. These are issues that Giddens can be forgiven for ignoring, certainly in his early writings, as the works which have done most to draw attention to their theoretical significance emerged during the 1980s and 90s. See, for example, Callon and Latour, 1981; Callon, 1986 and Latour, 1986; 1993; Haraway, 1992, and the review in Thrift, 1996, pp. 23–9.
3. Things are further complicated, of course, by the consideration of technologically manufactured parts that become part of the human body itself, from prosthetics to microchip implants.
4. For other illustrative examples of the mediating significance of hermeneutic frames of meaning see Stones, 1988, chapter 6, 1991, 1996, chapter 2, and 2002a.
5. An additional discerning observation made by Urry is that Giddens tends to concentrate upon the structural effects of temporal and spatial relations upon human action at the expense of an emphasis on their production and their symbolisation (see Urry, 1991, p. 170).
6. For an elaboration of the distinction between internal and external structures see chapter 3.
7. For the ways in which Giddens does employ structuration theory, albeit at a relatively abstract and generalising level, in some of his later work see Stones, 2004a, cf. Stones, 1996, chapter 4.

2   *Critics of Structuration: Friends or Foes?*

1. See also Crothers, 2003, on post-structuration.
2. This account of Archer's critique draws on my article 'Refusing the Realism-Structuration Divide', *European Journal of Social Theory* 4 (2), 2001, pp. 177–97.
3. See Craib (1992), Thompson (1989) and Layder (1981).
4. Mouzelis is here using a term coined by Habermas where the 'natural/performative' attitude is contrasted with the 'hypothetical-reflective' one. See J. Habermas, 1984, pp. 80–1 and 122–3.
5. This is a dimension of analysis that falls within the scope of the form of methodological bracketing that I have labelled 'agent's context analysis' which will be discussed in chapter 4.
6. Mouzelis uses the terms 'paradigmatic duality' and 'paradigmatic dualism' to denote, respectively, the habitual 'natural/performative' attitude and the 'hypothetical/reflective' one with greater critical distance. Consistent with Giddens's usage, I wish to retain the notion of duality to refer to all types of the duality of structure and agency.
7. By 'macro actors' Mouzelis means 'agents (individual or collective) whose decisions "stretch" widely in time and space' (1991, p. 45 and pp. 106–7).
8. More precisely it refers, at least in part, to external structures. It can also refer to aspects of the agent's own self that he or she cannot alter either at all or within a specific time period.
9. When and whether it is useful to divide them up like this into two or three different types of constraint will depend entirely on the particular question or problem to be addressed at any one time. My own inclination when dealing with questions about social relations is to treat material and social aspects of the external context as part and parcel of each other – as mutual constituents of the external structures and structuration processes – unless there is an overriding reason for not doing so.
10. In *Practical Sociology* (1995, p. 98) Bryant makes some parallel points emphasising that a commitment to realism, in this general sense, is logically entailed by structuration theory's adherence to structures as enabling and constraining.
11. The notion of 'emergent properties' raises a whole series of points about the precise nature of 'emergence' in the social sciences as opposed to the natural sciences, and it would take me too far off track to go into really sufficient detail in the present context. Suffice to say that I believe that the commitment to a conception of structure such as the one I argue for here is shared by both realist social theory and structuration theory and clearly requires some conception or other of emergence. Hence, I do not agree with Anthony King's 'individualist' critique of Archer's commitment to emergence (King, 1999, pp. 199–227). With Archer I would want to argue that the structural context of action for any particular individual or collective actor has, under certain descriptions, its own ontological autonomy, pre-existence and causal power. Archer would not want to dispute King's point that the social context of action includes individuals, but I believe she would want to argue, *pace* King, both that this context cannot be 'reduced' to individuals (that is, there are emergent physical, architectural, temporal-spatial, organisational, and textual – including legal and accounting

texts – legacies of past actions) and that, even if it could be reduced to individuals (which it can't) then it would still have an ontological autonomy, pre-existence and causal efficacy that could be distinguished from the actions of the particular actors in focus at times 2 and 3. None of this is undermined by King's rather different argument (plausible for many cases, but extremely indeterminate) about the vulnerability of any structural constraint (such as the distribution of wealth in society) to transformation if 'everyone or vast numbers of individuals' altered their interpretations and their actions (King, 1999, p. 222). It seems to me that a sufficiently sophisticated notion of emergence can also withstand the criticisms made of certain conceptions of emergence by Ira Cohen (1990, pp. 42–3) who emphasises praxis and the disappearance and reappearance of social properties as they are intermittently drawn upon by agents. There are no emergent social properties, he argues, that 'do not disappear and reappear because they exist above and beyond the reproduced seriality of social processes' (Cohen, 1990, p. 42). I would argue that the actuality of disappearance and reappearance does not rule out emergence. Consciousness of memories, for example, can disappear and reappear but the memory traces that give rise to these – which are the emergent properties of past experiences – must, as I have argued, have a virtual (pre-)existence for agents to be able to draw on them (voluntarily or involuntarily). Memory traces, in turn, are clearly necessary preconditions for the reproduction of the kinds of position-practice relations that Cohen describes, and so are the many infrastructural and material constituents of these relations. All of these are emergent properties of past practices.

12. This is when understood at the ontological/ontic level. Clearly there may be epistemological and methodological difficulties that prevent or inhibit the identification of particular position-practice relations.

13. Mouzelis uses the term syntagmatic dualism to refer to 'situations where a subject's participation in a game does not seriously affect its outcome' whereas syntagmatic duality 'refers to situations where the opposite is true' (Mouzelis, 1995, p. 156; see also 1991, pp. 37–9).

14. On this point see Archer's critique of Sewell's unnecessary and misleading assignment of 'publicly fixed codifications of rules' to the realm of resources (Sewell, 1992, p. 8; Archer, 1995, pp. 109–10).

15. Sewell writes that it is surprising that Giddens does not seems to have considered the point. In fact, Giddens does seem to have recognised a tension here but without satisfactorily addressing it (see chapter 1, p. 18); Giddens, 1984, p. 377).

16. For other aspects of the virtual see chapter 1, pp. 21–4.

3　Strong Structuration 1: Ontology

1. The notion of ontology-in-general as it is used here encompasses both 'philosophical ontology' and social 'scientific ontology' as this is distinguished, for example, in the realist literature (see Outhwaite, 1987, p. 46). Both are to be distinguished from the ontic level, although the distinction is useful precisely because an ability to make sense of the ontic is greatly enhanced through an appreciation of its ontological dimensions, hence ontology-*in-situ*.

2. The works of both Simmel and Merton are full of sociological concepts that could be developed in this manner. There is much in Simmel's work on specific forms that is relevant here (Simmel in Wolff [ed.] 1950) whilst Merton's analysis of reference groups contains many categories defined by variability in terms of degrees, extents, durations, relative characteristics, and so on (see Merton, 'Continuities in the Theory of Reference Groups and Social Structure', in Merton, 1957b, pages 281–386).

3. Also see Horne, 1996, for an interesting critical engagement with figuration studies from a structurationist perspective.

4. For the sake of fluency I will often use a variety of short-hand terms referring to these different kinds of internal structures. Thus, I will refer to 'specific' or 'conjunctural' internal structures when referring to *conjuncturally-specific internal structures*. I will also refer to 'general' or 'dispositional' internal structures or to habitus when referring to *general dispositional internal structures*.

5. At other times, both Crossley (2001, p. 110) and Jeffrey Alexander (1995, pp. 128–217) agree, that Bourdieu has a tendency to *over-emphasise* this aspect of agency.

6. These usages ('positions' and 'inter-related roles') closely parallel Merton's terminology of 'status' for teacher, for example, and 'role relationships' to indicate the link between roles associated with a given status such as teacher and the other positional agents/roles whom one is thereby brought into contact with (see chapter 1, p. 26).

7. For the classic account and critique of MacDonaldization see Ritzer, 1993.

8. The following account of the case study draws heavily on Stones, 1990, pp. 32–55.

9. 'The City' refers to the financial institutions of the City of London, and more widely to British financial institutions.

10. On 'ideal normative agreement' see Held, 1984, who draws creatively on Habermas's work to produce a typology that has clear empirical implications.

11. The term is from Rhodes, 1986, pp. 240–1, but is also entirely compatible with points made by Mouzelis with respect to hierarchies, and also to the nexus of position-practice relations.

12. Although, to take just one example, Spybey's analysis, recounted in chapter 1, should make us wary of too simple an equation of previous forms of management with a simple search for profit maximisation.

13. See Whittington, 1997/1992, p. 378, table II.

14. Archer also includes the notion of 'natural necessity' in this characterisation. I have left this aside as whilst I can see the importance of having some sort of notion of internal relations I have reservations about the way Archer uses the notion. To discuss this further in the present context would take me too far away from the central concerns of the book.

15. Archer makes a terminological distinction between actors and agents. I prefer not to do this and so have not followed Archer's conventions. I use the two words interchangeably both in general and when discussing Archer's work in particular. I don't believe this affects any of the specific things I have to say about Archer's approach.

4   *Strong Structuration 2: The Research Focus and the Wider
     Picture*

1. The phrase 'conventional notions of structure' is clearly not a precise one. It can
    embrace a variety of different notions of structure. Thompson, himself, hints
    even within the critique of Giddens that he is dealing with at least two different
    notion of 'conventional structures', one that deals with institutional practices
    and substantive distributions of options, and another one he refers to as 'social
    structure' and which seems to indicate the sort of dynamic entity captured by
    Marx in his account of the capitalist system. Ian Craib, in agreeing with
    Thompson on the need for such conventional notions, notes that three different
    conventional accounts of structures emerge quite clearly from the critical
    literature: that associated with Archer's morphogenetic approach; the 'Marxist
    notion of underlying structures that is in Bhaskar's work', and the notion of
    structure in a modified functionalism (Craib, 1992, p. 155). José Lopez and John
    Scott provide a valuable schematic overview of this whole domain in their recent
    thematic survey of different approaches to social structure within the
    sociological literature (Lopez and Scott, 2000). What I have called 'internal
    structures' is very roughly analogous to what Lopez and Scott call 'embodied
    structure', whilst the meso-level of position-practice relations within strong
    structuration fits closely with their analysis of 'relational structures'. Their
    category of 'institutional structures' should be seen as one possible dimension of
    what, following Thompson, I have called 'conventional structures'.
2. As will be evident from the discussion of question-types, there can be sub-forms
    within these two forms of bracketing (and probably other broad forms that it
    would be useful to develop) but, as far as I can see, all substantively directed
    questions incorporating duality and/or the quadripartite process of structuration
    will have at least to include one or both of these forms of bracketing.
3. Giddens himself uses the label 'strategic conduct analysis' for this bracket but, as
    I have argued elsewhere (Stones, 1996), there are good reasons for relinquishing
    the overly narrow connotations of the term 'strategic'.
4. Of course, a reverse situation will often exist, in which a participating agent may
    be aware of independent causal powers that she can't affect whilst a researcher
    remains unaware of them.
5. See Andrew Sayer, 1984, pp. 108–11 and *passim* on open systems and on
    falsification.
6. Also see the other aspects of agent's conduct outlined in chapter 3.
7. See chapter 3, pp. 109–15.
8. In outlining this fifth form of research strategy I also have in mind parallels with
    the kind of explanatory strategy associated with retroduction and open systems
    within realism. See Sayer, 1984, pp. 94–106.
9. I have in mind here the necessary methodological correlatives to the points made
    by Urry referred to in chapter 1, pp. 31–2.
10. The quotation is from *La Voix des Femmes*, 10/11 April 1848
11. For an extended engagement with Eleni Varikas's (1995) social historian's
    critique of *Gender and the Politics of History*, and an argument for 'Refusing the
    Post-structuralism–Social History Divide' that is based on the ontology of
    structuration theory see Stones, 2004b.

12. For Archer on 'situational logics' see 1995, pp. 218ff; also see Stones, 2001, pp. 190–2.
13. Cf. my *Sociological Reasoning*, 1996, pp. 106–9.

5 Case Studies in Structuration: Morawska's Insecure Prosperity and Ibsen's A Doll's House

1. Morawska's own conceptualisation of this is led astray by attempting to employ Sewell's reformulation of structuration theory as consisting of a duality of schemas and resources. I have explained in chapter 2 why I think this reformulation is unhelpful and confusing. A close look at Morawska's attempt to apply it to a complex empirical case confirms this. She places folk wisdom in the sphere of 'cultural' or 'mental schemas' whilst placing the Jews' know-how in countryside trading, familiarity with the peasant economic partners of the rural shtetls, and their strong sense and practice of communal bonds and collective responsibility upheld by religious precepts and effective social control in the realm of 'resources' (pp. 22–3). This is too simple a conceptual division to do justice to the empirical reality, for schemas are also involved in the perception and performance of resource-related practices (most practices are, in one way or another, resource-related, although clearly more or less 'purely theoretical' or contemplative practices are much less so). Schemas will often contain a phenomenology of resources within them, a phenomenology that is involved in the production and reproduction of practices. Thus, the folk wisdom that Morawska places within 'schemas' will no doubt itself be involved in orientations towards the various things she lists under resources. It is better to conceptualise structuration processes in terms of a duality of structure in which agents and their schemas are involved in each turn of the cycle. Resources, for their part, may be conceptualised separately, in terms of their bare physical distribution, movement, nature and potential, but any dynamic role they have within the structuration cycle cannot be conceptualised apart from their role within hermeneutic schemas. The kind of division that Morawska is attempting between a more general popular worldview and immediate everyday practical activities is better effected with the aid of the distinction between the general-dispositional and the conjuncturally-specific aspects of overall schemas. Even here, however, as one would expect, the distinction cuts across Morawska's resources example so that the Jews' sense of 'communal bonds and collective responsibility', and the 'religious precepts' that underpin this sense, should clearly be seen not just as having conjuncturally-specific effects but also, of course, as having a 'general-dispositional' existence of a kind that, like popular worldviews, will enter into practical social relations whilst also transcending the specifics of that particular interaction.
2. See chapter 3.
3. See chapter 1.
4. It seems to me, for example, that Archer's conception and presentation of interaction is under-developed in relation to its immanent relationship to structures, and consequently conveys, without wanting to, a sense of interaction sequences taking place in a space inadequately integrated or related to the

structural milieu within and without the agent. See, for example, Archer, 1995, pp. 165–94.

5. The children, as far as we can tell, are more completely at the mercy of a sum total of causal influences that are independent of their actions than anyone else in this causal sequence.

6 Conclusion

1. This is an argument for inter-disciplinarity. The debate about post-disciplinarity takes things one step further than this. For two different positions on this see Sayer (2000b) and McLennan (2003).

Further Reading

The literature specifically relevant to strong structuration is cited in the appropriate places within this book, including the references for the major critics of structuration in chapter 2. The classic secondary account of Giddens's version of structuration theory is Ira J. Cohen's excellent *Structuration Theory: Anthony Giddens and the Constitution of Social Life* (1989). Of the book length accounts that set out explicitly to cover the breadth of Giddens's writings, including structuration theory, Kaspersen (2000) provides a clear and concise introduction, Craib (1992) takes a more critical and reflective approach, and Tucker's account (1998) is marked by the thought-provoking connections and comparisons it makes between Giddens's later work and other theorists of modernity, democracy and public life. Christopher Pierson's interviews with Giddens (1998) provide a lively and engaging entrée into the different aspects of his thinking, whilst Bryant and Jary's recent edited collection *The Contemporary Giddens* (2001a, b, c, d) brings things up to date whilst providing a good sense of some of the continuities and the transformations in emphases and orientations over the past four decades. The extensive and meticulously presented bibliographies at the end of the latter books include sections covering the literature on 'The principles of structuration theory' (section 7, pp. 296–301) and on 'Uses of structuration theory by others' (section 9, pp. 303–11). Section 8 of Volume 4 of Bryant and Jary's four volume edited collection of articles related to the work of Giddens (1997) contains some of the best of these 'extensions and applications of structuration theory', several of which have been referred to in the present text. Steven Loyal's recent work *The Sociology of Anthony Giddens* (2003), although often more critical than I would want to be, provides a perceptive analysis of many aspects of Giddens's writing based on a close and intelligent engagement with his work. For the philosophical background relevant to structuration theory see Doyal and Harris (1986), Outhwaite (1987), and Benton and Craib (2001). Outhwaite's book is notable for its precise and systematic discussion of structuration theory's relationship to both the hermeneutic and critical realist traditions, whilst Doyal and Harris present their text explicitly as a self-conscious attempt to provide the philosophical underpinnings for Giddens's version of structuration.

Bibliography

- When making a reference within the text to articles in Bryant and Jary's edited collection *Anthony Giddens: Critical Assessments* I have cited both the original date of publication and the date of the edited collection. The date of the publication directly referred to is always placed first in the citation within the main body of the text, and in placing the item within the bibliography.
- References to English language translations cite the date of translation first followed by the date of the first publication in the original language.
- When referring to second or subsequent editions of a publication within the text I cite the date of the publication used followed by the date of the original publication.

Alexander, J. (ed.) *Neofunctionalism*. London: Sage, 1985.

Alexander, J. *Fin de Siecle Social Theory*. London: Verso, 1995.

Althusser, L. *For Marx*. London: Allen Lane, 1969/1965, trans. Ben Brewster.

Anderson, P. A Culture in Counterflow – 1. *New Left Review*, no. 180, 1990, pp. 41–78.

Archer, M. 'Morphogenesis versus structuration', *British Journal of Sociology*, vol. 33, 1982, pp. 455–83.

Archer, M. *Culture and Agency: The Place of Culture in Social Theory*. Cambridge: Cambridge University Press, 1988.

Archer, M. *Realist Social Theory: The Morphogenetic Approach*. Cambridge: Cambridge University Press, 1995.

Archer, M. Social integration and system integration: developing the distinction. *Sociology*, vol. 30, no. 4, November, 1996, pp. 679–99.

Archer, M. *Being Human: The Problem of Agency*. Cambridge: Cambridge University Press, 2000.

Archer, M. *The Internal Conversation: Mediating Between Structure and Agency*, Cambridge: Cambridge University Press, 2004

Armstrong, P. 'Engineers, management and trust', *Work, Employment and Society*, vol. 1, no. 4, 1987, pp. 421–40.

Bagguley, P., Mark-Lawson, J., Shapiro, D., Urry, J., Walby, S., and Warde, A. *Restructuring: Place, Class and Gender*. London: Sage, 1989.

Bank of England, *Bank of England Quarterly Bulletin (BEQB)*, London (various issues).

Banker, The (various issues).

Bauman, Z. Hermeneutics and modern social theory', in D. Held and J.B. Thompson (eds) *Social Theory of Modern Societies: Anthony Giddens and his Critics*. Cambridge: Cambridge University Press, 1989.

Bendelow, G and Williams, S.J. *Emotions in Social Life: Critical Themes and Contemporary Issues.* London: Routledge, 1998.

Benton, T. *The Rise and Fall of Structural Marxism: Althusser and his Influence.* London: Macmillan, 1984.

Benton, T. and Craib, I. *Philosophy of Social Science.* Basingstoke: Palgrave, 2001

Berger, P. and Luckmann, T. *The Social Construction of Reality.* Garden City, NY: Doubleday, 1966.

Bernstein, R. 'Social theory as critique', in D. Held and J.B. Thompson (eds) *Social Theory of Modern Societies: Anthony Giddens and his Critics.* Cambridge: Cambridge University Press, 1989, pp. 19–33.

Bhaskar, R. *The Possibility of Naturalism: A Philosophical Critique of the Contemporary Human Sciences.* Brighton: Harvester, 1979.

Blank, S. 'Britain: the politics of foreign economic policy, the domestic economy, and the problem of pluralist stagnation', in P. Katzenstein (ed.) *Between Power and Plenty.* Madison: University of Wisconsin Press, 1978.

Bottomore, T and Nisbet, R. (eds) *A History of Sociological Thought.* London: Heinemann, 1976.

Bourdieu, P. *Outline of a Theory of Practice.* Cambridge: Cambridge University Press, 1977/1972, trans. Richard Nice.

Bourdieu, P. *The Logic of Practice.* Cambridge: Polity Press, 1990/1980, trans. Richard Nice.

Bourdieu, P. *On Television and Journalism.* London: Pluto Press, 1998/1996, trans. Priscilla Parkhurst-Ferguson.

Bourdieu, P. 'Scattered remarks. Contribution to a symposium on Pierre Bourdieu's "Meditations Pascaliennes"', *European Journal of Social Theory,* vol. 2, no. 3, 1999, pp. 334–40.

Bourdieu, P. and Wacquant, L. J. D. *An Invitation to Reflexive Sociology.* Cambridge: Polity Press, 1992.

Brandon, H. *In the Red: The Struggle for Sterling 64/66.* London: Andre Deutsch, 1966.

Brett, E. *International Money and Capitalist Crisis: The Anatomy of Global Disintegration.* London: Heinemann, 1983.

Bryant, C. 'The dialogical model of applied sociology', in C. G. A. Bryant and D. Jary (eds) *Giddens' Theory of Structuration: A Critical Appreciation.* London, Routledge, 1991, pp. 176–200 [Reprinted in C. Bryant and D. Jary (eds) *Anthony Giddens: Critical Assessments,* vol. IV. London: Routledge, 1997, pp. 161–185]

Bryant, C. 'Sociology without philosophy? The case of Anthony Giddens' structuration theory. *Sociological Theory,* vol. 10, pp. 137–149, 1992 [Reprinted in C. Bryant and D. Jary (eds) *Anthony Giddens: Critical Assessments,* vol. I. London: Routledge, 1997, pp. 388–405].

Bryant, C. *Practical Sociology: Postempiricism and the Reconstruction of Theory and Application.* Cambridge: Polity Press, 1995.

Bryant, C. 'The uses of Giddens' structuration theory', Vienna: Institute for Advanced Studies', *Sociological Series,* no. 37, 1999.

Bryant, C. and Jary, D. (eds) *Giddens' Theory of Structuration: A Critical Appreciation.* London: Routledge, 1991.

Bryant, C. and Jary, D (eds) *Anthony Giddens: Critical Assessments,* 4 volumes. London: Routledge, 1997.

Bryant, C. and Jary, D. 'Anthony Giddens: a global social theorist', in C. Bryant and D. Jary (eds) *The Contemporary Giddens: Social Theory in a Globalizing Age*. Basingstoke: Palgrave Macmillan, 2001a, pp. 3–39.

Bryant, C. and Jary, D. 'The uses of structuration theory: a typology', in C. Bryant and D. Jary (eds) *The Contemporary Giddens: Social Theory in a Globalizing Age*. Basingstoke: Palgrave Macmillan, 2001b, pp. 43–61.

Bryant, C. and Jary, D. 'The body, self-identity and social transformation', in C. Bryant and D. Jary (eds) *The Contemporary Giddens: Social Theory in a Globalizing Age*. Basingstoke: Palgrave Macmillan, 2001c, pp. 115–29.

Bryant, C. and Jary, D. 'The reflexive Giddens; Christopher G.A. Bryant and David Jary in dialogue with Anthony Giddens', in C. Bryant and D. Jary (eds) *The Contemporary Giddens: Social Theory in a Globalizing Age*. Basingstoke: Palgrave Macmillan, 2001d, pp. 229–67.

Bryant, C. and Jary, D. 'Anthony Giddens', in G.Ritzer (ed.) *The Blackwell Companion to Major Contemporary Social Theorists*. Oxford: Blackwell, 2002, pp. 247–73.

Cairncross, A. and Eichengreen, B. *Sterling in Decline: The Devalutaions of 1931, 1949 and 1967*. Oxford: Basil Blackwell, 1983.

Callaghan, J. *Time and Chance*. London: Collins, 1987.

Callon, M. 'Some elements of a sociology of translation', in J. Law (ed.) *Power, Action and Belief. A New Sociology of Knowledge*. London, Routledge & Kegan Paul, 1986, pp. 196–232.

Callon, M. and Latour, B. 'Unscrewing the big Leviathan: how do actors macrostructure reality?', in K. Knorr-Cetina and A. V. Cicourel (eds) *Advances in Social Theory and Methodology: Toward an Integration of Macro and Micro Sociologies*. London, Routledge, 1981, pp. 277–303.

Carrabine, E. 'Discourse, governmentality and translation: towards a social theory of imprisonment', *Theoretical Criminology*, vol. 4, no. 3, 2000, pp. 309–31.

Carrabine, E. *Power, Discourse and Resistance: A Genealogy of the Strangeways Prison Riot*. Dartmouth: Ashgate, 2004.

Castle, B. *The Castle Diaries 1964–70*. London: Weidenfeld & Nicolson, 1984.

Castells, M. *The Rise of the Network Society*, volume 1 of *The Information Age: Economy, Society and Culture*. Oxford: Blackwell, 2000/1996.

Clark, J. Modgil, C. and Modgil, S. *Anthony Giddens: Consensus and Controversy*. London: Falmer Press, 1990.

Coates, D. *The Labour Party and the Struggle for Socialism*. Cambridge: Cambridge University Press, 1975.

Cohen, B. J. *The Future of Sterling as an International Currency*. London: Macmillan, 1971.

Cohen, I. J. 'Structuration theory and social praxis', in A. Giddens and J. H. Turner (eds) *Social Theory Today*. Cambridge: Polity Press, 1987, pp. 273–308.

Cohen, I. J. *Structuration Theory: Anthony Giddens and the Constitution of Social Life*. London: Macmillan, 1989.

Cohen, I. J. 'Structuration theory and social order: five issues in brief', in J. Clark, C. Modgil, and S. Modgil (eds) *Anthony Giddens: Consensus and Controversy*. London, Falmer Press, 1990, pp. 33–45.

Cohen, I. J. 'Anthony Giddens', in R. Stones (ed.) *Key Sociological Thinkers*. London: Macmillan, 1998, pp. 279–90.

Cooper, J. *A Suitable Case for Treatment: What to do About the Balance of Payments.* Harmondsworth: Penguin, 1968.

Craib, I. *Psychoanalysis and Social Theory: The Limits of Sociology.* Hemel Hempstead: Harvester, Wheatsheaf, 1989.

Craib, I. *Anthony Giddens.* London: Routledge, 1992.

Craib, I. *The Importance of Disappointment.* London: Routledge, 1994.

Crossley, N. *Intersubjectivity: The Fabric of Social Becoming.* London, Sage, 1996.

Crossley, N. *The Social Body: Habit, Identity and Desire.* London, Sage, 2001.

Crossley, N. *Making Sense of Social Movements.* Buckingham, Open University Press, 2002.

Crothers, C. 'Technical advances in general sociological theory: the potential contribution of post-structurationist sociology', *Perspectives: the American Sociological Association Theory Section Newsletter,* July 2003, pp. 3–6.

Dawson, P. *Provincial Magistrates and Revolutionary Politics in France, 1789–95.* Cambridge, Mass.: Harvard University Press, 1972.

Doyal, L. and Harris, R. *Empiricism, Explanation and Rationality: An Introduction to the Philosophy of the Social Sciences.* London: Routledge & Kegan Paul, 1986.

Doyle, R. *The Woman who Walked into Doors.* London: Vintage, 1998.

Doyle, W. *The Origins of the French Revolution.* Oxford: Clarendon Press, 1980.

Dreyfus, H. *Being-in-the-World: A Commentary on Heidegger's Being and Time, Division 1.* Cambridge, Mass.: MIT Press, 1991.

Erikson, E.H. *Childhood and Society.* London: Triad/Paladin, 1977 [original publication 1963].

Fuchs, S. 'Second thoughts on emergent interaction orders', *Sociological Theory,* vol. 7, 1989.

Furet, F. and Ozouf, J. *Reading and Writing: Literacy in France from Calvin to Jules Ferry.* Cambridge: Cambridge University Press, 1982.

Gambetta, D. 'Were They Pushed or Did They Jump?', PhD thesis, University of Cambridge, 1982.

Garfinkel, H. *Studies in Ethnomethodology,* Englewood Cliffs, NJ: Prentice Hall, 1967.

Gellner, E. *Relativism and the Social Sciences.* Cambridge: Cambridge University Press, 1985.

Giddens, A. *Capitalism and Modern Social Theory: an Analysis of the Writings of Marx, Durkheim and Max Weber.* Cambridge: Cambridge University Press, 1971.

Giddens, A. *New Rules of Sociological Method: A Positive Critique of Interpretative Sociologies.* London: Macmillan, 1976 (second edition, Cambridge: Polity Press, 1993).

Giddens, A. *Studies in Social and Political Theory.* London: Hutchinson, 1977.

Giddens, A. *Central Problems in Social Theory: Action, Structure and Contradiction in Social Analysis.* London, Macmillan, 1979.

Giddens, A. *A Contemporary Critique of Historical Materialism: vol 1: Power, Property and the State.* London: Macmillan, 1981.

Giddens, A. *Profiles and Critiques in Social Theory.* London: Macmillan, 1982.

Giddens, A. *The Constitution of Society: Outline of the Theory of Structuration.* Cambridge: Polity Press, 1984.

Giddens, A. *The Nation-State and Violence: Volume Two of A Contemporary Critique of Historical Materialism.* Cambridge: Polity Press, 1985.

Giddens, A. 'Erving Goffman as a systematic social theorist', in A Giddens, *Social Theory and Modern Sociology*. Cambridge: Polity Press, 1987, pp. 109–39.

Giddens, A. 'A reply to my critics', in D. Held and J. B. Thompson (eds) *Social Theory of Modern Societies: Anthony Giddens and His Critics*. Cambridge: Cambridge University Press, 1989, pp. 249–301.

Giddens, A. *The Consequences of Modernity*. Cambridge: Polity Press, 1990a.

Giddens, A. 'Structuration theory and sociological analysis', in J. Clark, C. Modgil, and S. Modgil (eds) *Anthony Giddens: Consensus and Controversy*. London: Falmer Press, 1990b, pp. 297–315.

Giddens, A. *Modernity and Self-Identity: Self and Society in the Late Modern Age*. Cambridge: Polity Press, 1991a.

Giddens, A. 'Structuration theory: past, present and future', in C. G. A. Bryant and D. Jary (eds) *Giddens' Theory of Structuration: A Critical Appreciation*. London: Routledge, 1991b, pp. 201–21.

Giddens, A. *The Transformation of Intimacy: Sexuality, Love and Eroticism in Modern Societies*. Cambridge: Polity Press, 1992.

Giddens, A. *Beyond Left and Right: The Future of Radical Politics*. Cambridge: Polity Press, 1994.

Giddens, A. *The Third Way: The Renewal of Social Democracy*. Cambridge: Polity Press, 1998a.

Giddens, A. and Pierson, C. *Conversations with Anthony Giddens: Making Sense of Modernity*. Cambridge: Polity Press, 1998b.

Giddens, A. *Runaway World: How Globalisation is Reshaping our Lives*. London: Profile Books, 1999.

Goffman, E. *Behaviour in Public Places: Notes on the Social Organisation of Gatherings*. Glencoe: Free Press, 1963.

Gramsci, A. *Selections from the Prison Notebooks*. London: Lawrence & Wishart, 1971.

Grant, W. *Business and Politics in Britain*. London: Macmillan, 1987.

Gregory, D. 'Space, time and politics in social theory: An interview with A. Giddens', in C. Bryant and D. Jary (eds) *Anthony Giddens: Critical Assessments*, vol. III. London: Routledge, 1997, pp. 23–35. [source: *Environment and Planning D: Society and Space*, vol. 2, 1984, pp. 123–32].

Gregson, N. 'On the (ir)relevance of structuration theory to empirical research', in D. Held and J. B. Thompson (eds) *Social Theory of Modern Societies: Anthony Giddens and His Critics*. Cambridge, Cambridge University Press, 1989, pp. 235–48.

Groarke, S. 'Psychoanalysis and structuration theory: the social logic of identity', *Sociology*, vol. 36, no. 3, 2002, pp. 555–72.

Habermas, J. *The Theory of Communicative Action, Volume One: Reason and the Rationalization of Society*. London, Heinemann, 1984/1981, trans. T. McCarthy.

Habermas, J. *The Theory of Communicative Action, Volume Two: Lifeworld and System: A Critique of Functionalist Reason*. Cambridge: Polity Press, 1987/1981, trans. T. McCarthy.

Hägerstrand, T. 'Space, time and human conditions', in A Karlqvist, *Dynamic Allocation of Urban Space*. Farnborough: Saxon House, 1975.

Hägerstrand, T. *Innovation as a Spatial Process*. Chicago: Chicago University Press, 1976.

Hall, S. 'Popular-democratic vs. authoritarian populism', in A. Hunt (ed.) *Marxism and Democracy*. London: Lawrence & Wishart, 1980, pp. 157–85.

Haraway, D. J. 'The promises of monsters: a regenerative politics for inappropriate/d others', in L. Grossberg, C. Nelson and P. Treichler (eds) *Cultural Studies*. New York: Routledge, 1992, pp. 295–337.

Held, D. 'Power and legitimacy in contemporary Britain', in McLennan, G., Held, D. and Hall, S. (eds) *State and Society in Contemporary Britain*. Cambridge: Polity Press, 1984.

Held, D., McGrew, A., Goldblatt, D. and Perraton, J. *Global Transformations: Politics, Economics and Culture*. Cambridge: Polity, 1999.

Held, D. and Thompson, J. B. (eds) *Social Theory of Modern Societies: Anthony Giddens and his Critics*. Cambridge: Cambridge University Press, 1989.

Heritage, J. *Garfinkel and Ethnomethodology*. Cambridge, Polity Press, 1984.

Hindness, B. and Hirst, P. *Mode of Production and Social Formation*. London: Macmillan, 1977.

Hirsch, F. *The Pound Sterling: A Polemic*. London: Victor Gollancz, 1965.

Horne, J. 'The sociology of Anthony Giddens, structuration theory and sport and leisure', *North American Society of the Sociology of Sport, Annual Conference, Birmingham, Alabama*, 13–16 November 1996.

Ibsen, H. *A Doll's House* London: Nick Hern Books, 1994/1879, trans. Kenneth McLeish.

Ignatieff, M. *The Needs of Strangers*, London: Chatto & Windus/Hogarth Press, 1984.

Ingham, G. *Capitalism Divided? The City and Industry in British Social Development*. London: Macmillan, 1984.

Jary, D. ' "Society as time-traveller": Giddens on historical change, historical materialism and the nation-state in world society', in C. Bryant and D. Jary (eds) *Giddens' Theory of Structuration: A Critical Appreciation*. London: Routledge, 1991, pp. 116–59.

Jary, D. and Jary, J. 'The transformations of Anthony Giddens', in C. Bryant and D. Jary (eds) *Anthony Giddens: Critical Assessments*, vol. IV. London: Routledge, 1997, pp. 137–52 [source: *Theory, Culture and Society*, vol. 12, no. 2, 1995, pp. 141–60].

Jessop, B. *The Capitalist State: Marxist Theories and Methods*. Oxford: Martin Robertson, 1982.

Jessop, B. *Nicos Poulantzas: Marxist Theory and Political Strategy*. London: Macmillan, 1985.

Jessop, B. *State Theory: Putting the Capitalist State in its Place*. Cambridge: Polity, 1990.

Kaspersen, L. B. *Anthony Giddens; An Introduction to a Social Theorist*. Oxford: Blackwell, 2000, trans. Steven Sampson (updated from original Danish edition, published by Hans Reitzels Forlag A/S, Copenhagen, 1995).

Kilminster, R. 'Structuration theory as a world-view', in C. G. A. Bryant and D. Jary (eds) *Giddens' Theory of Structuration: A Critical Appreciation*. London, Routledge, 1991, pp. 74–115.

King, A. 'Against structure: A critique of morphogenetic social theory', *The Sociological Review*, vol. 47, no. 2, 1999, pp. 199–227.

Kong, T. 'The Voices in Between: The Body Politics of Hong Kong Gay Men', PhD thesis, University of Essex, 2000.

Laclau, E. and Mouffe, C. *Hegemony and Socialist Strategy.* London: Verso, 1985.

Laing, R.D. *The Divided Self.* Harmondsworth: Penguin, 1960.

Latour, B. 'The powers of association', in J. Law (ed.) *Power, Action and Belief. A New Sociology of Knowledge.* London, Routledge & Kegan Paul, 1986, pp. 88–111.

Latour, B. *We Have Never Been Modern.* Hemel Hempstead: Harvester Wheatsheaf, 1993.

Layder, D. *Structure, Interaction and Social Theory.* London: Routledge & Kegan Paul, 1981.

Lindblom, C. E. *Politics and Markets.* New York: Basic Books, 1977.

Longstreth, F. 'The city, industry and the state', in C. Crouch (ed.) *State and Economy in Contemporary Capitalism.* London: Croom Helm, 1979.

Lopez, J. and Scott, J. *Social Structure.* Buckingham: Open University Press, 2000.

Loyal, S. *The Sociology of Anthony Giddens.* London: Pluto Press, 2003.

Lukes, S. *Power: A Radical View.* London: Macmillan. 1974.

Mann, M. *The Sources of Social Power, volume I: A History of Power from the Beginning to AD 1760.* Cambridge: Cambridge University Press, 1986.

Mann, M. *The Sources of Social Power, volume II: The Rise of Classes and Nation-States, 1760–1914.* Cambridge: Cambridge University Press, 1993.

Manning, P. *Erving Goffman and Modern Sociology.* Cambridge: Polity Press, 1992.

Massey, D. *Spatial Divisions of Labour.* London: Macmillan, 1984.

McLennan, G. 'Critical or positive theory? A comment on the status of Anthony Giddens' social theory', *Theory, Culture and Society*, vol. 2, no. 2, 1984, pp. 123–9.

McLennan, G. 'Post-Marxism and the "four sins" of modernist theorizing', *New Left Review*, vol. 218, 1996, pp. 53–74.

McLennan, G. 'Sociology's complexity', *Sociology*, vol. 37, no. 3, 2003, pp. 547–64.

McNally, R. and Wheale, P. 'Environmental and medical bioethics in late modernity: Anthony Giddens, genetic engineering and the post-modern state', in C. Bryant and D. Jary (eds) *The Contemporary Giddens: Social Theory in a Globalizing Age.* Basingstoke: Palgrave Macmillan, 2001, pp. 97–112.

Merton, R. K. 'The role-set: problems in sociological theory', *The British Journal of Sociology*, vol. 8, 1957a, pp. 106–20.

Merton, R. K. *Social Theory and Social Structure*, rev. and enl. edn. Glencoe, Ill.: Free Press, 1957b.

Merton, R. K. 'On sociological theories of the middle range', in R. Merton, *On Theoretical Sociology: Five Essays, Old and New.* New York: Free Press, 1967, pp. 39–72.

Mills, C. Wright. *The Sociological Imagination.* Harmondsworth: Pelican, 1970 (original publication 1959, Oxford University Press).

Moffitt, M. *The World's Money: International Banking from Bretton Woods to the Brink of Insolvency.* New York: Simon & Schuster, 1983.

Morawska, E. *For Bread with Butter: Lifeworlds of the East Central Europeans in Johnstown, Pennsylvania, 1890–1940.* New York: Cambridge University Press, 1985.

Morawska, E. *Insecure Prosperity: Small-Town Jews in Industrial America 1890–1940.* Princeton: Princeton University Press, 1996.

Mouzelis, N. *Back to Sociological Theory: The Construction of Social Orders.* London: Macmillan, 1991.

Mouzelis, N. *Sociological Theory: What Went Wrong? Diagnosis and Remedies.* London: Routledge, 1995.

Mouzelis, N. The subjectivist-objectivist divide: against transcendence. *Sociology*, vol. 34 (4), 2000, pp. 741–762.

Nussbaum, M.C. *Cultivating Humanity: A Classical Defence of Reform in Liberal Education.* Cambridge, MA: Harvard University Press, 1997.

Offe, C. *Industry and Inequality.* London: Arnold, 1970.

Opie, R. 'Economic planning and growth', in W. Beckerman (ed.) *The Labour Government's Economic Record: 1964–70.* London: Duckworth, 1972.

Orlikowski, W. J. 'The duality of technology: rethinking the concept of technology in organizations', *Organization Science*, vol. 3, 1992, pp. 398–427. [Reprinted in C. Bryant and D. Jary (eds) *The Contemporary Giddens: Social Theory in a Globalizing Age.* Basingstoke: Palgrave Macmillan, 2001, pp. 62–96.]

Orlikowski, W. J. and Yates, J. 'Genre repertoire: the structuring of communicative practices in organizations', *Administrative Science Quarterly*, vol. 39, 1994, pp. 541–74.

Outhwaite, W. *New Philosophies of the Social Sciences: Realism, Hermeneutics and Critical Theory.* London: Macmillan, 1987.

Outhwaite, W. 'Agency and structure', in J. Clark, C. Modgil and S. Modgil (eds) *Anthony Giddens: Consensus and Controversy.* London, Falmer Press, 1990, pp. 63–72.

Palmer, R. R. *The Improvement of Humanity: Education and the French Revolution.* Princeton, NJ: Princeton University Press, 1985.

Parker, J. *Structuration Theory.* Buckingham, Open University Press, 2000.

Parsons, T. *The Social System.* London: Routledge, 1991/1951.

Pettigrew, A. *The Awakening Giant: Continuity and Change in ICI.* Oxford: Blackwell, 1985.

Plummer, K. (ed.) *Symbolic Interactionism: 2 volumes.* Aldershot: Edward Elgar, 1991.

Plummer, K. 'An Invitation to a Sociology of Stories', in K. Plummer. *Telling Sexual Stories: Power, Change and Social Worlds.* London, Routledge, 1995.

Poulantzas, N. *Political Power and Social Classes.* London: New Left Books, 1973, trans. Timothy O'Hagan *et al.*

Poulantzas, N. *State, Power, Socialism.* London: Verso, 1978, trans. Patrick Camiller.

Pred, A. 'Context and bodies in flux: some comments on space and time in the writings of Anthony Giddens', in J. Clark, C. Modgil and S. Modgil (eds) *Anthony Giddens: Consensus and Controversy.* London, Falmer Press, 1990, pp. 117–29.

Rhodes, R. A. W. 'Power-dependence theories of central-local relations: a critical reassessment', in M. Goldsmith (ed.) *New Research in Central–Local Relations.* London: Gower, 1986.

Rhodes, R. A. W. *Beyond Westminster and Whitehall.* London: Unwin Hyman, 1988.

Ritzer, G. *The McDonaldization of Society: An Investigation into the Changing Character of Contemporary Life.* Thousand Oaks, Cal.: Pine Forge Press, 1993.

Rule, J. *Theory and Progress in Social Science.* Cambridge: Cambridge University Press, 1997.

Sayer, A. *Method in Social Science: A Realist Approach*. London: Hutchinson, 1984 [second edition, 1992, London: Routledge].

Sayer, A. *Realism and Social Science*. London: Sage, 2000a.

Sayer, A. 'For postdisciplinary studies: sociology and the curse of disciplinary parochialism and imperialism', in J. Eldridge, J. MacInnes, S. Scott, C. Warhurst and A. Witz (eds) *For Sociology: Legacies and Prospects*. Durham: Sociology Press, 2000b.

Schutz, A. 'Commonsense and scientific interpretations of human action', in A. Schutz, *Collected Papers*, vol. 1, The Hague, Martinus Nijhoff, 1962.

Schutz, A. *The Phenomenology of the Social World*, Evanston, Ill., Northwestern University Press, 1967, trans. G. Walsh and F. Lehnert (original publication, 1932).

Schutz, A. *Reflections on the Problem of Relevance*. New Haven, Yale University Press, 1970.

Scott, J. W. *Gender and the Politics of History*. New York: Colombia University Press, 1988.

Sewell, W. 'A theory of structure: duality, agency and transformations', *American Journal of Sociology*, vol. 98, 1992, pp. 1–29.

Shilling, C. 'Reconceptualising structure and agency in the sociology of education: structuration theory and schooling', in C. Bryant and D. Jary (eds) *Anthony Giddens: Critical Assessments*, volume IV. London: Routledge, 1997, pp. 342–64 [source: *British Journal of Sociology of Education*, vol. 13, no. 1, 1992, pp. 69–87].

Shilling, C. 'Towards an embodied understanding of the structure/agency relationship', *British Journal of Sociology*, vol. 50, no. 4, 1999, pp. 543–62.

Shilling, C. and Mellor, P. A. 'Embodiment, structuration theory and modernity: mind/body dualism and the repression of sensuality', in C. Bryant and D. Jary (eds) *The Contemporary Giddens: Social Theory in a Globalizing Age*. Basingstoke: Palgrave Macmillan, 2001, pp. 130–46.

Smith, M. *Pressure, Power and Policy: State Autonomy and Policy Networks in Britain and the United States*. Hemel Hempstead: Harvester Wheatsheaf, 1993.

Smith, M. *The Core Executive in Britain*. London: Macmillan, 1999.

Spybey, T. 'Traditional and Professional Frames of Meaning in Management. *Sociology*, vol. 18, no. 4, 1984, pp. 550–62 [Reprinted in C. Bryant and D. Jary (eds) *Anthony Giddens: Critical Assessments*, volume IV. London: Routledge, 1997, pp. 213–28].

Stones, R. 'The Myth of Betrayal: Structure and Agency in the Non-devaluation of the Pound 1964–7', PhD thesis, University of Essex, 1988.

Stones, R. 'Government–finance relations in Britain 1964–67: a tale of three cities', *Economy and Society*, vol. 19, no. 1, 1990, pp. 32–55.

Stones, R. 'Strategic context analysis: a new research strategy for structuration theory', *Sociology*, vol. 25, no. 3, 1991, pp. 673–95. [Reprinted in C. Bryant and D. Jary (eds) *Anthony Giddens: Critical Assessments*, volume IV. London: Routledge, 1997, pp. 186–219].

Stones, R. 'Labour and international finance, 1964–67', in D. Marsh, D. and R. A. W. Rhodes (eds) *Policy Networks in British Government*. Oxford, Oxford University Press, 1992.

Stones, R. *Sociological Reasoning: Towards a Past-Modern Sociology*. London, Macmillan, 1996.

Stones, R. 'Refusing the realism-structuration divide', *European Journal of Social Theory*, vol. 4, no. 2, 2001, pp. 177–97.

Stones, R. 'Social theory, the civic imagination and documentary film: a past-modern critique of the Bloody Bosnia season's *The Roots of War*', *Sociology*, vol. 36, no. 2, 2002a, pp. 355–76.

Stones, R. 'Social theory, documentary film and distant others: simplicity and subversion in *The Good Woman of Bangkok*',. *European Journal of Cultural Studies*, vol. 5, no. 2, 2002b, pp. 217–37.

Stones, R. 'Anthony Giddens', in G.Ritzer (ed.) *Encyclopaedia of Social Theory*. Thousand Oaks, Cal.: Sage, 2004a.

Stones, R. 'Refusing the poststructuralism-social history divide', 2004b.

Storey, J. *Managerial Prerogative and the Question of Control*. London: Routledge & Kegan Paul, 1983.

Sydow, J. and Windeler, A. 'Managing inter-firm networks: a structurationist perspective', in C. Bryant and D. Jary (eds) *Anthony Giddens: Critical Assessments*, vol. IV. London: Routledge, 1997, pp. 455–95.

Thompson, J. B. *Critical Hermeneutics: A Study in the Thought of Paul Ricoeur and Jurgen Habermas*. Cambridge: Cambridge University Press, 1981.

Thompson, J. B. *Studies in the Theory of Ideology*. Cambridge: Polity Press. 1984.

Thompson, J. B. 'The theory of structuration', in D. Held and J. B.Thompson (eds) *Social Theory of Modern Societies: Anthony Giddens and his Critics*. Cambridge: Cambridge University Press, 1989, pp. 56–76.

Thrift, N. 'Bear and mouse or bear and tree? Anthony Giddens' reconstitution of social theory', *Sociology*, vol. 19, no. 4, 1985, pp. 609–23.

Thrift, N. *Spatial Formations*. London, Sage, 1996.

Tomlinson, J. *Globalization and Culture*. Cambridge: Cambridge University Press, 1999.

Tucker, K. H. 'Aesthetics, play and cultural memory: Giddens and Habermas on the postmodern challenge', in C. Bryant and D. Jary (eds) *Anthony Giddens: Critical Assessments*, vol. IV. London: Routledge, 1997, pp. 61–84 [source: *Sociological Theory*, vol. 11, no. 2, 1993, pp. 194–211].

Tucker, K. H. *Anthony Giddens and Modern Social Theory*. London: Sage, 1998.

Tugendhat, G. 'American Opinion and the Dollar', *The Banker*, April, 1965.

Turner, J. H. 'Giddens's analysis of functionalism: a critique', in J. Clark, C. Modgil, and S. Modgil (eds) *Anthony Giddens: Consensus and Controversy*. London, Falmer Press, 1990, pp. 103–14.

Urry, J. 'Time and space in Giddens' social theory', in C. G. A. Bryant and D. Jary (eds) *Giddens' Theory of Structuration: A Critical Appreciation*. London, Routledge, 1991, pp. 160–75.

Urry, J. 'Sociology of Time and Space', in B. Turner (ed.) *The Blackwell Companion to Social Theory*. Oxford, Blackwell, 1996, pp. 369–95.

Urry, J. *Sociology Beyond Societies: Mobilities for the Twenty-First Century*. London: Routledge, 2000.

Urry, J. *Global Complexity*. Cambridge: Polity Press, 2003.

Varikas, E. 'Gender, experience and subjectivity: the Tilly-Scott disagreement', *New Left Review*, May/June, no. 211, 1995, pp. 89–101.

Wacquant, L. 'Pierre Bourdieu', in R. Stones (ed.) *Key Sociological Thinkers*. London: Macmillan, 1998, pp. 215–29.

Walby, S. *Theorizing Patriarchy*. Oxford: Blackwell, 1990.

Whittington, R. 'Putting Giddens into action: social systems and managerial agency', in C. Bryant and D. Jary (eds) *Anthony Giddens: Critical Assessments*, vol. IV. London: Routledge, 1997, pp. 365–86 [source: *Journal of Management Studies*, vol. 29, no. 6, 1992, pp. 693–712].

Willis, P. *Learning to Labour*. Farnborough: Saxon House, 1977.

Willmott, H. C. 'Unconscious sources of motivation in the theory of the subject: an exploration and critique of Giddens' dualistic models of action and personality', *Journal for the Theory of Social Behaviour*, vol. 16, 1986, pp. 105–21.

Willmott, R. 'Structure, culture and agency: rejecting the current orthodoxy of organisation theory', *Journal for the Theory of Social Behaviour*, vol. 27, no. 1, 1997, pp. 94–123.

Willmott, R. 'Structure, agency and the sociology of education: rescuing analytical dualism', *British Journal of Sociology of Education*, vol. 20, no. 1, 1999, pp. 5–21.

Wilson, H. *The Labour Government 1964–70: A Personal Record*. London: Weidenfeld & Nicolson and Michael Joseph, 1971.

Winkler, J. T. 'Corporatism', *Archives Europeenes de Sociologie*, vol. 17, 1976, pp. 100–36, 1976.

Wolff, K. (ed. and trans.). *The Sociology of Georg Simmel*. Glencoe, Ill.: Free Press, 1950.

Index

Breinigsville, PA USA
03 March 2010

233509BV00001B/133/P